Black American Women's Writing

In memory of my mother, Florence Gertrude Lennox,
who made everything possible

Black American Women's Writing

A Quilt of Many Colours

Eva Lennox Birch

HARVESTER WHEATSHEAF

New York   London   Toronto   Sydney   Tokyo   Singapore

First published 1994 by
Harvester Wheatsheaf
Campus 400, Maylands Avenue
Hemel Hempstead
Hertfordshire HP2 7EZ
A division of
Simon & Schuster International Group

© Harvester Wheatsheaf 1994

Typeset in 10/12pt Plantin
by Hands Fotoset, Leicester

Printed and bound in Great Britain by
Biddles Ltd, Guildford and King's Lynn

British Library Cataloguing in Publication Data

A catalogue record for this book is available from
the British Library

ISBN 0-7450-1612-X

---

1 2 3 4 5   98 97 96 95 94

Contents

Introduction

A woman wrote a book on women writers, and she has an apology in
the preface in which she explains why the book doesn't include any
black women writers. I think that's dishonest scholarship. I may be
wrong but I think so, and I took the trouble to tell her that. I feel
perfectly qualified to discuss Emily Dickinson, anybody for that
matter, because I assume what Jane Austen and all those people have
to say has something to do with life and being human in the world.
(Toni Morrison)[1]

'Dishonest scholarship' aptly describes any exclusion of books by
black writers on literature courses in institutions of learning that cater
for a predominantly white population, and it applies with equal force
to those white critics who avoid offering critical comments on that
work. Morrison's words stand as my own answer to those who
interpret any examination of the writing of black women by white
women, as an insidious attempt at appropriation. If Morrison defends
the right of a black American to study and enjoy Austen and
Shakespeare on the grounds that any literature worth reading has
something to say to us all about being human, then a conscious
avoidance by whites of the work of black writers is indefensible. It
also leaves the white critic vulnerable to the accusation that avoidance
is simply a deliberate ignoring, identified by Barbara Smith in her
challenging essay 'Towards a black feminist criticism'[2] as a product
of racism. Smith equates white avoidance of black concerns with
blindness 'to the implications of any womanhood that is not white
womanhood' and challenges 'ostensible feminists' and 'acknowledged
lesbians' to 'Struggle with the deep racism in themselves that is the
source of their blindness' (p. 3). In that same essay Smith castigates
Elaine Showalter for her failure to mention any black or third world

writer in her essay for *Signs* in 1975.[3] Yet almost twenty years on in her work tracing tradition and change in American women's writing, Showalter includes both Zora Neale Hurston and Alice Walker as significant participants in that process.[4] Such an inclusion is a measure of the recognition of the contribution made by black women writers to the culture of America, but it also marks a shift in the perspective from which literature is viewed in academia. Showalter's own repositioning stems from her engagement with the constant challenge to the canon offered by white and black feminists, and is contained in her questioning of whether 'in the multi-cultural reality of the present we can continue to assume a monolithic national identity' (p. 5). In an America where many inhabitants do not have English as their first language, or in a Great Britain wherein exist thriving communities of Asian and West Indian citizens, the challenge to a notion of an exclusive white male Eurocentric cultural dominance cannot go ignored.

The press for audience of the hitherto muted voices of women, black and white, has produced an ongoing, sometimes vituperative, debate concerning the ways in which their writings should be approached. In discussion of white women's writing, white women critics have found tools of analysis in feminist theory, whether it be from the disparate locations of the theoretical positions of Michèle Barrett[5] or Hélène Cixous,[6] with which they felt comfortable. When it comes to an approach to the work of black women, they have experienced a deep unease. Ever conscious of the accusation of 'cultural imperialism' that was levelled by Smith at Showalter, white women teachers have been only too aware of the truth of Smith's observation that 'When white women look at black women's works they are of course ill-equipped to deal with the subtleties of racial politics'.[7] This is a self-evident truth but will only become an impassable barrier to understanding if the *only* way of looking at that work is from the viewpoint of race. It would be facile and dangerous, however, to suggest that because the writers and critics are women, communication is effected without effort or is uncomplicated by the real experience of race and class. Showalter in *Sister's Choice* warns against the dangers of reductivism inherent in any assumption of a monolithic national identity which ignores these factors in the production or the reading of literature. She also alerts us to the danger of assuming that all writings by women have a universal sameness. To embrace such a position is to move towards an over-simplified acceptance of an essentialism based on theories of woman's biological and psychological constitution which are under constant interrogation by women in literary, medical and psychological discourse. My own position is akin to Showalter's in that, like her, I believe that all writing must be seen and approached as the product of a particular historical conjuncture within a particular national context. Such an approach is possible only if we begin by expecting difference and will be productive only if we do not allow the difference to produce and perpetuate division.

So what is my own subject position when I approach the writing of black American women as reader and teacher? I am white, female and, by virtue of education and occupation though not family origins, now regarded as 'middle class'. I am quite definitely middle-aged. I have spent my working life teaching literature to children and adults who have approached that study with a variety of motives and degrees of commitment. In my teaching at the Metropolitan University of Manchester where my students have *chosen* to follow particular courses, there is a special pleasure in designing programmes of study that are negotiated between staff and students. Over the last decade students and teachers have shared an enthusiasm for the study, discussion and examination of an increasing body of texts by black women writers. Students, male and female, welcome the opportunity to discuss texts they themselves have discovered in bookstores, and that have hitherto remained outside the prescribed male, white, literary canon. My own teaching is focused on two areas: one is the teaching of the American novel, in which one term is devoted entirely to the teaching of black American literature, including the works of Zora Neale Hurston; the other is women's writing over the last two centuries, where texts from Europe and America are studied. It can be argued that it is a sad reflection of our society's attitude towards race and gender that either of these expressions of experience have to be singled out for special study. On the other hand, perhaps their value can best be assessed as steps towards recognising and hopefully eradicating any oppression which is founded on the rejection of difference, for although Manchester has a large black population, black students are not fully represented in our higher education institutions. New access courses are hopefully, if slowly, correcting this underrepresentation in the student body, and the recent appointment of two black teachers in the School of English at my own institution promises radical alteration in the content and the thrust of some courses.

In the light of conditions that would seem unpropitious for extensive engagement with the work of women from another culture, we must ask *why* do students ask for books by black American writers to be included, and why do we as white teachers feel the need to teach these? I think the obvious answer to the first question is that they enjoy them as literature, but there are other, more profound reasons. In answer to the second question, honest scholarship provides another easy response. In any sustained study of the American novel it would be ludicrous to neglect examination of the work of black women writers who have received acclaim and whose work commands so much interest outside America. To exclude such works because they have emerged from a different culture in which the writers' colour is significant, is inherently a racist exclusion. Teachers of literature have both opportunity and responsibility to facilitate the building of racial bridges by joining students in serious reading of writers whose cultural and historical roots are significantly different to those of white British *and* white American writers. This is particularly pressing in Britain, where our need is to give positive support to the development of a truly multi-racial society in which the term 'ghetto' should have no place.

'Ghettoism' is the inevitable product of a refusal to accept and examine difference, which exacerbates suspicion and mistrust of that difference. Hence white teachers should be encouraged to include black writing on their literature courses at all levels in the education process. The important consideration to bear in mind, however, is that literature that has been shaped by cultural forces that differ from our own, must not then be judged by critical criteria that are themselves sexist or racist. Any approach to black American women's writing demands an awareness of the historical and cultural forces that shaped it, and any criticism should be, in my opinion, from a feminist standpoint. Yet I am aware that even this statement is not uncontentious. Because I am not black I cannot have complete identification with the body of black feminist critics such as Barbara Christian or Barbara Smith who have successfully encouraged the development of black feminist theory. Nor can I pretend that real divisions have not arisen within the feminist movement because of the perceived racism of white members. One has only to read bell hooks' impassioned account of racism and feminism in American society in *Ain't I a Woman*[8] to have any idealistic notion of automatic sisterhood between black and white women dismissed. She reminds us that 'sisterhood cannot be forged by the mere saying of words' (p. 157) and stresses that the onus for real change lies with the individual whose self-examination will reveal that 'labelling ourselves feminists does not change the fact that we must consciously work to rid ourselves of the legacy of negative socialisation'. Here hooks was speaking specifically of American women but her comment could be applied with equal veracity to women in British society, who have inherited the same legacy of 'negative socialisation' within patriarchal, capitalist structures. This perhaps provides a valid starting-point for a feminist approach to black American women's writing.

Just as there is productive debate amongst feminists about the politics of their movement, so the whole field of feminist literary critical theory teems with approaches that compete for our attention. Some theorists would have us ground our examination of women's literature on the biological determinant of sex, and whilst agreeing that women have been undervalued in patriarchal societies both as writers and as individuals, would still urge that we evaluate the creativity of women artists as examples of this 'natural' difference. We have seen, however, that acceptance of 'essentialism' simply perpetuates notions of female inferiority. As Newton and Rosenfelt argue in their introduction to *Feminist Criticism and Social Change,*[9] this essentialism 'subsumes women into the sisterly category of "woman" despite real differences of race, culture, class and historical condition, or posits women's nurturing and relational qualities as in themselves a counter to male domination' (p. xvii). Other theorists would have us see racial difference as the single platform from which to evaluate the writing of women from different cultures. Yet the whole concept of racial difference in a multi-cultural society is problematic, especially as interbreeding has blurred the supposed difference between the races. In the field of black American writing in the late nineteenth and early twentieth centuries, exemplified in Harper's *Iola Leroy* and Nella Larsen's *Passing* and *Quicksand*, this problem was embodied in the 'tragic mulatto' who was to be a dominant preoccupation of black writers for a few decades. Other Marxist feminist critics might emphasise the economic circumstances of production and consumption as paramount considerations in our approach to women's writing. Yet others direct our attention to the 'negative socialisation' of women as the result of gender ideology, and it is this position in particular that I find offers most productive access to literature written by women. As Foucault argues, gender is a social construct designed to limit the range of life choices available to humankind for the convenient operation of social institutions. This has resulted in the inscription and imposition of immutable gender positions in Western society. The position of women as the 'other' and 'inferior', as Simone de Beauvoir defined it, as well as the imposition of compulsory heterosexuality resultant from this ideology of gender, are responsible for that 'negative socialisation' which all women share.

The clearest view of the ways in which sexuality, class, race and gender have become encoded in social institutions in America and Great Britain, is to have a vantage point that is positioned outside, in the position of the 'other', which is where feminist criticism begins. Jonathon Culler in his essay 'The power of division' in *The Difference Within: Feminism and critical theory*[10] poses the question: 'Is feminist criticism the study of women writers as a separate activity, or is it a perspective on literature of all sorts, and other discourses as well?' (p. 150). I would argue that it is too limiting to see it only as a function of a separatist activity; a feminist critical perspective is not limited in application only to the texts of women, and is equally useful as a means of opening up male texts. It also functions most productively in the opportunities it provides for the deconstruction of other discourses as well as the literary. Like Culler I see the strength and the dynamics of a feminist critical approach resting on the very diversity of perspectives that it embraces. Some critics devoted to a single critical approach would suggest that a divided mind is no mind; I would suggest that only division allows for growth, and that a lack of plurality, or the facility to recognise the benefits of plurality, are phallocentric and authoritarian. Nevertheless from the ferment of opinion and the variety of philosophical bases on which such criticism rests, a consensus can be found concerning the fundamental aims of feminist criticism. These can be identified as the need to interrogate the literary canon; the need to identify a tradition in the writing produced by women; and the need to investigate the possible distinctiveness of women's expression. Taking these as guidelines enables teachers and students alike to analyse *why* they are so drawn to the writing of black American women.

Upon analysis of questionnaires, designed to gauge student response to the content of courses within the Department of English in which I teach, it emerges that the areas with which greatest engagement is professed by the majority of students are those outside the white, male canon. This is partly explained by the preponderance of female over male students in the degree programmes for which the English section is responsible within the Humanities faculty. However, further questioning elicits particularly eager responses to the writing of black women, sometimes on the grounds that they are 'different' and therefore interesting, but most usually because the women students feel that they are engaging with texts that have something to say to them about being female, irrespective of the racial and national divide between the writers and the readers. My experience of teaching this literature has revealed that women readers feel nearer in spirit to the works of black women writers, whose experiences are of our time, than they are to the 'greats' of the white, male canon. Perhaps one reason for this is that black women writers speak of and from a position of marginalisation that in itself is recognisable to women of any colour. The examination of racial and sexual oppression in their writing inevitably starts with, but crosses the bounds of race, and emphasises the universality of women's sense of the constraints with which a socially constructed gender position burdens them.

The focus of attention in the writing by black women is not single. Indeed, Barbara Christian points to this specifically in her essay 'Trajectories of self-definition'[11] in which she says:

> For what Afro-American women have been permitted to express, in fact to contemplate, as part of the self, is grossly affected by other issues. The development of Afro-American women's fiction is, in many instances, a mirror image of the intensity of the relationship between sexism and racism in this country. (p. 234)

The personal struggle of Afro-American women against marginalisation in America, channelled into establishing for themselves a self-definition in which their beauty, strength and individuality is recognised, is not just one of race, but of gender too. In examining racial prejudice black women writers expose the cultural constraints of class, gender and religion with which white women can also identify. White women cannot, as Barbara Smith points out, share the experiential reality of white racism suffered by black women, but by being exposed to a literature expressing that reality, they can move towards an understanding of their own culturally shaped prejudice, confront their own fear of difference, and realise that there is more that joins black and white women than should ever keep them apart.

One area in which both black and white women writers experienced exclusion, though admittedly to a different degree and on different grounds, was the right to a place in the literary canon. Because of their unique historical roots as enslaved people in American society, black women were excluded much more firmly from engagement in discourse than were their white sisters. Alice Walker in *In Search of Our Mothers' Gardens*[12] testifies to the white, male domination of the literary canon throughout most of her formal education, which kept her ignorant of her own black literary heritage. Paul Lauter's research into the production and perpetuation of the American canon led him to the conclusion that:

By the end of the 1950s, one could study American literature and read no work by a black writer, few works by women except Emily Dickinson and perhaps Marianne Moore and Katherine Anne Porter, and no work about the lives or experiences of working-class people. (p. 23)[13]

This echoes my own experience as an undergraduate in the mid-1950s in England. Taking an Honours degree in English at an all-women's college of London University, I was never *once* offered the work of a woman as part of the canon (except the meditations of a medieval nun written in Anglo-Saxon). No woman novelist was studied as the course content did not include the novel, presumably in the belief that it was a 'bastard' production. I did not hear of Aphra Behn for many years.

If, as Paul Lauter sums up in the above-quoted essay, the canon is 'A means by which culture validates social power', it follows that in a social organisation in which women are held to be subordinate to men, the culture validated by that society will be a male construct. Lauter goes on to identify the forces which shaped the American canon as political in aim: to create a 'usable' past and to lay claim to an American literary tradition which was not merely a copy of the European. In this construction women in general and blacks in particular were excluded. This was despite the obvious fact that the only indigenous American expression – apart from the American Indian oral culture – free from the desire to ape a European culture, came from the African people brought to America as slaves, and which is inscribed in their folklore, songs and inventive use of the English language. Yet their culture was silenced, ignored and devalued. In her discussion of women's writing in the American tradition, Showalter asks the question: 'Does a muted culture have a literature black s are themselves a within the parameter dedicated by the conventions of the dominant culture

of its own, or must it always revise the conventions of the dominant?'[14] The answer is not simple, for although black women writers have displayed remarkable ingenuity in their re-visioning and re-working of established literary forms, they are still working within the parameters dictated by those forms. They have nevertheless a literature of their own in the sense that they have constantly addressed issues of which only they, as black women, had any knowledge. In their challenging of the negative stereotypical presentation of black men and women found – if they are there at all – in the writing of white writers, they are engaging in debate with canonical assumptions. They have entered this debate after centuries of struggle to be recognised as full members of American society, during which time social forces were determined to silence them.

In the very act of writing at all, black women writers have interrogated the validity of the American canon in a more positive way than perhaps white European women can be said to have questioned theirs. In her essay *A Room of One's Own*,[15] published in 1929 (when Zora Neale Hurston and Nella Larsen were achieving published success), Virginia Woolf identifies British women's lack of education and their economic dependence on men as significant reasons for their non-representation in the English canon. She also defines white women writers as suffering the constraints imposed by their having only male language, male sentences at their disposal. She has nothing to say about the language of black women writers whose previous exclusion from literary discourse on the grounds of race as well as economic impoverishment, had done nothing to dull the vitality of their expression, or their rendering of experience. Of course, as the wife of Leonard Woolf and the daughter of Lesley Stephens and a member of the Bloomsbury literati, Virginia Woolf was writing from within a privileged, intellectually stimulating and – compared to most of her compatriates – an economically sound circle, and we cannot castigate her for the accident of birth. However, although Woolf urges women to 'write as a woman', one suspects that she took for granted that this writing would still be in the standard English which she associated with literary production. Perhaps what she could not at that time envisage was a woman's writing, such as that of the black American woman, which owed its lyrical power to its use of the oral heritage of its author's people. ✳

Writing within a dominant white male culture, black women writers have not only entered with the richness of their own linguistic heritage, but as the research of many black and white scholars has increasingly shown, have developed a literary tradition of their own. In the discussion of the work of Jean Toomer and Toni Morrison, in his essay 'When Lindbergh slept with Bessie Smith',[16] Houston A. Baker Jr concludes that 'What is compelling about comparison of the two works is that Morrison would, indeed, seem to emanate from a tradition different from that of Wright and Ellison' (p. 94). The result is a literary tradition that is not only black, but also distinctively female, characterised by a celebratory embracing of the writer's African cultural heritage, and a determined retrieval of their mothers' stifled creativity. They speak and write out of themselves, practising, without an avowed awareness of it, the process described by Hélène Cixous in 'The laugh of the Medusa' (see note 6) as necessary if women are to 'write as woman':

> If a woman has always functioned 'within' the discourse of man, a signifier that has always referred back to the opposite signifier which annihilates its specific energy and diminishes or stifles its very sounds, it is time for her to dislocate this 'within', to explode it, turn it round, and seize it, taking it in her own mouth, biting that tongue with her very own teeth to invent for herself a language to get inside of it. (p. 257)

I believe that in the writing of black women we do see this dislocation of the 'within' because they were positioned so firmly on the outside of that 'within'. As such, although they undoubtedly speak as, for and to black women, they also speak much more clearly to white women than do some white writers. What we find in their writing is what Marjorie Pryse describes as 'The strategies by which individual women overcame every conceivable obstacle to personal evolution and self-expression'.[17] Victims of 'negative conditioning', their writing reveals a complete rejection of this process to which all women have been subjected. In questioning the fictional stereotyping of black women, they question all such stereotyping, and in celebrating their own language they challenge the hegemony of white male language. In this developing tradition they have also freed themselves from many novelistic and literary conventions, allowing space to experiment with form, narrative time and theories of genre. Above all, their writing challenges the received orthodoxy of the dominant culture, in which are inscribed those ideas on race, gender, class and religion on which oppression is built.

This book is not offered as, nor is it capable of being, a comprehensive survey of black women's writing in America. What I hope to do is to examine certain distinctive elements in early black writing and oral culture, such as spirituality, political awareness, community, creativity and the effects of slavery, which have been identified by black scholars as distinctive determinants in the creation of a specifically black women's literary tradition. These elements, as American black scholars have demonstrated, are the products of particular social, political and historical circumstances, which white students have to recognise in their approach to black writing. I then intend to discuss from a feminist critical viewpoint a few writers whose work I believe has developed these cultural strands in a particularly interesting way. Because of the particular focus of my argument, many favourite writers have had to be excluded and those examined are offered as exemplars of the richness of the literary tradition of black American women writers. To avoid diffusion I have also limited my focus to black women as writers of prose, although some of those chosen have also reputations as poets.

I hope to demonstrate that the tradition under discussion was consolidated to a great extent in the published work of Zora Neale Hurston, whose research and writing is now accessible, and to whom later twentieth-century black women writers frequently acknowledge a respect and debt. The other writers have been selected because I judge them to have built strongly upon particular foundation-stones in Hurston's work. Audre Lorde and Paule Marshall I consider as exemplifying and celebrating the variety and difference in black women which Hurston was at pains to point out; Maya Angelou as revealing the beauty, power and inspirational force of autobiography; Toni Morrison as a writer who 'puts it all together' in novels which emphasise community and a cleaving to ancestral history as the path to racial – and human – health; Alice Walker as exploring a female spirituality born of political involvement. All, I think, are positive and optimistic writers. Their protest against racial and sexual division is not directed by hatred, but by a loving desire for an holistic society that can accommodate all differences.

I take my subtitle from the quilt as a symbol of the co-operative creativity celebrated in so much of the writing by black women. Their literary tradition has indeed bright and startling flashes of colour and texture provided by the work of particular writers, but it is not a tradition built simply of stars. It is one that celebrates black womanhood and pays homage to the foremothers whose creativity has gone unsung. In Edith Wharton's *The House of Mirth*[18] Lily Bart experienced 'an odd sense of being behind the social tapestry, on the other side where the threads are knotted and the loose ends hung' (p. 279). Lily did not find this a pleasant experience because this location emphasised her exclusion from the New York society for which she had been 'negatively conditioned' to belong. In the quilting together of the tradition of black women writers, their ancestors are the enabling 'threads knotted behind the loose ends'. They are not hidden, however, but recognised for the part they played.

— 1 —

Pioneering voices

It is beyond my present competence and scope to offer anything other than a selective sampling of particular modes of black address from the nineteenth century. Those chosen have been identified by black critics as the foundation stones on which a black American women's literary tradition was built, and consist of slave narratives, spiritual autobiographies, autobiographical as well as sentimental novels, and oral culture. None of these cultural manifestations was the preserve of females alone, but subsequent women writers have used them differently from men.

Any white reader who approaches black American literature must start by recognising that the experiential reality described is a unique one. Black roots in American history were planted in institutionalised slavery. To this fact white readers of black writers must constantly return, for it is the source of the gulf which lies between our history as white imperialists, and theirs as the oppressed. Individual voices from slavery, in the form of slave narratives, unite in clear testament to the inhumanity of enslavement. Their importance lies in the fact that they express the only area of a slave's life over which the slave could exercise control: her thoughts and feelings. Consequently the autobiographical statement in black literature has acquired such significance for critics that Selwyn R. Cudjoe describes it as 'the quintessential literary genre',[1] allowing insight into the psyche of the black American in slavery. The black scholar Stephen Butterfield also identifies slave narratives as the building bricks of black American literature:

> And little by little, book by book, they construct the framework of a black American literature. Autobiography in their hands becomes so powerful, so convincing a testimony to human resource, intelligence,

endurance, love in the face of tyranny, that, in a sense, it sets the tone for most subsequent black American writing.[2]

Those qualities of resourcefulness, intelligence, love and endurance described by Butterfield, survive and are celebrated still in the writing of black American women today, echoing the thoughts and struggles of their ancestors.

There has been an endless procession of books about slavery, though few written by slaves, which is why the authentic voices of the slave narratives demand our attention. Some of these accounts were collected in slave times at the prompting of active Abolitionists who used them as evidence in their struggle to rid the South of slavery, and the circumstances of their production mean that they speak of collective physical and emotional suffering. Almost three-quarters of a century after Abolition had been achieved, in the 1920s and 1930s, over two thousand former slaves were interviewed, whose oral statements were transcribed by willing researchers.[3] These accounts remained largely unpublished until the 1960s, when the Second Black Renaissance in art, writing and music coincided with the Civil Rights Movement. Previous historians had expressed doubt about the historical accuracy of recollections of people considered too old to remember reliably. Now that we have access to these accounts of lives spent in disparate geographical locations in the South, an undeniable common truth emerges about the conditions endured. Particularly poignant are the shared concerns and anguish of the female slaves who, although ignored by history, were not silent and whose oral accounts of their enslaved condition, as Marjorie Pryse suggests, 'enlarge our conventional assumptions about the nature and function of literary tradition', in that they force us to recognise the oral as an integral part of that tradition.[4] These narratives record how the female slave had to endure the same harsh physical working conditions as her male counterpart, as well as those accorded to her because of her sex. Her additional burdens were sexual exploitation – which could mean rape – and the demands of child-bearing. A reading of these accounts dispels any doubt that black women were vulnerable to physical, sexual and emotional abuse at any time from their white owners. Regarded by the worst of the owners as livestock, some were bred for sex and sale, put to work as children, and lived lives of unremitting toil.

Black women were considered to be 'naturally' sexually available, more passionate than white women, more willing to have sexual intercourse. With such an opinion of their sexuality, it is not surprising that the rape of a black woman by a white man was not considered a crime. The vulnerability of female slaves to sexual ambush and exploitation is that which marks off their experience as being different to that of the men. It also marked them off from white women who were the untouchable wives and mothers of the white owners. The definition of the black woman in terms of rampant sexuality and the denial of that same sexuality to the white women, did nothing to foster sisterly bonds between them. As Harriet Jacobs shows in her autobiographical account *Incidents in the Life of a Slave Girl*,[5] such a distinction added further trials to the already harassed slave girl. Not only did Jacobs have to endure constant sexual attacks from her master Flint, but she had to contend with the vicious jealousy of his wife. The 'jealous mistress' became a vindictive and relentless persecutor who vented her own sense of sexual inadequacy and marital betrayal on the defenceless object of her husband's lusts. Harriet Jacobs explains her taking of a white lover to free herself from Flint's attentions, but even the birth of her children did nothing to alleviate her situation. Many slave narratives attest to the vehemence of the attacks made upon black women by white mistresses driven to desperation on the birth of their slaves' half-white children, whose arrival faced them with the unpalatable fact that their own husbands and sons had fathered them. The slave narratives also reveal that maternal bonding could be emotionally catastrophic for women whose children could be sold away from them, with no account taken of the parent's or child's anguish. Harriet Beecher Stowe's stand against this in *Uncle Tom's Cabin*[6] is conveyed in a narrative consisting of 'mother' stories, in which the inevitable evil of separation of mother from child is castigated as being even more destructive than physical violence. The enslaved mother was denied what nineteenth-century domestic ideology deemed to be the most sacred duty of the white mother: that of providing constant physical care and moral guidance to her children. Yet these black women survived, quickly learning strategies for survival for themselves and their children. Moreover, the enforced sundering of maternal ties intensified the bonding, particularly between mothers and daughters, through whom family history is traditionally passed on. Over a century after Abolition Toni Morrison re-creates the intensity of a slave mother's maternal feelings in her flight for freedom, and her determination to have her own children out of bondage, in her novel *Beloved*, which is a fictive rendition of a history found in the slave narratives.

Actual slave narratives are testaments describing appalling physical and emotional cruelty, and as such are addressed to the white oppressors. They stand as indictments of an horrendous evil and detail both resistance and reaction to that evil. In them, women record their abuse, men their anger and frustration at their own impotence to change the situation. In his work on black autobiography, Butterfield identifies the voice of the 'mass' in these narratives as dominant:

> [The black autobiographer] is not an individual with a private career, but a soldier in a long, historic march towards Canaan. The self is conceived as a member of an oppressed social group, with ties and responsibilities to the other members.[7]

Butterfield traces the links between the slave narratives and twentieth-century black autobiographers, and in his analysis of the autobiographical voices of male writers this connection is affirmed, but he admits that the female autobiographer, exemplified in Maya Angelou, was writing out of a different, female tradition in autobiographical statement. Many black male slave narratives, like that of Frederick Douglass[8] who was born in slavery in 1818 and who rose to prominence to become a federal administrator, were inspirational 'success stories', written as protest, accusation, defiance and intention: to shake dominant white society into effecting social change. The informing impulse in these is social rather than personal. The black woman, perhaps reflecting the position of women in the white, patriarchal society from which she was excluded, ponders the personal, expresses the intimate, salvages the emotional highs and lows of female experience. Even in those narratives written by women at the instigation of Abolitionists there is an insistent demand for self-fulfilment, in their expressed desire for work that would provide economic independence. The perceived need for self-definition through work is as strong in these narratives as is the cry from Charlotte Brontë's *Shirley*.[9] This novel challenges and questions the ideology of gender in the West which had rendered the middle-class white British woman impotent and often redundant within her society. The demand of such white women was for an education and economic independence which would enable them to escape from the confines of the domestic sphere. How more challenging to this ideology was the very existence of enslaved women who could demand nothing, and for whom 'escape' meant something very different. For black women the idea of female exclusion in the supposed safety of the domestic sphere was an unimagined luxury. The narratives they have left constantly interrogate those notions of gender which, although inscribed in the social institutions of British and American society, were applicable only to white women. Sojourner Truth summed this up in her gesture at the Seneca Falls Convention in 1848 when, addressing a racially mixed audience, she bared her breast and asked 'Ain't I a woman?' Clearly Sojourner Truth was demanding an examination of the construction of gender in American society, and asking why it excluded black women. Yet despite their perceived 'inferiority' to white women, what emerges from a reading of these narratives is a refusal of the female slave to accept victim status. Many detail attempts to escape, to find work as free women, and to buy relatives out of bondage.

That the slave narratives are at the root of much of the black writing which followed, as protest and witness to black status in America, cannot be denied. However, not all blacks were slaves. Some had been freed, some had bought freedom, some had escaped. As early as the 1830s in Boston and Philadelphia black women were forming their own literary societies, thus giving opportunity and encouragement to those amongst their number who wanted to write. That some black women *could* write and manipulate the English language more skilfully than could many whites had already been shown in the eighteenth century in the writing of Phyllis Wheatley, whose devotional poetry disproved the white assumption that the blacks were incapable of ever aspiring to the same level of literacy as their masters. Other challenges to notions of white intellectual and moral supremacy came in the shape of the spiritual autobiographies, the earliest of which pre-date the fugitive slave narratives by some fifty years. This is not surprising in the light of the enforced illiteracy of the slave, and the access to literacy of free blacks. The slave narratives express in particular the narrators' awareness of a physical self, the spiritual autobiographies an awareness of the spiritual self. William L. Andrews, in his introduction to three nineteenth-century spiritual autobiographies by women, comments that 'Like the fugitive slave narrator, the black spiritual autobiographer traced his or her freedom back to the acquisition of some sort of saving knowledge and to an awakening from within'.[10]

Of the women whose autobiographies are edited by Andrews, Jarena Lee (born in 1783) and Zilpha Elaw (born in 1790) were the daughters of free parents, whilst Julia Foote (born in 1823) was the child of former slaves who had bought freedom. Their autobiographies express a common demand for individual female self-hood, through spirituality. This is still extant, and is a predominant concern expressed in the writing of Alice Walker today, although she rejects Christianity as a channel for that spirituality. Paradoxically, although Elaw, Lee and Foote demanded a freedom to preach a religion now depicted by their twentieth-century literary descendants as a factor in women's oppression, their demands can be recognised as an expression of a 'womanism' with which Walker could not argue.

In her excellent essay on 'Adding Color and Contour to Early American Self-Portraitures; Autobiographical Writings of Afro-American Women'[11] Frances Smith Foster argues that the life stories by Afro-American women in the nineteenth century 'present protagonists who transcend the images of the victimised slave woman and the home-bound True Woman' (p. 35). They present themselves as pioneers in the struggle of the black woman for self-definition and independence. It is interesting to examine the personal histories of Lee, Elaw and Foote in the light of this comment. All three found voice through their commitment to the Christian religion, and an organisation which because of its hierarchical and patriarchal structure seemed an unlikely breeding-ground for female independence. Yet the black African Methodist Episcopal church to which they belonged had allowed, as did the slave narratives, an expression of group humanity, and had provided opportunity for cohesion amongst the blacks. In *Long Black Song*,[12] Houston A. Baker argues convincingly that the violent disruption of the Africans' identity in slavery had been exacerbated by their enforced abandonment of native gods. Christianity was imposed upon them. When the first abducted Africans were landed in the Americas as slaves in 1619, the English Church was eager to convert them to Christianity, and slave baptismal records go back as far as 1641, although the African slaves were initially loath to embrace the religion of their oppressors. Evangelicising of slaves began in earnest in the early eighteenth century through the agency of the Society for the Propagation of the Gospel, newly formed in London. Such efforts were not always welcomed by the Southern whites, who feared the opportunity provided by communal worship for possible slave insurrections. So great was the concern of some States that they enacted measures to prevent the gathering together of slaves on the Sabbath. What they could not legislate against, however, was the great tide of non-conformist religious movements that swept through the colonies in the 1730s, a time now referred to as 'The Great Awakening', to which blacks as well as whites responded. By 1775 blacks comprised nearly one-quarter of the colonial population, and had been recruited in large numbers to the Baptist Church.

This alien religion offered Africans of disparate tribal origin a common focus. Victims of a diaspora, they were quick to embrace a religion which promised liberation – albeit only in a spiritual sense – personal redemption, and eventual retribution for their oppressors. They were particularly attracted to Old Testament stories where they were able to find identity with the enslaved Israelites. Yet whilst they accepted the Christian message, they were forced to worship in a church where physical segregation of blacks from whites emphasised their supposed inferiority. They were not allowed to sit in the body of the church, nor to take Communion with white worshippers. There was an obvious contradiction in a church which preached that humankind was made in God's image, yet was unable to conceive of a humankind that was not white. Some whites justified enslavement as a natural consequence of innate racial inferiority, or as 'a punishment resulting from sin or a natural defect of the soul'.[13] Some even argued that blacks had no souls. Jarena Lee found difficulty in convincing her employer of her religiosity until a time when he 'seemed to admit that colored people had souls' (*Sisters*, p. 47).

The first black man to be granted a licence to preach was George Leile, a slave in the ownership of a Baptist deacon. Leile assisted in the founding in 1780 of the first Negro congregation in America – the African Baptist Church in Savannah. In the same decade another ex-slave, Richard Allen, was finding a mission in Christianity. Allen was born into slavery in 1760 in Philadelphia where attitudes towards manumission were more tolerant than those in the deep South, and by the age of 17 he had bought his freedom. He then began a career as an itinerant Methodist preacher – as did Elaw, Lee and Foote, who followed him – but, unlike theirs, his mission was recognised in his appointment to the Old St George's Methodist Episcopal church in Philadelphia. Here he drew large congregations of black as well as white worshippers, until the racism of the whites erupted. They demanded that the seats be reserved for the whites, while the blacks should stand around the walls of the church. Animosity reached its height in 1787 when white deacons seized and forced to their feet the praying Richard Allen and an associate minister Absalom Jones. Outraged at this act, Allen decided upon separation from the whites. Allen and Jones established the Free African Society, to which Jarena Lee belonged, but by 1794 the two ministers had gone their separate ways. Jones formed the African Episcopal Church which later affiliated with the mainstream white church, and Allen founded the African Methodist Episcopal Church which has remained separate from the white. By 1815 Allen had been elected as the first black bishop of America, and the AME remains today as one of the largest black American denominations.

The AME afforded the blacks the opportunity to join in worship and to come to enlightenment in their own way. As testified to in the spiritual autobiographies, this involved a conventional path to God via conversion, prophetic dreams, trances and visions. Hurston, in *The Sanctified Church*,[14] notes: 'The vision is a very definite part of Negro religion. It almost always accompanies the call to preach' (p. 85). This call to preach, however, was only acceptable in black men. The American church was clearly racist, but the black church was equally sexist. Richard Allen's only response to Jarena Lee's request for permission to be ordained, was that church rules would not allow it. In seeking to preach, women were interrogating patriarchy with questions that could not be answered. Lee asks: 'And why should it be thought impossible, heterodox, or improper for a woman to preach? Seeing the saviour died for woman as well as the man?' (*Sisters*, p. 36). In a church that was devoutly served by women (in the capacity of cleaners, fund-raisers, needlewomen and carers), such a challenge to male authority was met with hostility. Although Bishop Allen gave Lee permission to hold prayer meetings in her own house, and later allowed her to take her mission abroad, she was never granted a licence to preach.

Lee's autobiography was published in 1849, after which she seems to have disappeared into obscurity. She does record, however, meeting with Zilpha Elaw, another itinerant woman preacher with whom she spent some time on a joint mission. Zilpha Elaw published her memoirs in 1846, and then like Lee disappears from public record, but she has left us a full account of her many travels, which in 1842 took her as far as the north of England. In her autobiography she records that so great was the hostility aroused in English men at the sight of a woman who dared to preach, that they offered her physical abuse: 'In one of their large chapels in which I preached, a number of young men conspired together, and came to hear me, with their hands full of stones' (*Sisters*, p. 132).

Although the avowed purpose of Lee and Elaw was to disseminate the Christian message, their life journeys as black women were implicit demonstrations of the injustices of the slave system, and certainly Elaw gave support to English Abolitionists. Their triumphs as preachers and their efforts to gain official recognition within their church show that black women were demanding the right to be part of a hierarchy that had been appropriated by black men. In Julia Foote's account of her own ministry published in 1879, the same sexism is apparent in the church's threat of excommunication and her husband's threat to have her locked away: 'He said I was getting more crazy every day, and getting others in the same way, and that if I did not stop he would send me back home or to the crazy-house' (*Sisters*, p. 197).

Clearly Foote's husband was not making an empty threat here, nor was he suggesting an unusual course of action in his proposed 'disposition' of his recalcitrant wife. The then current medical discourse had identified female defiance of male dominance as a form of mental disorder, to be dealt with by incarceration. Because of the rigidity of gender construction in the nineteenth century, women who regularly disobeyed the dictates of father, husband or brother could easily find themselves committed to an asylum for the insane. Not surprisingly the asylums for the mentally 'ill' suddenly had more female than male inmates.

In their autobiographies Elaw, Lee and Foote implicitly reveal the social injustices arising from racism and sexism. They also expose a dichotomy in patriarchal attitudes about women's social role as insoluble as that which had forced the black and white churches to split. As wives and mothers they were confined to the domestic sphere, yet as women they were regarded as 'naturally' more spiritual than men. In the preface to Foote's autobiography she is described as being 'guilty' of three crimes: 'colour', 'womanhood' and 'evangelicism'. The injustice of exclusion as preachers within the church hierarchy is the price of those 'crimes'. Perhaps another 'crime' of which the three women could have been accused – for it seems to be a subtext in the hostility they aroused – was their foregrounding of their religious over their domestic missions as wives and mothers, which was in defiance of gender ideology of the time. In spite of their undoubted religious devotion they were seen by the church as difficult and defiant members. For such defiance Foote was threatened with excommunication, which prompted her to write a letter pleading against this punishment. The letter was dismissed as being of no importance: 'My letter was slightly noticed, and then thrown under the table. Why should they notice it? It was only the grievance of a woman, and there was no justice meted out to women in those days' (*Sisters*, p. 207). Foote's, Elaw's and Lee's autobiographies express a protest against the double standards arising from the artificial imposition of gender separation which echoes still, and to which black women writers of today give added voice.

Although the organisation of church hierarchy placed constraints upon these women as preachers, it nevertheless provided an opportunity for self-definition, in that it gave them access to language. These spiritual autobiographies, unlike the slave narratives, are couched in formal register, shaped by Biblical rhetoric, and are expressed in delicately refined and restrained language. They provided literary models for other women who felt impelled to publish their life histories. This facility with a language designed to be decorous, as befitted the female gender, is apparent in Harriet Wilson's *Our Nig*,[15] published in 1859, and now claimed as the first novel by a black American woman. The language in this text is formal, drawing on sermonical rhetoric and moral rectitude with phrases such as 'disgrace and calumny', 'her fall', 'misdeed'. To avoid giving offence, Nig's white mother's loss of virginity is euphemistically expressed as the sacrifice of a 'priceless gem', 'the delicate virginity of May' (*Nig*, p. 6). Only occasionally does the vernacular obtrude, in Fredo's black father's use of 'dis' for 'this' or 'I's' for 'I have'. Henry Louis Gates Jr describes this text as the 'missing link' between black autobiography and a distinctive black voice in fiction.[16]

Wilson's semi-autobiographical story of a life in the North as a free black was written to raise money she needed for the nursing of her sick child, but it is also an exposure of Northern racism. The uncertain narrative stance comes from contradictory authorial aims, where an account of a true life, reminiscent of a slave narrative, is rendered within the formulaic framework of the popular sentimental novel. Wilson makes appeals to her 'gentle reader' for sympathy and support in the fashion typical of the nineteenth-century novel, and structurally *Our Nig* is conventional, with linear time charting the life journey of an abandoned child into adulthood, in chapters bearing apt literary epigraphs. Gates identifies formulaic conventions which ally *Our Nig* with the then popular sentimental novel, but points to departures from that mode as evidence of the distinctiveness of Wilson's text. He notes there is no veneration of mothers in *Our Nig*, unlike the popular novel, nor does it end with a happy marriage. At times the author's chapter headings suggest autobiography: 'Mag Smith: my mother', 'My Father Dies', 'A New Home for Me'; at others the narrator distances herself from the narrative by adopting a third-person narrative voice, discussing the persona of 'Frado', nicknamed 'Nig'.

Life for 'Nig' in the North is little better than that of her enslaved sisters in the South. She too is subjected to overwork, physical and verbal abuse, 'all because I am black' (*Nig*, p. 75), although she makes no mention of being the victim of sexual abuse. The inequalities of a racist society are questioned in Frado's wondering why God has not made her white. Wilson describes how 'Nig', like the spiritual autobiographers, had sought solace in the church. Even this was touched by the cruelty of her mistress who, on discovering 'Nig' reading the Bible, echoed the white hostility already discussed towards black female preachers: 'I found her reading the Bible today, just as though she expected to turn pious nigger and preach to the white folks' (*Nig*, p. 88). Wilson allows Frado to be sceptical of a segregated religion – 'Her doubt was, *is* there a heaven for the black?' (*Nig*, p. 84), when her mistress emphasises constantly that it was not meant for 'niggers'. In this Wilson is holding up to examination the fabric of American religious practice and polemic, to reveal that both were shot through with inconsistency and bigotry. Eventually, Frado rebels against Mrs Bellmont's vicious tyranny and is turned out of the house with little confidence in her ability to survive. Her self-esteem at this time is at rock-bottom. Having been described as ugly by Mrs Bellmont, she feared that 'everyone thought her so. Then no-one would take her. She was black, no-one could love her' (*Nig*, p. 108). Like Morrison's Pecola Breedlove in *The Bluest Eye* and Alice Walker's Celie in *The Color Purple* the black woman-child had been persuaded that her unworthiness and her ugliness were mutually inescapable. 'Nig's' childhood had been blighted by her rejection by her white mother, who, having 'ruined' her chances of marriage to a white man, had accepted a marriage proposal from a black one. This in itself was an unusual miscegenation, for the most common alliance was between a white master and his black slave. In 'Nig's' account, her mother remarried following the death of her black husband, and promptly decided to give away her children, her 'black devils', with no thought of the bitter hardships this would cause them. This is an ironic reversal of the lot of black slave mothers who were made desolate by the separation from a child, even if it was half-white. By dint of her innate good nature, and some friendly assistance, Fredo/ Nig finds work and later marries, only to be deserted by her husband who leaves her to bring up and support their sick child.

Gates' research verifies Wilson's existence and marriage, and the possible death of the child for whose benefit *Our Nig* had been penned. He also suggests that the interracial marriage of Nig's parents might have caused the novel to have remained in obscurity for over a century. Undoubtedly *Our Nig* raises questions about racism, sexism and religious experience which become dominant preoccupations in the literature of black American women writers in the twentieth century. Wilson's text may be primitive, shaky in execution and contradictory in impulse, but it is clearly important for the tradition it established. Harriet Wilson's penning of *Our Nig* was a desperate measure to raise money, and shows an entrepreneurial impulse uncharacteristic of her early life, which had been structured simply on survival. Her effort can be compared with that of another woman of colour, Mrs Seacole, whose *Wonderful Adventures of Mrs Seacole in Many Lands*[17] had been published in 1858, one year before *Our Nig*, and was similarly written to raise much-needed money. Mrs Seacole was attempting to make good financial losses sustained in the Crimean War, for unlike Wilson she had devoted a life to commercial enterprise. She, like Wilson, was of mixed blood, having a Creole mother and a Scottish father. Born 'free' in 1805 into a Jamaica that supported an estimated population of 300,000 African slaves, as well as 60,000 free and enslaved 'coloured' people and between 20,000 and 30,000 Europeans, her mixed parentage limited the opportunities open to her. The Jamaican mulatto community was barred from voting, entering professions or inheriting large fortunes. Because the white ruling class feared the consequences of a possible alliance between the free coloured and the African slaves, as had happened when Haiti had struggled for their independence (gained in 1803), they jealously guarded the curbs placed on coloured advancement. As a result Jamaica evolved a strict class system with whites at the top, Africans at the bottom and the coloureds sandwiched in between.

This social organisation differs from that of the newly independent American colonies where any drop of black blood denoted black status. The strategy of the British colonisers in Jamaica, desirous of ensuring their safety from foreign attack or slave insurrection, was to form segregated militia units comprising coloureds and free blacks which served as an arm of the British army. In this manner the British were able to encourage an identification with the British colonial power as members of the British Empire. It is interesting to note, however, that when the 2nd West India regiment volunteered for service in the Crimean War their offer was rejected, just as was Mrs Seacole's offer to serve as a nurse, which tells us much about British racism.

It was into this West Indian society that Mrs Seacole was born and this explains her undoubted sense of being British. She followed her mother's occupation as hotelier, and learned from her the skills of tropical medicine, much of which had been brought to the Caribbean by African slaves. I think that Mrs Seacole's memoirs are important in that her adventures as root healer and entrepreneur establish her as the literary forebear of the enterprising capitalist adventurers from the Caribbean acknowledged by Paule Marshall as her West Indian ancestors. Like Silla Boyce in Marshall's *Browngirl, Brownstones*, Mrs Seacole kept a boarding house, having imbibed the self-help ethic considered essential for material success: 'Indeed, my experience of the world . . . leads me to the conclusion that it is by no means the hard, bad world which some selfish people would have us believe it' (Seacole, p. 60).

Clearly Wilson's and Seacole's perceptions of the world were very different. Seacole suggests that fortune favours the brave and hard-working and had no time for 'weakness'. Mrs Seacole diminishes her black blood in favour of the white. She condemns the slave system of America, yet gives no weight to the fact that British colonialists had held slaves in the West Indies. She attempts to distance herself from the slaves as 'niggers' at the same time as castigating white Americans who considered themselves 'superior' to herself. Mrs Seacole is in fact a perfect example of the contradictory impulses which are at war in the mulatta.

Mrs Seacole expresses pride in the West Indians who had rebelled against colonial rule to establish a republic. A century later Audre Lorde, another American descendant of West Indian ancestors who had migrated to the North American States, speaks of her own intense pride in her Grenadian forebears for the same reason. Indeed in her travels to New Grenada Mrs Seacole was full of admiration for the self-freed blacks of that island, who had been joined in their successful bid for independence by fugitive slaves from America, saying that, 'as they were generally superior men – evinced perhaps by their hatred of their old condition and their successful flight' (p. 100), they soon rose to positions of eminence. Those who ran for freedom were, in her eyes, 'superior' to those who did not. Presumably she considered that in her own ancestry there was the blood of African slaves of this 'superior' kind, for she is at pains to minimise the consequence of miscegenation. She avoids any reference to herself as negroid, preferring to describe herself as 'a little yellow' or 'brown'. When in London, seeking to join Nightingale's nurses, she is rejected in spite of her proven nursing skill, she yet refuses to believe that her colour could have been a factor in this decision. Nevertheless she could not have been unaware of British racism as she recounts how street urchins mocked herself and a friend in a London street. This, she explains, was because her friend had a darker complexion and so was 'a fair subject for their rude wit'. This expression of colorism is ridiculed by Hurston in the character of Mrs Turner in *Their Eyes Were Watching God*, as it is in Morrison's depiction of Geraldine in *The Bluest Eye*, yet clearly it is the inevitable result of an inscription of black inferiority upon which enslavement depended. The schizophrenic result of colorism is seen in Mrs Seacole, who rails against American women onboard ship in the Panama for refusing to share accommodation with her because of her colour, yet still seeks identification with them in her efforts to present herself as a Victorian Englishwoman.

Mrs Seacole is the product of the colonial impulse to exploit, an impulse that is strong in her and her family. Although barred from nursing in an official capacity in the Crimea, she sets up a business, 'Seacole and Day', to act as provisioner and hotel-keeper for officers at the front. She became a well-known figure in that war, reported by *The Times* war correspondent for her fearless ministering to soldiers wounded on the battlefield. However, peace left her business bankrupt, and Mrs Seacole's memoirs – addressed to British wives and mothers whose menfolk in the Crimea had known her as 'Mother Seacole' – are an attempt to cash in on her undoubted service as medical comforter to the British soldiers. Like Wilson, Mrs Seacole tried to sell her story; unlike Wilson, she succeeded. This perhaps illustrates the different backgrounds of the two women. Wilson's mixed parentage meant she would be forever deemed and treated as black in American society, whereas Seacole's was less disadvantageous to her in the West Indies. Seacole saw nothing wrong in claiming to be, as Hurston would have said, 'a rooster's egg'. She identifies herself as 'a Creole' with 'good Scottish blood coursing in my veins. My father was a soldier of an old Scotch family' (p. 55). To Mrs Seacole the adjectives of 'good' and 'old' mean 'superior'. Nevertheless she was an intrepid and enterprising woman, and Paule Marshall's depiction of the entrepreneurial skills of West Indian emigrants in Brooklyn can be identified with the same courageous spirit that informed Mrs Seacole. What Marshall warns against in her writing, is Mrs Seacole's denial of her blackness in order to live 'white'. Seacole, the 'Crimean heroine', spent the last twenty years of her life commuting between London and Jamaica, and died in modest luxury. A plaque can now be seen on the house in which she lived in George Street, Marylebone, bearing the legend 'Mary Seacole Crimean Nurse'. Her book cannot be seen as part of the anti-slavery tradition which fed the literary imagination of writers like Walker, Morrison and Angelou, but I suggest it is a useful introduction to the writing of black Americans of West Indian descent.

Our Nig and Mrs Seacole's text deal with the problem of the mulatta child, as does Frederick Douglass's autobiography, and all three emphasise that the very existence of the mulatta/o throws into question the notion of race itself. The 'tragic' mulatta who was the recurring subject of so much fiction, including Nella Larsen's *Passing* and *Quicksand* in the late 1920s, is the embodiment of the absurdity of racial construction. Such a protagonist was the vehicle chosen by the redoubtable campaigner for Abolition and later women's rights, Ellen Harper, in her novel *Iola Leroy or Shadows Uplifted*,[18] first published in 1893. So many years after Abolition Harper still resorts to the treatment of the mulatta as an indication of American attitudes to race. In her 'sentimental' novel Harper deconstructs the image of the black woman as someone less capable of delicate refinement than the white, in the figure of her heroine the mulatta Iola Leroy. Although brought up as a rich and privileged white woman, Iola is the daughter of a beautiful octoroon and former slave who was loved, freed and married by her white owner. On the death of Iola's father the legality of his wife's manumission is denied by his distant cousin who had disapproved of the match, and the widow and children are deemed to be slaves. This narrative strategy allows Harper to reveal the real horror of racism as Iola, removed from white into black society, has to confront the same sexual and social exploitation as so many black women. Experience is to change Iola's conception of slavery. We are told that 'Iola, being a Southern girl and a slave-holder's daughter, always defended slavery when it was under discussion' (p. 97). Her sudden change in status with the revelation of her mother's drop of black blood soon changes her attitude: 'I used to say that slavery is right. I didn't know what I was talking about' (p. 106). Using the sentimental novel as a vehicle in the knowledge that this mode of address was assured of a large white female audience, Harper enables the reader to confront the consequences of racism. Iola, who could have 'passed' for white, as can Nella Larsen's heroines, chooses to be black, but the necessity for choice exposes the illogicality of racial division. In her discussion of this novel Barbara Christian considers Harper's strategy of creating a black heroine who had believed herself to be white, as a clever one.[19] It allowed Harper the chance to interrogate racism, but perhaps the price paid by the novelist in this is that Iola emerges as a 'black' white woman, rather than a black one. Christian suggests that this results from the form chosen and the intended middle-class audience, both of which placed restraints upon the writer.

It is clear that black women in the nineteenth century were entering into literary discourse in a significant way, and that what they have left in the form of slave narratives, spiritual autobiographies, and early fictionalised life accounts provided a rich legacy for later writers. Yet the most pervasive of the shaping forces of black literature was surely that which was not recorded: the oral culture of a largely illiterate people. The richness of their dialect and the inventiveness in language and story-telling are detailed in the researches of Zora Neale Hurston, and are now integral in the writing of black women writers who use black language with pride and delight. The retrieved folklore and the music of the blacks are part of the fabric of their literary tradition and account for much of its distinctiveness. LeRoi Jones (Baraka)[20], in his work on Negro music, emphasises the input of music into the black literary tradition. Black music, he says, can be traced to the field holler, an African call and response that enabled field workers to communicate, or acted as a verbal autograph. The slaves also developed work songs that eased the burden of communal labour. When plantation economy disintegrated after the Civil War, and black plantation communities dissolved, the old work songs were an inadequate response to the changed situation, and gave way to the distinctive solo performance of the Blues. Whereas African songs recorded tribal events, American Blues expressed the sorrows and triumphs of the individual. The solitary black experience in which life is viewed as a difficult road, was the mainspring of the Blues, and this metaphor for experience was fed into literature. Hurston, whose work did much to retrieve black oral culture, reflects the influence of the Blues in her autobiography. Her tracks – sometimes difficult, often solitary, sometimes joyous – are always her own. Similarly, Alice Walker talks of wanting to find a prose style imitative of jazz music, improvisational and harmonious.[21] Altogether, music as a shaping force, as a source of solace and delight, is never far from the surface in the writing of Toni Morrison, Audre Lorde or Maya Angelou.

Arna Bontemps said of the literature of the Harlem Renaissance: 'it required apologies. It was not first rate, but it was an anticipation of what was to come'. The same can be said of the pioneering black voices that feed into the Harlem Renaissance. It is on those that the writers who came to dominance during the Harlem Renaissance drew for example and inspiration, and on which the ever-strengthening distinctiveness of a black female literary tradition has been built. In my next chapter I will go on to discuss some of the features of that time in Harlem that were both to encourage as well as to hamper the development of that tradition.

— 2 —

Harlem and the
First Black Renaissance

The abolition of slavery after the Civil War had not brought automatic acceptance of the black people into the family of white America. The war's cessation in 1865 was the point at which the blacks' struggle for their full participation in and enjoyment of the promises enshrined in the Declaration of Independence was begun in earnest. Various spokespeople for the American blacks emerged, the most notable of whom was Frederick Douglass. Born into slavery in 1818, and spending half of his life in that condition, Douglass was the first black leader to capture the respect and attention of white Americans, and he progressed to become a federal administrator and eventually Consul-General to Haiti before his death in 1895. His guiding ideal, pursued without compromise throughout his life, had been the assimilation of his people into American society by the assertion of their political rights. This was not facilitated during the post-war period of reconstruction when efforts to repair the devastated Southern economy were accompanied by a hardening of the Southern whites' attitudes towards blacks, expressed in the violence of Ku Klux Klan lynchings and a determined move to disenfranchise the emancipated Negro. Douglass died in 1895 with his dreams for his people unrealised and the mantle of black leadership fell on the shoulders of a younger man, Booker T. Washington, who believed that black social and economic improvement would come gradually and naturally through accommodation and compromise rather than self-assertion, and only if the blacks were educated.

In his ghosted autobiography, *Up From Slavery*, first published in 1901 (from which date it has never been out of print), Washington describes his own rise from a slave childhood begun in 1856, to an unlooked-for position as leader of his people. A man of prodigious determination and diligence, his rise to prominence came not through the pulpit or the legislature, but through an education at Hampton Normal Institute, a school for the industrial training of blacks, established and administered by a Northern ex-general of the Civil War. Having imbibed and embraced the self-help ethic of the Victorian Samuel Smiles on which Hampton was founded, Washington perpetuated it in his principalship of the Tuskegee Institute, which was the first industrial school for blacks to be run by a black man. His aim – to educate the freed black to fulfil a productive role in the reconstruction of the South – was a laudable one, although later leaders like W. E. B. DuBois and Alain Locke were to point to the self-set limitations of such an education, based as it was on transforming the black male at least into a tradesman and the black woman into a proficient laundress. Washington tirelessly sought white patronage as well as the donations of poor blacks to establish and maintain Tuskegee, confessing to 'a strong feeling that what our people most needed was to get a foundation in education, industry, and property, and for this I felt that they could better afford to strive than for political preferment' (*Up From Slavery*, p. 93). Tuskegee encouraged industry, self-reliance and a faith in the power of materialism which Washington astutely recognised as becoming the dominant creed in late nineteenth-century America. In Washington's system of education, the Puritan ethics of labour and thrift went hand-in-hand with the use of a toothbrush and regular bathing, as essential requirements for the Negro who was to make himself indispensable to a Southern community through his 'skill, intelligence and character' (p. 202). Washington was convinced that industrial education would enable the blacks to become 'fit' members of the larger, white society whose approval they would slowly win. His autobiography stresses that such a gradual improvement of his people's condition would reassure the Southern whites and secure friendly interracial relations. His was a policy of conciliation rather than confrontation taken to such an extent that of the Ku Klux Klan he could write at the turn of the century: 'Today there are no such organisations in the South, and the fact that such ever existed is almost forgotten by both races. There are few places in the South now where public sentiment would permit such organisations to exist' (p. 79). Such seeming sycophancy was the product of his determination to placate Southern hostility and so afford his people an opportunity and a space to acquire the skills he believed they needed for social and economic advancement. His address in 1895 to a mixed audience in Atlanta was a masterly exercise in verbal tightrope-walking, designed to encourage the blacks without alarming the whites. It was such a summation of his policy of conciliation that the whole of his speech is now known as 'The Atlanta Compromise'. In this very carefully manipulated address, whilst stressing the advantages to both black and white of an educated black people, he promised that 'In all things that are purely social we can be as separate as the fingers, yet one as the hand in all things essential to mutual progress'. What he seemed to be promising was an undemanding, unthreatening, segregated and submissive black people who would gradually earn, rather than demand as a right, their place in American society.

With hindsight it is easy to diminish Washington's real achievements in his role as race leader, and to describe his deference to whites as demeaning, but this would be to ignore the deftness of a political strategy that had succeeded in giving his people a sense of purpose and belief in their own potential which two centuries of slave experience had sapped and stifled. Inevitably his educational aims were limited by their tailoring to his own experience of the condition of the rural black in the South where Tuskegee was founded, and which could not satisfy the different demands made by life in the industrial North to which many blacks were attracted. Seeking an imagined opportunity for economic and political improvement in the expanding industrial cities of the North, many Southern blacks migrated there. In the early 1900s, those who flooded into New York followed the typical pattern of migrating groups, gravitating towards areas where people of their own culture have already established themselves. In New York that place was Harlem. Similar groupings of racially different communities are found in many European cities where migrants were initially welcomed as a convenient labour force. British society is changing under the impact of Commonwealth immigrants whose contribution has been recognised as not simply economic, but cultural. What we see is a struggle by immigrants to preserve their own culture as a sign of identity, this being a necessary step towards a multi-cultural society. However, the struggle of blacks born in America was different. Their need was to find an identity previously denied them. Harlem offered them a place to do this.

Nathan Huggins[1] describes the twenties in Harlem as 'a point of change' (p. 3). Certainly this time is identified with a burgeoning of black creativity in what has retrospectively become known as the

Harlem Renaissance, the vanguard of which was literary in nature. Harlem represented a spirit of advancement, at source motivated by the political impulse to improve the social position of all blacks, founded on a dream of possibilities rather than a cohesive creed. Artists, musicians and writers found in Harlem a climate congenial to their creative energy, and were encouraged by the philosophies of previous as well as emerging race leaders. As the demographic disposition of the American blacks changed in their move from agrarian to industrial occupations, so there was a plethora of often conflicting black voices advocating different routes to black self-expression and political power. The ideas of Booker T. Washington still commanded popular appeal, and his autobiography was a source of inspiration to his people, although even before his death in 1915 these ideas had been challenged and questioned by younger black intellectuals. In 1903 W. E. B. DuBois was to write:

> Mr Washington distinctly asks that black people give up, at least for the present, three things. –
> First, political power,
> Second, insistence on civil rights,
> Third, higher education of Negro youth, –
> and concentrate all their energies on industrial education, the accumulation of wealth, and the conciliation of the South.[2]

In 1905 W. E. B. DuBois founded the Niagara Movement which was dedicated to outspoken protest against racial injustice, the active pursuit of civil rights and an implicit rejection of the accommodationist impulse of Washington's philosophy. Although it started with only 250 members this movement marked a shift in political strategies for black advancement. By 1909 some of Washington's white allies had deserted him to join the Niagara Movement blacks in their formation of the National Association for the Advancement of Colored People, an organisation which Washington steadfastly refused to join. Clearly Washington's strategies could not be accommodated successfully into the political aims of the Northern, urban black.

On Washington's death, the banner he dropped was raised anew by Alain Locke, who proclaimed hopefully that blacks could be reborn, and take their rightful place in twentieth-century American society. Locke was one of the emerging political thinkers whose analysis of the new social structure which transformed rural blacks into urban, industrialised citizens, emphasised that in transplantation the Negro had been transformed. Removed from their place of Southern enslavement, the new Northern blacks sought a new social identity. Harlem afforded a space in which this self-definition could develop, and also gave black intellectuals and political leaders a chance to raise the consciousness of people drawn from all over the South. The concept of the 'New Negro' was born and articulated by Alain Locke who wrote in the periodical *The New Negro*, published in 1925, that 'the younger generation is vibrant with a new psychology; the new spirit is awake in the masses'.[3] This 'new' psychology focused on the problem of identity, recognising that blackness was not simply a colour, but a state of mind engendered by generations of institutionalised slavery given justification, sought from science and religion, by the supposed racial inferiority of blacks. The uprooting and replanting of Southern blacks into the expanding industrial centres in the North did not dispel white opinion that even the educated black was their racial or intellectual inferior. The blacks were relegated to the lowest socio-economic strata in American society, but even those black union leaders who foregrounded class rather than race as a determinant in their people's disadvantaged state, and advocated a joining with the white proletariat in the class struggle, were forced to recognise the racism of the equally dispossessed, poor whites. A. Philip Randolph sadly admitted that such a union was an impossible dream because 'Black America is a victim of both class and race prejudice and oppression'.[4] The continuance of slavery in the South had depended upon the assumption of the racial inferiority of blacks and, despite the work done by the anthropologist Franz Boas to show that environmental and not hereditary factors were cultural determinants, prejudice was deep-seated. It also survived by the denial of facts. White opinion was not to be changed by Boas who attacked the Jim Crow laws 'which are based simply upon public prejudice, without the shadow of knowledge of the underlying biological facts'.[5]

To disprove this inscription of black inferiority, black political leaders pointed to the black artists in Harlem as evidence of the mistaken white view. James Weldon Johnson was quick to grasp the propaganda potential of the Harlem writers, whom he charged with the serious task of re-educating white opinion:

> But these younger writers must not be mere dilettantes; they have
> serious work to do. They can bring to bear a tremendous force for

breaking down and wearing away the stereotyped ideas about the Negro, and for creating a higher and more enlightened opinion about the race.[6]

Johnson was convinced that art and propaganda were inextricably interrelated, a view with which today's literary critics who interrogate the canon – and question its validity as anything more than a perpetuation of vested interests – would not quarrel. He found support for his argument in W. E. B. DuBois, who urged the channelling of political energy into the arts. DuBois, along with other black intellectuals, subscribed to the idea of 'Negritude' as a celebration of the artistic and spiritual qualities of black Americans, which involved the recognition of experience encapsulated in black oral culture. Yet, conscious of white opinion, he wanted that oral tradition to be translated into a form that accorded with white cultural standards. Like many of the new black bourgeoisie, he did not want his people portrayed as 'low' characters. This attitude informed some black critics who rejected any unflattering depiction of the Negro. Arna Bontemps' novel *God Sends Sunday* was described by Alice Dunbar Nelson as having left a sour taste in her mouth, because 'The characters are low, loose in morals, frivolous in principles, and in many instances even criminal . . . Bontemps, undoubtedly has portrayed some ambitions of Negro life – but in my opinion Negro literature has not benefited thereby'.[7] The attitude expressed in this review suggests that in keeping with DuBois – who saw black art as one way of convincing the whites of the reality of black intellectual and imaginative power – Alice Dunbar Nelson's criticism was influenced by extra-aesthetic considerations. Houston A. Baker identifies this as being dependent upon race theories that when joined with 'the use of the word *culture* in a slanted manner have allowed Whites to state that Black men are part of an inferior race and possess no cultural capabilities'.[8] In truth, Alain Locke's concept of the 'New Negro' could only be realised if the artists were free to develop their own black aesthetic and not simply direct their efforts to achieving incorporation within dominant white culture. Black identity could not be affirmed if it entailed the rejection of the oral culture which was an expression of their shared experience, and which had been accorded no place of value within the dominant white culture – although Mark Twain's use of white vernacular in *Huckleberry Finn* had been acclaimed as an authentic American voice. According to Richard Ellison,[9] if black contribution to American culture was to be recognised, black artists needed to cherish, reclaim and build upon the oral culture which had preserved their sense of identity and self-esteem during their years of enslavement.

Searching for the roots that made their cultural inheritance unique, the Harlem Renaissance writers turned to the art and music of their African ancestors, in an effort to prove that the black American was not a cultural orphan. Some, like Hughes and Hurston, believed that the authenticity of their own voices depended upon their deliberate use of the hitherto 'non-literary' language and idiom of the blacks, as well as the standard English then associated with the literary. They argued that the exclusion from their writing of the particularly expressive use of English by black Americans would not only be a constraint upon their creativity, but also would give credence to the idea of white supremacy. Although hailed by Alain Locke as part of the 'talented tenth' of the black population whose responsibility it was to speak for the silenced majority, these writers resisted this idea of an artistic elite. At a time when 90 per cent of black Americans lived in poverty in the Deep South, the philosophy of the 'talented tenth' was not without dangers. The elevation of the intellectual above the ordinary person can lead to a separation of the artist from the roots of experience. In his article on 'The Negro Artist and the Racial Mountain' in *The Nation* in 1926, Langston Hughes warned that the 'urge within the race towards Whiteness' – to be as little Negro and as much American as possible – was a self-denying, suicidal aspiration. With Wallace Thurman and Zora Neale Hurston he founded a magazine called *Fire!* In this, Harlem writers voiced their resistance to white standardisation as well as their fears that art founded on a propagandist or elitist base would become vitiated. They, too, wanted the advancement of the Negro, yet at the same time attempted to resist an over-politicising of their work which could lead to the loss of personal recognition for themselves as individual artists. In the aforementioned article in *The Nation*, Hughes expressed the aims of these Harlem writers:

> We younger Negro artists who create now intend to express our individual dark-skinned selves, without fear or shame. If White people are pleased, we are glad. We know we are beautiful. And ugly too. . . .
> if colored people are pleased, we are glad. If they are not, their displeasure doesn't matter either. We build our temples for tomorrow, strong as we know how, and we stand on top of the mountain free within ourselves.[10]

In the same article, Hughes identified the double-bind in which the Harlem writers found themselves. They were constrained by political pressures from black leaders, and by their financial dependence upon white patrons. Hughes and Hurston both depended upon the financial assistance of a rich white woman, Mrs Osgood Mason. She gave money to support their writing; in return she insisted upon being called 'Godmother', as well as claiming editorial rights to their work. It is not surprising that in her autobiography Hurston refers to the Renaissance in Harlem as 'so-called'. The 'rebirth' was limited. In *The Big Sea*, Hughes describes the gradual appropriation of Harlem by whites coming in droves to the Cotton Club to listen to black musicians. Moneyed whites brought Jim Crow to the very heart of Harlem, 'flooding the little cabarets and bars where formerly only colored people laughed and sang, and where now the strangers were given the best ring-side tables to sit and stare at the Negro customers – like amusing animals in a zoo'.[11]

Arna Bontemps reminisced to the scholar Robert E. Hemenway about that particular period in black cultural history when black artists were 'shown off and exhibited and presented' to all sorts of white people.[12] The terms used here can be applied to valuable works of art, but also to freaks or performing animals. This feature of the Renaissance, when blacks were lionised and petted, illustrates the constraints under which the writers worked. As 'exhibits' they were 'owned', or at least controlled, by their own political leaders or by rich white patrons. What had begun in the Harlem of the 1920s as an exciting, vibrant explosion of black creativity, with the possibility of regeneration and self-definition, had become considerably muted by the mid-1930s. The race riots of 1935 were both an expression of black discontent and an acknowledgement that Booker T. Washington's dream of full and equal status for the blacks in American society was still just that – a dream.

Yet despite its constraints, the Harlem Renaissance was an important seed-bed for the black writers who came later. In that brief period, certain preoccupations and ideas took root that were seminal to the literature that followed. The Renaissance gave substance to Marcus Garvey's pronouncement that 'Black is beautiful'; it expressed a pride in a hitherto ignored black identity; it established a black aesthetic founded on suppressed and hitherto discounted Afro-American culture; it gave voice to a 'talented tenth' that included women as well as men. Of the women writers who came to prominence at that time, I have singled out Zora Neale Hurston for sustained discussion, believing that her efforts to record the richness of black life and culture were a significant advance in the development of a distinct literary tradition. She was not the only woman writer in Harlem, and she certainly shared with Nella Larsen a concern about the clash in cultures that Harlem witnessed. Like Larsen, Hurston pondered and explored the dilemma of the educated mulatta and her search for a meaningful place in American society; engaged with sexual and racial politics; and opened up the problematic area of the ambiguous nature of female sexuality. Both Hurston and Larsen came to prominence in Harlem within a literary milieu that was male dominated, and both had to combat the sexism and racism in their lives which they used as the stuff of their fictions. Both died in relative obscurity in the middle of this century. Larsen had abandoned a sustained career in writing and returned to nursing, after being accused of plagiarism in 1922, from the shock of which it is said she never recovered. Hurston, having combated in a court of law an accusation that she had sexually corrupted a juvenile, was still writing at the end of her life, although she was reportedly working as a chambermaid to survive financially. It is strange and sad that these women who had received so much early acclaim as writers, should have been forced eventually by adverse circumstances into the stereotypical roles of carer and cleaner to others which had been the lot of so many black women.

Unlike Jean Toomer, whose *Cane* was heralded as the black masterpiece of the Harlem Renaissance, Hurston never denied her allegiance to her own black people, and yet literary history was to silence her voice far more effectively than it did Toomer's. Perhaps Hurston's cynical dismissal of the black literati as the 'niggerati' is a significant comment, revealing her shrewd assessment of those intellectuals who were in danger of losing contact with the roots of black experience. I feel she deserves particular attention in this limited review because, above all else, her work is a sustained celebration of the rich inventiveness of black creativity and the will to survive which characterises much of the writing by black women who came later. Her engagement with the Harlem Renaissance was significant too, because it illustrated that her position as a black woman and aspiring writer was one of extreme vulnerability. In many ways she was like Booker T. Washington, whose strategies for survival in a white world she had learned well. She too was an accommodationist when it suited, and like him she would have one opinion for white consumption and another for black. She emerges as a complex, tragic and talented figure; a woman who had to combat the societal pressures exercised by class, race, gender and religion. Langston Hughes, her friend at that time, has left a personal record:

> Of this 'niggerati' Zora Neale Hurston was certainly the most amusing. Only to reach a wider audience, need she ever write books – because she is a perfect book of entertainment in herself. In her youth she was always getting scholarships and things from wealthy White people, some of whom simply paid her just to sit around and represent the Negro race for them, she did it in such a racy fashion. She was full of side-splitting anecdotes, humorous tales and tragicomic stories, remembered out of her life in the South as a daughter of a travelling minister of God, she could make you laugh one minute and cry the next. To many of her White friends, no doubt, she was a perfect 'darkie', in the nice meaning they gave the term – that is a naive, childlike, sweet, humorous and highly colored Negro. But Miss Hurston was clever too – a student who didn't let college give her a broad 'a' and who had a great scorn for all pretensions, academic or otherwise.[13]

Her laughter was remembered, but it was a laughter born of the pain of being poor, black and female.

—— 3 ——

Zora Neale Hurston
(b. 1891?/1901? – d. 1961)
The search for a black female self

In her article 'Looking for Zora'[1] Alice Walker uncovers the perplexing circumstances of Zora Neale Hurston's final years spent in St Lucie County Welfare Home in Florida, and her eventual burial by public subscription in an unmarked grave. Walker's discovery of Hurston's years of impoverishment and institutionalised living is particularly surprising considering that Hurston was the most productive Afro-American woman writer of her time. Her published material includes two collections of folklore, four novels, over a dozen short stories, one libretto for a folk-opera, two original musicals, numerous magazine articles, and an autobiography. As Toni Cade Bambara points out in her introductory remarks to Hurston's *The Sanctified Church*, 'Now there was a woman who worked'.[2] Her writing career spanned a quarter of a century, and yet Walker refers to her as 'one of the most significant unread authors in America'.

Until she embarked on a university course in black literature, where she found Hurston's name appended like a 'verbal footnote' to the 'illustrious all-male list' that constituted the body of the syllabus, Walker had been unaware of Hurston's work. The question immediately raised by Walker's memory of this is what had happened to allow Hurston to all but disappear from the conscious awareness of her own people? Could it be possible that she was in fact a minor talent undeserving of critical attention? Had her writing possessed significance only for her contemporaries? Yet Walker's own importance within the black female literary tradition demands a respect that makes us hesitate to reject the praise she affords Hurston as a writer, as does the epitaph Walker composed for inscription on the headstone she erected in her memory. It reads:

Zora Neale Hurston
'A Genius of the South'
Novelist Folklorist
Anthropologist
1901   1960

The reasons for previous critical neglect of Hurston can be found in the underrepresentation of women in general and the marginalisation of black writers in particular, within the American literary canon. Her determined retrieval of the lore and language of her people, whose cultural contribution had gone largely ignored by dominant white society, and her use of black dialect and mythology in her creative writing, offered a direct challenge to that canon. In *Shadow and Act*,[3] the protest novelist Ralph Ellison suggests that folklore is valuable both as a mediating agent between the folk and the harsh reality of their experience, and as a basis for creative writing. Hurston's anthropological fieldwork had brought her to the same conclusion and had made her examine how best she could fulfil her aspirations as both scholar and artist. Had she never trained as an anthropologist, the folk material known to her from the 'earliest rocking' of her cradle would still have been accessible to her. Inevitably some commentators, who perceived a conflict between academic study and artistic retrieval of that material, criticised her dual approach. On both counts Hurston encountered partisan criticism. In particular, she was accused of exploiting folklore to further her career as a writer. However, Hemenway in his insightful and sympathetic literary biography of Hurston,[4] argues that no such conflict was experienced by Hurston for whom a line between fiction and folklore could not be drawn. Her anthropological study proved that the rich complexity of black oral culture could stand examination through the 'spy-glass' of anthropology, and gave her the analytical tools needed to investigate the process of myth-making. Hurston was to put her findings to use in her writing, in which she began to deconstruct myths about religion, race and gender which had contributed to the negative socialisation of black men and, in particular, women.

Only now, as the result of twenty years of black feminist critical research, has Hurston been retrieved from critical oblivion, and the importance of her contribution to the tradition of black women's writing recognised. That she possessed more than a minor talent as a writer is revealed in a careful examination of her work, a record of which, as well as an insight into her life, one might expect to find in her autobiography *Dust Tracks on a Road*.[5] This work, despite the many delights to be found there, is also infuriatingly ambiguous and evasive. It is a tense, uneven text, full of contradictory, unresolved impulses, leading Walker to describe it as 'the most unfortunate thing Zora ever wrote' (*In Search of*, p. 91). One exasperating feature of Hurston's autobiography is the apparent sycophancy of her attitude towards white patrons, or indeed white readers – attitudes which become less contemptible when contextualised. She has to be seen as a remarkable product of her times. A poor black girl from a motherless home, she struggled to win an education, and learned through experience that her career could be made or marred by white people. Hurston's battle to 'wrassle me up a future' involved her in a struggle with internalised contradictions exacerbated by racism in America, and sexism amongst the blacks. The exasperating ambiguities these pressures produced are at the root of all her writings, and generated the same ongoing productive ferment which provided the dynamics of black folklore:

> Negro folk-lore is not a thing of the past. It is still in the making. Its great variety shows the adaptability of the black man: nothing is too old, or too new, domestic or foreign, high or low, for his use. (*S. Ch.*, p. 56)

Substitute 'Zora Neale Hurston' for 'black man' and we have an account of the process that produced Hurston the writer. It would be unfair now to blame her for the strategies she employed in the pursuit of her ambitions. After all, she did not write in a vacuum. As a woman and a writer, she was the product of the black experience shaped by the pressures exerted by race, class, religion and gender. This last factor might explain something of her decline in popularity as a writer, as her contemporary male critics expressed little sympathy for her aims or preoccupations. Similarly, her awareness of her position as an Afro-American daring to find voice in a society with Jim Crow laws, must at times have caused her to err on the side of caution when the issue of race arose.

Hemenway's biography consistently points to the conflict Hurston perceived between her claim for individuality and her strong racial pride. *Dust Tracks* is a tragic illustration of how these two urges fragmented Hurston. In her autobiography she remembers the advice of her white friend, after whom she had been called 'Neale', not to 'be a nigger': 'I knew without being told that he was not talking about my race when he advised me not to be a nigger. He was talking about class rather than race' (p. 43).

Hurston knew that to 'be a nigger' was to be uneducated, poor, underprivileged and segregated from the mainstream of white American society. Although Hurston had been born into the unique all-black town of Eatonville, which she recalls with pride, she knew that to be born black in America was a disadvantage. Consciousness of the inscription of power, privilege and white aesthetics in dominant white society is perhaps reflected in her childhood fantasies about the doll she had improvised from a corn-cob. 'Miss Corn Shuck', as Hurston called her, was a desirable, marriageable love-object with the long, straight, yellow hair thought by the young Hurston to be an essential ingredient in female beauty. In her article, 'A Black Feminist's Search for Sisterhood',[6] Michelle Wallace describes how she and her own sister would, when playing, cover their black braids with a long, trailing scarf, pretending that it was long, straight hair: 'There was a time when I would have called that wanting to be white, yet the real point of the game was being feminine. Being feminine *meant* being white.'

Wallace's own memory perhaps illuminates Hurston's early perception of self which she shared with other black women, the majority of whom, like her, lived in the Southern States where there still persisted the peculiar ideal of womanhood originating from eighteenth-century plantation society. Barbara Christian describes what this entailed for a Southern 'lady': 'She was expected to be beautiful in an ornamental way, chaste, pious, married and eventually a mother. She was obviously, white: a respectable woman, she did not work.'[7]

This ideal of Southern womanhood established a standard to which white women might aspire as a norm, but from which all black women were excluded. Theirs had been a history of sexual abuse, they certainly had had to work and, judged by a white aesthetic, they could not even be deemed beautiful. Clearly Hurston, in common with other Afro-Americans, had an image of self composed of a myriad of negative perceptions, all of which she took with her when she went to New York in 1925.

In Harlem she established herself as a 'character', a vivid member of the group that included Langston Hughes. In spite of lasting estrangement resulting from a sad quarrel between Hughes and

Hurston, she kept faith with the confidence in their jointly proclaimed artistic intentions: 'We know we are beautiful and ugly too . . .'[8] In her own writing Hurston reveals both the beauty and the ugliness of her people – and herself – and by locating most of her fiction within black communities, resists what she felt could be a burdensome necessity of engaging in the race war: 'Negroes were supposed to write about the Race Problem. I was and am thoroughly sick of the subject. My interest lies in what makes a man or a woman do such-and-so, regardless of his color' (*Dust Tracks*, p. 38). This defiant assertion springs more from hope than experience, and illustrates the paradox in Hurston that complicates our understanding of her. As a student of anthropology she had become associated with the world of 'high culture'. Although her background had given her first-hand knowledge of a living black culture, she had been opened to white middle-class values by virtue of the acculturation that is part of the education process. This combination made her unique amongst her Harlem peers. Acknowledging that the source of her creativity lay in her folk-heritage, her artistic aim was to reconcile the 'high' culture of the educated black with the rich, oral, but 'low' culture of her people. In the collection and dramatic presentation of the folk-tales Hurston learned – as well as revealed – much about herself. Particularly, as Hemenway says, she realised that 'the type of reportorial precision required of the scientific folk-lorist bored Hurston' (*ZNH*, p. 101). This does not diminish the value of the folklore, but it convinced Hurston that her real interests lay in the field of creative writing. In this she was determined to keep inviolate her individual artistic integrity, at the expense of the minimising of the importance of racial identity. Her initial success as a Harlem writer came when she won a prize for her story 'Drenched in Light' (later reprinted as 'Isis' in *Spunk: The Selected Stories of Zora Neale Hurston* – see Bibliography, p. 257), which expresses her belief that to be female, poor and black was *not* an automatic tragedy. To have admitted anything other would have been to accept defeat before she had even started on a career. The spirit of this story, which is a constant in her writings, confirms her faith in the power of the individual. This individualism, however, was focused on as a weakness by those who felt she neglected the race problem.

Yet without question both Hurston's academic success and her writing career sprang from her exploration of the culture of rural black community life. Her original intention as a student at Barnard

College was to major in literature, but her excellence as a student of anthropology persuaded her to pursue academic study in that subject. Undoubtedly a factor in that decision was the tutelage of the renowned anthropologist Franz Boas, who fired her with both an enthusiasm for the subject and a commitment to his own stance as a cultural anthropologist. Hemenway recounts how she idolised Boas and referred to him as 'the greatest anthropologist alive' (*ZNH*, p. 63). Perhaps the extravagance of this claim can be explained by reference to the theoretical basis of Boas's anthropological work, which, although contentious, was appealing to a young black American. The polyglot population of North America had afforded Boas a rare opportunity to pursue anthropological interests which included the study of language, folklore and miscegenation. He concluded that racial groups could not be differentiated on the grounds of intelligence, personality or emotional stability, and proposed that racial discrimination was founded on social, not genetic factors:

> No matter how weak the case for racial purity might be, we understand its social appeal in our society. Whilst biological reasons that are adduced may not be relevant, a stratification of society in social groups that are racial in character will always lead to racial discrimination. As in all other sharp social groupings, the individual is not judged as an individual, but as a member of his class.[9]

Boas's approach to anthropological study was an holistic one, stressing the need to understand a group's culture, and as such must have been compelling to Hurston, herself a member of a socially deprived group. It might also have given further fostering to her demand to be regarded as an individual, rather than as a member of that group.

With Boas's encouragement, Hurston set out to collect the oral folklore of rural blacks, no doubt bearing in mind her tutor's teachings about the importance of such an undertaking as 'the source(s) of a true interpretation of human behaviour' (Boas, *Race*, p. 258). Hemenway describes how 'She [Hurston] believed that an aesthetically oriented black subculture provided a striking contrast to the imaginative wasteland of white society' (*ZNH*, p. 162). Hurston believed her mission was to retrieve the black oral subculture which was the living triumph of her people over white oppression. Embodied in their Blues, spirituals, 'lying', sermons and folk-tales

was an expression of racial and cultural health. Hurston feared that
this would be undermined if white Americans were allowed to extend
their colonisation into black culture, a process already in operation
with the appropriation of jazz and Blues musicians. The white
cultivation of an 'exotic primitivism' in Harlem, which sometimes
Hurston played up when it suited her, was nevertheless an
interference she resented. She had seen how even the most spiritual
of black experiences had been diluted for public performances for
whites: 'Glee clubs and concert singers put on their tuxedoes, bow
prettily to the audience, get the pitch and burst into magnificent song
– but not *Negro* Song' (*ZNH*, p. 56). Hurston wanted to halt this
process of cultural appropriation and dilution. Accordingly, as Toni
Cade Bambara says in her introduction to *The Sanctified Church* (see
Note 2), Hurston's writing put into practice the theoretical
underpinning of the Harlem Renaissance: that all great art is founded
upon the 'fecundating matrix' of folk-art. Bambara claims that
Hurston never ever cut those critical ties with the 'lowly down under'.

Although young and untried as either an anthropologist or a writer,
Hurston recognised that the value of black folklore lay in its
distinctiveness from white culture. An illuminating discussion of this
is to be found in Houston A. Baker's *Long Black Song*.[10] He says that
whereas white American culture is characterised by stories of pioneers
and the frontier, of which blacks were never a part, black lore was
engendered and shaped by slavery. He argues that the enslaved
Africans welded into a new race in America, as separate tribal
identities were dissolved, merged and found expression in a culture
which had evolved from shared American experience. This opinion
is endorsed by Richard Dorson in *Negro Folk-Tales in Michigan*:

> United States Negro tales form a distinctive repertoire separate from the
> narratives of west Africa, the West Indies, Europe, the British Isles and
> White America. Southern negroes have drawn upon all these lores, and
> added materials from their own environment and experience, to pro-
> duce a highly diversified and culturally independent folk-tradition.[11]

Black scholars have identified three main types of stories within black
folk-culture, concerning animals, trickster slaves and ghosts. Each of
these is fully represented in Hurston's collection *Mules and Men*,[12]
and as genres they are in no way unusual. Animal tales are prevalent
in any folklore where primitive peoples are trying to make sense out
of the natural world. There is an abundance in most cultures of folk

heroes whose exploits the underprivileged applaud. Ghost stories satisfy a psychological need that is not peculiar to black people. Nevertheless, the interest of the stories collected by Hurston is in their inscription of the distinctiveness of the black experience in America. As such, the animal stories are more than explanations of physical phenomena, and can be seen as sly and subversive expressions of how the enslaved Africans felt in an alien world. Particularly significant are the stories about rabbits whose only means of defence are alertness and speed. J. Mason Brewer in *American Negro Folklore*[13] suggests that the hare of African folklore stories is translated into the rabbit in Afro-American tales:

> The animal tales told by Negro slaves with Brer Rabbit as the hero have a meaning far deeper than mere entertainment. The rabbit actually symbolised the slave himself. Whenever the rabbit succeeded in proving himself smarter than another animal the slave rejoiced secretly.

The smart rabbit capable of outwitting physically superior animals takes on huge and palpable form in the many stories about John, or Jack, and 'Ol' massa' that emerged after the Civil War. This cycle is characterised by a contest between John and his master in which John succeeds in making his master look foolish and at the same time wins his own freedom. In many of the 'John' stories collected by Hurston the teller begins with the assertion that 'Ol' massa lakted John' whom he regarded as a 'pet nigger', and upon whose affection John plays for his own ends. Yet not all of these stories present a reciprocal affection from the slave, and many embody rejection of white paternalism. One such tells how John was rewarded with freedom for saving Ol' massa's children from drowning. As he is freed by a reluctant owner John leaves the plantation with his erstwhile master's voice ringing in his ears:

> Fur as John could hear 'im down de road he was hollerin' 'John, oh John! De children loves you. And I love you. De Missy *like* you'. John would holler back, 'Yassuh'. 'But member youse a nigger, tho'. Ole massa kept callin' 'im and his voice was pitiful. But John kept on steppin' to Canada. (*M&M*, p. 98)

As a story set in slavery times, but recounting post-bellum experience, the hollowness of the supposed freedom is in 'member youse a nigger'. The incipient sexual fear is found in the master's expression of love, but the admonition that 'Missy' only *likes* John. Such stories destroy any notion that the emancipated slave was naive enough to believe unreservedly the Abolitionists' promises of equality under Recon-struction. Above all, John, a product and survivor of enslavement, knows he cannot trust the white man. This mistrust is revealed in Cliff's tale about the rabbit who was unconvinced by the dog's assurance of safety because the dogs' convention had passed a law stating that rabbits would be unmolested. Perhaps there is a veiled reference to the Ku Klux Klan in the rabbit's observation, 'Yeah, but all de dogs ain't been to no convention' (*M&M*, p. 119).

Just as many of the stories are expressions of wish fulfilment, so some have encoded apocalyptic futures for oppressors. Such is the one that explains how the alligator, once 'pure white all over', becomes black. One of Hurston's contributors, Big Sweet, recounts how this transformation results from an encounter with Brer Rabbit who was always bemoaning his 'trouble'. Asked by the alligator to explain what 'trouble' was, the rabbit persuades the alligator to venture on to land, where the rabbit lights a fire:

De 'gator run from side to side, round and round. Way after a while he broke thru and hit de water 'ker ploogum'. He got all cooled off but he had done got smoked all up befo' he got to de water, and his eyes is all red from de smoke. And dat's how come a 'gator is black today – cause de rabbit took advantage of him lak dat. (*M&M*, p. 116)

There is particular significance in the reference to fire in the light of the blacks' constantly reiterated faith in 'Fire next time'. One day the whites will be overturned and they will know for certain 'Dat's trouble'. Even the ghost and 'han't' stories recounted were significant to the enslaved, for they owe as much to African sympathetic magic as to any belief in life after death. Not surprisingly, people whose destinies are controlled by others will enlist the aid of magic to help them to control events. In this way Ol' Massa's maiden sister Miss Pheenie can be miraculously transformed into a 'squinch owl', and animals can talk.

Hurston emphasised in her introduction to *Mules and Men*, published in 1935 but containing materials collected between 1928 and 1931, that she did not collect as an outsider: 'From the earliest rocking of my cradle, I had known about the capers Brer rabbit is apt to cut and what the Squinch Owl says from the house top' (p. 3). She was, however, a pioneer in that she was the first black scholar to attempt such an undertaking. Armed with a degree in anthropology, she set out in the footsteps of previous white collectors. Her advantage over her white predecessors was that she as a black woman would be better able to represent black values. These had not been the concern of the most famous of these collectors, Joel Chandler Harris, who in 1880 had published *Uncle Remus: His songs and sayings*,[14] in which the narrator was a creation of the collector. As Arthur Huff Fauset demonstrates in his essay on 'The New Negro' in *The New Negro Renaissance*,[15] Uncle Remus is a white projection of an unthreatening avuncular black man who is a stereotypical faithful, ante-bellum black retainer, child-like and dependent. So powerful is this characterisation of Uncle Remus that he survived to be immortalised by Walt Disney in the film 'Song of the South'. Alice Walker recalls how she and her siblings hated that film because an old black man was telling 'their' stories to white children.

Hurston rightly doubted the effectiveness of any white person's efforts to collect stories which were never intended for white consumption, because 'They all got a hidden meanin' jus' like de Bible. Everybody can't understand what they mean' (*M&M*, p. 134). Moreover, as Hurston herself was to admit, 'folk-lore is not so easy to collect as it sounds'. The complete physical domination of the Africans in slavery had produced in them a fierce determination to keep the domain of the mind and imagination intact. If, as has been argued, the value of these stories was that they kept alive a sense of black identity and pride in the face of adversity, it was unlikely they would willingly surrender them to non-blacks. Hurston explains this in her introduction to *Mules and Men*:

> The theory behind our tactics: 'the white man is always trying to know into somebody else's business. All right, I'll set something outside the door of my mind for him to play with and handle. He can read my writing but he sho' can't read my mind'. (*M&M*, p. 5)

Although she identifies herself with the tale-tellers in the reference to 'our' tactics, she also knew that as an educated black she was already set apart from the ongoing experience of rural black people. Wherever she went in search of folk-tales she had to overcome the suspicion and win the confidence and acceptance of the community. Her anthropological scholarship had taught her that the study of a culture involved more than its literary and visual artefacts, but should encompass a whole way of life. She saw herself acting as historian and artist, whose duty it was to represent the dramatic articulation of the contributors. In her letter to Franz Boas asking him to introduce *Mules and Men* she begged his forbearance that her approach had not been purely scientific. This acknowledgement illuminates a dichotomy at the root of her endeavours, and leads us to question whether Hurston the anthropologist was going to be subordinated to Hurston the creative writer. Her first attempts at fieldwork had not been successful, and Hemenway records how Boas had advised her 'particularly to pay attention, not so much to content, but rather to the form of diction, movements and so on' (*ZNH*, p. 91). Nevertheless Boas gave *Mules and Men* his formal approval by writing the introduction, saying in it that Hurston's collection 'throws into relief . . . the peculiar amalgamation of African and European traditions which is so important for understanding historically the character of American Negro life'. He knew that *Mules and Men* was intended to be a popular book and not an analytical anthropological study. Hurston had discovered that without the narrative framework she provided for the tales, publishers had found the collection 'monotonous'. To achieve the 'atmosphere' for her collection she devised a framework which is as informative about the life and culture of the rural blacks as are the tales themselves. She offers no analysis or theoretical explanations of these tales, preferring to 'show' rather than to 'tell', and allows the stories to speak for themselves. To enhance their dramatic impact she presents them in a coherent arrangement in which the tales appear to be prompted by actual situations, so that when for instance a marital quarrel seems to be brewing, a story about the balance of power between the sexes is inserted.

   Black writers who have followed Hurston and who have expressed a debt to her for the retrieval of their oral culture, assert that in *Mules and Men* she captures the richness of black imagination and idiom in the reported conversations with individual storytellers, which is thrown into greater relief by the formal register of the narrative exposition. Hurston's paper on the 'Characteristics of Negro Expression', written in 1930 and published in the journal *Negro* in 1934, acknowledges her people's gift for mimicry but repudiates the then current belief that the intellectual inferiority of the black limited them simply to imitation of whites. Her observations on the complexity and inventiveness of Negro expression refute the assumption that the Afro-Americans' language is evidence of their inability to master a complex Western language. In *Mules and Men* her named narrators, who delight in linguistic exercise, deconstruct the literary stereotype of the eye-rolling, infantile 'darkie'. That the

African slave was aware of the power of language invested in naming, is demonstrated in a story about the euphemistic explanation of naming by a master to his slave. The slave is told the fire is a 'flame vaperator', a bed a 'flowery bed of ease', the stairs a 'jacob ladder', a barn a 'mound', a donkey 'July, de God dam', and the cat 'a round head'. When a fire erupted, the slave roused his master, explaining the situation with the words he had been taught to use, and is not understood. Exasperated, John, who was 'gittin tired', said:

> 'Aw, you better git up out dat bed and come down stairs. Ah done set dat ole cat afire and he run out to de barn and set it afire and dat ole Jackass is eatin' up everything he get his mouf on.' (*M&M*, p. 86)

Such a story could not emanate from a linguistically unsophisticated people.

Hurston's paper on Negro expression explains how the blacks, deprived of a written language, vivified their nouns by the affixing of an 'action' word, as in 'cookpot', 'sitting chair', and created new verbal nouns such as 'jooking' and 'bookooing'.[16] She notes their facility for intensifying descriptions by double descriptions such as 'kill-dead', 'high-tall', 'little-tee-nichy', and the vivid amalgamations of 'knee-bent' and 'body-bowed', as well as their invention of new words like 'bodacious' and 'schronchuns', all of which are to be found in *Mules and Men*. She ascribes this richness to the Afro-Americans' 'will to adorn', which characterised their language as it did the humblest of their dwellings. Hurston describes the blacks' interpretation of English as a pictorial one, making full use of simile and metaphor usually drawn from the natural world. The vividness and humour of the language is seen in Big Sweet's threat to her philandering lover that she intends to 'take my Tampa switch-blade knife, and Ah'm goin round de hambone lookin' for a meal' (*M&M*, p. 147), or the dismissal of Gene by Gold: 'Aw, shut up, Gene. You ain't no big hen's biddy if you do lay gobbler eggs. You tryin' to talk like big wood when you ain't nothin' but brush' (*M&M*, p. 26).

Alice Walker believes that Hurston does more than simply affirm that the rural blacks have their own culture, for in her foreword to Hemenway's biography of Hurston, Walker claims to be 'soothed by her [Hurston's] assurance that she was exposing not simply an adequate culture but a superior one' (p. xi).

The lyrical beauty of black language is displayed in their sermons, two of which are recorded in *Mules and Men*. In her study of sermons delivered by black preachers, Hurston notes how they are free of dialect expressions. In *The Sanctified Church* she says of black worship, 'The truth is, that the religious service is a conscious art expression', and that 'In the mouth of the Negro the English language loses its stiffness yet conveys its meaning accurately' (*S. Ch.*, p. 8). Pa Henry's prayer at Eatonville illustrates the simple dignity of such expression:

> 'You cut loose my stammerin' tongue; You established my feet on de rock of salvation and yo' voice was heard in rumblin' judgement. I thank thee that my last night's sleepin' couch was not my coolin' board and my cover was not my windin' sheet.' (*S. Ch.*, p. 28)

Intent upon conveying the ritualised and dramatic experience of the sermon, she notes in *The Sanctified Church* that the black preacher *performed* his sermon:

> The well known 'Ha!' of the Negro preacher is a breathing device. It is the tail end of the expulsion just before inhalation. Instead of permitting the breath to drain out, when the wind gets too low for words, the remnant is expelled violently. (*S. Ch.*, p. 82)

The sermon of the itinerant preacher who arrives in Polk County exemplifies both this method of delivery and the rich texture of the language:

> 'Look at dis woman God done made,
> But first thing, ah hah!
> Ah wants you to gaze upon God's previous works.
> Almighty and arisen God, hah!
> Peace-giving and prayer-hearing God,
> High riding and strong armded God
> Walking acrost his globe creation, hah!
> Wid de blue elements for a helmet
> And a wall of fire round his feet
> He wakes de sun every morning, from his fiery bed
> Wid de breath of his smile.' (*M&M*, p. 148)

We can *hear* the preacher in this sermon as well as see him with his travelling bag and 'dog-eared' bible as he slowly commands the attention of the people. The concentrated epithets 'high riding' and 'strong armded' portray a God who is presented vividly as an elemental warrior king. He 'molds' the mountains, 'melts' the skies into oceans. This God is not abstracted out of existence as He is in

Milton's *Paradise Lost*, but is a palpable and visible entity without being diminished in the process.

In her autobiography, *Dust Tracks on a Road*, Hurston recalls her childhood delight, relived in *Mules and Men*, when she lingered on Joe Clarke's porch to hear the stories and 'capping' of the townspeople. One does not have to be black to smile at the hyperbolic exaggeration of 'ugliness' in Clifford Ulmer's statement that 'Ah knowed one so ugly till you could throw him in the Mississippi river and skim ugly for six months' (p. 73). The delight for the reader, and we assume for the speakers, is in the knowledge that the whole purpose of a 'lie' was to overtop another in inventiveness. As such, no one could ever presume to designate the black American as 'inferior' in verbal wit or imagination. Nor, as Hurston presents them, do these exchanges emanate from two-dimensional characters. The reader is encouraged into a shared intimacy with people we have no doubt actually lived. Hurston gives them all 'a local habitation and a name': 'Yes, there was George Thomas, Calvin Daniels, Jack and Charlie Jones, Gene Brazzle, B. Moseley and "Seaboard". . . . Mutt . . . and Ellis. . . . her husband whose house stands under the huge camphor tree on the front street' (*M&M*, p. 9).

She began researching in her home town of Eatonville where she knew that, as 'Lucy Hurston's daughter', she would encounter less hostility to her project. Her pride in her home town is conveyed in her determination to present the Eatonville community as whole and healthy. She notes that nearby Woodbridge is different: 'It is lacking in Eatonville's feeling of unity. In fact a white woman lives there' (*M&M*, p. 15). Hurston rejects the notion that there is a phenomenon called 'The Negro' and portrays the townspeople as individuals who love, quarrel and gossip just as do whites: 'She and Bennie were step-brother and sister and they had had a lawsuit over the property of his late father and her late mother, so a very little of Bennie's sugar would sweeten Shug's tea and vice versa' (*M&M*, p. 40). The stresses and strains of personal relationships are captured in this 'between-story' conversation, convincing the reader of the actuality of the storytellers.

By adopting the role of mediator between narrators and readers, Hurston describes a whole way of life in the community of which she had been a part. To win confidence and to elicit stories she asks questions about customs she probably knew about, for the benefit of the reader. The Woodbridge 'tea party' is an example. She describes in detail the party food; the practice of sending an envoy to ask a girl to dance; the 'coon-dick' alcohol; the music; tense card games and party clothes. This perhaps is why *Mules and Men* had a mixed reception. Critics complained that Hurston was doing nothing to reveal the misery or economic privation of the blacks. Sterling Brown in particular felt that 'the portrait of the South was incomplete' and he concluded '*Mules and Men* should be more bitter: it would be nearer the total truth' (*ZNH*, p. 219). But this attack is to ignore two facts: firstly, that Hurston had no desire to show her people 'down' in spirit, although she noted at a party that, 'I looked about and noted the number of bungalow aprons and even the rolled down paper bags on the heads of several women' (*M&M*, p. 69). The other fact is that these parties would occur on weekend pay-days, and her most profitable collecting time would be at leisure-hours gatherings. Her decision not to show the misery which is the lot of any economically deprived group, black or white, was a deliberate one. In *Mules and Men* she celebrates the unquenchable spirit of her people, who had survived and overcome the inhumanity of their enslaved American past. She rejoices in their capacity to sing, dance, eat, drink and laugh wherever and whenever possible, but rejects the stereotype of the Negro who laughs foolishly. Laughter, she says, was often a defence mechanism:

> The brother in black put a laugh in every vacant place in his mind. His laugh has a hundred meanings. It may mean amusement, anger, grief, bewilderment, chagrin, curiosity, simple pleasure or any other of the known or undefined emotions. (*M&M*, p. 67)

Many of the tales she collected reveal the blacks' ability to laugh at themselves – always a sign of the psychic health of people who have kept alive a sense of beauty and hope. We laugh with and not at them.

Hurston portrays her Eatonville female storytellers' 'will to adorn' in their desire to beautify their environment. Alice Walker recalls that whenever her own mother moved house she always took her purple petunias, and Hurston is remembered for her own desire for a garden of flowers. In *Mules and Men* the storyteller Bertha Allen is determined to keep her yard 'raked'.[17] Although not a foregrounded feature in Hurston's re-creation of Eatonville, there is a subtext which reveals much about the role of the women as cooks, cleaners and beautifiers in a community life which is organised around specific gender roles. We see that Mrs Allen loses out to her menfolk who prefer to go fishing rather than help her in the hard work of 'raking'.

Mrs Allen is too 'correct' to join them. Only Big Sweet, liberated by her determination to take what she can from life, goes fishing: 'Lemme tell *you* something, *any* time Ah shack up wid any man Ah gives myself de privilege to go wherever he might be, night or day. Ah got de law in my mouth' (*M&M*, p. 134).

There are many exchanges between men and women which reveal tensions in the relations between the sexes, particularly about the amount and nature of the work that each did, but in the rural society described there was no gender distinction in who could carry flick-knives. Women were prepared to engage men in physical as well as verbal battle, though the latter was usually sufficient. In the women Hurston depicts is revealed the same independence of spirit that characterised many of the female slave narratives, and she shows how they were prepared to challenge male dominance. An imagined exchange between Gene Brazzle and the woman Shug illustrates this. Gene says:

> 'Get off of us mens now. We *is* some good. Plenty good too if you get de right one. De trouble is you women ain't good for nothin' exceptin' readin' Sears and Roebuck's bible and hollerin' 'bout gimme dis and gimme dat as soon as we draw our pay.'
> [To which Shug's reply is:] 'Well, we don't git it by askin' you mens for it. If we work for it we kin git it. You mens don't draw no pay. You don't do nothin' but stand around and draw lightnin'.' (*M&M*, p. 26)

Hurston demonstrates that whilst the women recognise and sympathise with the men's inferior economic status in American society, they object to their sexism. Perhaps aping the white society, where men were 'bosses', the men were in danger of losing sight of the part played and suffered in their history by their women. In Angela Davis's *Women, Race and Class*, published in 1981,[18] the importance that black women had assumed during slavery is assessed:

> Precisely through performing the drudgery which has long been a central expression of the socially conditioned inferiority of women, the Black woman in chains could help to lay the foundation for some degree of autonomy both for herself and her men. Even as she was suffering under her unique oppression as a female, she was thrust into the centre of the slave community. She was, therefore, essential to the *survival* of the community. (p. 17)

In *Mules and Men*, eighty years after Abolition and fifty years before Davis's text, the black woman reminds the men that she had earned her right to their respect. Without theorising about it Hurston tacitly acknowledges the reality of sexual politics and was at pains to have no direct involvement in them.

Her neutrality is tested in Polk County where the men gather to look her over as a new 'addition', and the women see her as a potential rival for male attention. She claims that to allay suspicion and to meet approval, she passed herself off as a bootlegger on the run, a claim telling us something of Hurston the writer and woman. This assumed persona both adds suspense to the narrative framework and throws around Hurston a glamorous aura to which she was not averse. She admits to having flirted with the men – 'because of my research methods I had dug in with the male community' (*M&M*, p. 186) – which so upset the women that one threatened to kill her. Significantly Hurston did not look to a man, but to the Amazonian Big Sweet for protection. She needed Big Sweet's assistance and approval if her research was to succeed, and pays tribute to her help and fidelity: 'Big Sweet helped me to collect material in a big way. She had no idea what I wanted with it, but if I wanted it, she meant to see to it that I got it' (*Dust Tracks*, p. 188). Hurston's respect for Big Sweet, who proved to be as staunch in her defence of a friend as she was fierce to protect her man from sexual rivals, is clear, and that a friendship was formed between these two very different women is obvious. Big Sweet's sexual rival was the notorious Ella Wall, immortalised in a song about her sexual availability and power. Ella was much sought after because she offered good 'boody' (sex). This objectification of the women as sex objects, which the women do not like, is apparent in the exchanges between the men and women. Big Sweet takes offence when she thinks Jim Allen's reference to a cow might be a veiled reference to her size: 'Who you callin' a cow, fool? Ah know you ain't namin' my mamma's daughter no cow' (*M&M*, p. 134). She bridles knowing that the men judged women by their size and colour, a fact not lost on the woman Good Bread, who is sensitive to Mr Ford's sly interrogation of Hurston about women's sizes:

'Zora, why do you think dese li'l slim women was put on earth?'
'Couldn't tell you to save my life.'
'Well dese slim ones was put here to beautify de world.'
'De big ones musta been put here for de same reason.'
'Ah, now, Zora. Ah don't agree wid you there.'
'Well, then, what *was* they put here for?'
'To show dese slim girls how far they kin stretch without burstin'.'
(*M&M*, p. 70)

Hearing this, Good Bread leaves, threatening to cut her tormentors, but not before another adverse comment is made upon her wearing of overalls. This pressure on women to be slim and fashionably dressed is highlighted when Tookie Allen, wearing a 'shake-baby', parades in view of the men for their admiring attention, which was heightened because of her 'yellow' colour. It is interesting that even in all-black Eatonville, sensitivity about colour, and admiration for light skin, point to the colorism of the inhabitants.

Colorism and sexism are not glossed over in *Mules and Men* and *Tell My Horse*.[19] In neither text does Hurston eulogise her people as being without prejudice. In *Tell My Horse* she recounts a conversation with a young West Indian male who 'let it be known that he thought that women who went in for careers were just so much wasted material' (p. 16). Hurston's own life was a challenge to this attitude, and in her autobiography she attributes the failure of her one 'admitted' marriage to her own refusal to abandon a career for marriage. Nevertheless, here as in many aspects of Hurston's life and writings, there is an underlying ambivalence, seen when she describes the preparation for marriage of a West Indian girl who is instructed by older women that: 'The whole duty of a woman is love and comfort. Think of yourself in that way and no other' (p. 20). Intellectually Hurston despised this. Her own life had been a determined struggle to realise her own potential independent of a man. Yet emotionally she so hankers after a romantic love that there is expressed a sort of envy at the eagerness with which the young bride entered marriage.

Perhaps the most telling indication of sexism is to be found in the named narrators in *Mules and Men*. Only six of the seventy tales are told by women. At the root of this lies the relegation of the Afro-American woman to a private sphere that silenced them. In *Head Above Water*,[20] Buchi Emecheta tells how the honoured storyteller in African society is a woman. We can assume that the Afro-American male continued to be told traditional stories by his mother at home, yet public performance of these had been appropriated by the adult male. Perhaps this indicates the insidious influence of Western gender structure to which the blacks were exposed? Indeed the dominance of the male in the social hierarchy is stressed in *Mules and Men* when Old man Allen angrily demands 'respect for his grey hairs' from a youngster. No such respect seems to be accorded to women. Similarly, young Julian is encouraged by older males to tell a story, whilst the women have to *demand* audience, as Big Sweet does with 'When ah'm shellin' my corn, you keep out yo' nubbins, Sam' (p. 115). As Hurston reveals, the women had to allow the men to hold centre stage in storytelling, yet it is also clear that some women exercised tremendous power in particular spheres of communal life. In particular Hurston notes that the distinction of being a powerful Hoodoo doctor was shared by both sexes, as had been the case in their African ancestry. Hurston herself claims to have been initiated into Hoodoo mysteries. The accuracy of her descriptions of ritual practices is probably unquestionable, but as her text was intended for popular consumption there may be an element of sensationalism in her claims for herself in this. What is indisputable is that Frizzly Rooster, Eulalia and Kitty Brown were living practitioners of Hoodoo. Some conjurors, like Mother Catharine, practised a Hoodoo that was woman-centred: 'Mother Catharine's religion is matriarchal. Only God and the mother count. Childbirth is the most important element in her creed' (*S. Ch.*, p. 56).

Close examination of the culture Hurston describes reveals its complexity, as old and new experience was assimilated and reshaped in folklore. That Hurston deserved praise for careful collection of this lore has been admitted by many black scholars and writers, though not all have approved of what they saw as her consequential self-aggrandisement. That she herself wanted centre stage is probably true, but there is no reason to doubt the sincerity of her wish to instil self-pride into her people too. She saw what was happening in Jamaica: 'But a new day is in sight for Jamaica. The Black people of Jamaica are beginning to respect themselves. They are beginning to love their own things, like their songs, their Ansani stories, proverbs and dances' (*Tell My Horse*, p. 9).

Alice Walker, who, like Hurston, believes that racial pride is nourished by a recognition of cultural roots, admits to feeling pride and delight when she reads *Mules and Men*. She praises Hurston for her timely intervention, when traditional rural black society was being diminished by migration to urban centres. Narrative links in *Mules and Men* suggest that Hurston strove to facilitate communication between the rural and the new urban black like herself, often by pretending a story was unknown to her, to such a degree that one can understand the suspicion of her contributors who might have sensed the ambivalence in her purpose. Was she using their tales for her own creative ends, or for scholarship? In an article, 'How it feels to be colored me', written at the same time that she embarked on her fieldwork, it is clear that her desire to celebrate her people was no

stronger than her craving for personal success: 'At certain times I have
no race. I am me' and 'The cosmic Zora emerges. I belong to no race,
nor time. I am the eternal feminine with the string of beads.'[21]
Implicit in this is the paradox of the scholar who wishes to be the
archetypal 'adorned' female. She craved attention and recognition for
herself as a writer and woman in spite of, not because of, her race.

Hurston's work on black folklore successfully challenged the
literary canon and accelerated the process of the deconstruction of
negative black stereotypes initiated in the nineteenth century by those
of her people who had found access to publishing. Blyden Johnson
says:

> Hurston's folk-lore did not idolise common Negroes into noble
> savages. But neither did it turn them into Rastuses and Sambos; nor
> deprive their behaviour of logical and recognisable roots in the
> conditions of a regional culture whose impact had been distilled into
> Negro spirituals or the blues.[22]

Johnson's judgement makes a telling connection between religious
experience and black oral culture which, as Hurston's researches
showed, could comfortably accommodate both Brer Rabbit and
Moses; the Holy Ghost and a human one. Hurston's writing was
enabled and shaped by the twin forces of Christian religion and a folk
culture with deep African roots, and her first novel, *Jonah's Gourd
Vine*,[23] published in 1934, concerns the clash of cultures represented
in the Christianisation of her people. In this she was influenced by
two factors, her anthropological interests and her familial background. In a report made to Boas during her expeditions to collect
the material that made up *Mules and Men* she said: 'A careful study
of Negro churches, *as conducted by Negroes*, will show, I think, that
the Negro is not a Christian, but a pagan still . . . his concept of God
. . . pre-Christian' (quoted in *ZNH*, p. 93). This must have been a
startling conclusion for the daughter of a Baptist minister. *Jonah's
Gourd Vine* can be read as an attempt to reconcile her research findings
and her religious upbringing, although it is most often approached as
an autobiographical novel, based on the marriage of her parents.
Undoubtedly autobiographical influences are strong. The protagonist
John Pearson's background as a mulatto from 'the other side of the
creek' is similar to John Hurston's, and she gives to John Pearson's
wife the name of her own mother, Lucy Ann Potts. Her autobiography
tells of her encouragement from her mother to 'jump at de sun', advice

repeated by Lucy Pearson to her husband in *Jonah's Gourd Vine*: 'Cover de ground you stand on. Jump at de sun and eben if you miss it you can't help grabbin' holt uh de moon' (*JGV*, p. 156). Hurston's depiction of Lucy Pearson as a black mother who is not content to see her daughter accept second-class status and so urges her to get as much education as she can, echoes the determination for familial improvement seen in many nineteenth century female narratives.

As a very young girl Hurston's mother had married a handsome but poor share-cropper who rose to become a minister of the church and mayor of Eatonville. In that time she bore several children, and had to endure her husband's frequent sexual transgressions:

> My mother rode herd on one woman with a horse-whip about Papa, and 'spoke out' another one. . . . The woman who got 'spoken out' threatened to whip my mother . . . But when Papa heard of the threats against mama, he notified the outside woman that if she could not whip him too, she had better not bring the mess up. (*Dust Tracks*, p. 17)

In her examination of Pearson's philandering in *Jonah's Gourd Vine*, Hurston points to the operation of double standards towards infidelity which gender differentiation supported. When Pearson's wife says that if he were to leave her she could easily find another man, he is quick to remind her, 'Ah'm de first wid you, and Ah means tuh be de last. Ain't never no man tuh breathe in yu' face but me' (*JGV*, p. 179). Hurston records a similar exchange between her own parents in her autobiography, but insists that her father's 'meanderings' meant so little that her parents' love for each other was undiminished. Yet it is difficult to accept this assertion with unqualified belief, for however constant the relationship might have remained, her mother clearly suffered because of her husband's persistent infidelities. Whilst acknowledged, this anguish is strangely minimised by Hurston, in her determination to uphold her father's memory as a powerfully attractive man. This cannot be attributed entirely to a sense of family loyalty. Hemenway recounts how Hurston had craved her father's attention and been jealous of his preferment of her sister. It is interesting to note that in her autobiography the exuberant, unrepentant description of her merciless beating of her stepmother reads like the account of a fight between rivals of love. She unwittingly betrays a sense of pride in her father's sexual prowess, and presents him as a man worth fighting for. Perhaps the obsessive fictional reiteration of the circumstances of her mother's death point to an oedipal source of guilt in Hurston. What is apparent is that she was herself strongly attracted to the phallic power represented by her father, and which she extols in the person of John Pearson.

In *Jonah's Gourd Vine* Hurston defends John Pearson's behaviour by depicting him as a man held in the grip of powerful and conflicting demands: one produced by the constant struggle between his genuine spirituality and his carnal longings, the other by the enforced expression of that spirituality in a religious code alien to his African heritage. Christianity castigates as sin a behaviour that might not have troubled his African ancestors. John Pearson is a minister of the church who believes that a woman trapped him by using Hoodoo; a minister of the church and a confessed sexual profligate; a loving husband and a persistent adulterer. For this Hurston does not offer Christian condemnation. Rather she seeks the reader's understanding of Pearson as an Afro-American man who is not, as the whites would see him, simply a sexually rampant black male, but one whose Christianisation is a denial of his physicality. John Pearson is an intelligent if uneducated man, whose delight in sexuality is unashamed: 'Even the strong odor of their [women's] sweaty bodies was lovely to remember' (*JGV*, p. 41). His personal magnetism assures his success with women as well as his ministry, in which he personifies some of the characteristics of the archetypal black preacher in literature, as described by Nancy Tischler:

> The preachers were gradually to metamorphosize into aggressive race leaders, but the earlier stories showed them as mindless, selfish and over-sexed conjure men, preaching hell, fire and golden streets of Glory-land . . . and at times seducing the females in the congregation.[24]

It might seem from this that Hurston was endorsing this fictional stereotype, except that, unlike the archetypes Tischler describes, John Pearson is not mindless, nor does he hurt anyone wilfully. The person who suffers most is Pearson himself, as he is eventually destroyed by the deadly struggle between the flesh and the spirit.

Hurston explains the significance of the title of the novel in a letter to Langston Hughes:

> You see, a prophet of God sat up under a gourd vine that had grown up one night. But a worm came along and cut it down. Great and sudden growth. One act of malice and it is withered and gone.[25]

John Pearson is destroyed by what the church saw as his lust. Because

Christian orthodoxy could not differentiate between Pearson the preacher and Pearson the man, it assists in the act of destruction. No longer could the prophet of God sit under the gourd vine; no longer could John be a preacher, although Hurston defends Pearson by emphasising that sexual infidelity diminished him neither as a husband nor as a preacher. He was, she points out, still regarded as a 'Battle-axe' against sinners.

In her observations of Hoodoo practice and initiation in *Mules and Men* Hurston had identified a grafting of African religious practice on to Christianity, that the 'Christianisation' of the Negro was facilitated only because in Christianity the Afro-American was able to reclaim some 'borrowed' symbols:

> Hoodoo, or Voodoo, as pronounced by the whites, is burning with a flame in America, with all the intensity of a suppressed religion. It has thousands of secret adherents. It adapts itself like Christianity to its locale, re-claiming some of its borrowed characteristics to itself. (*M&M*, p. 193)

She identifies reclaimed 'borrowings' in candles as fire-worship, purifying water as baptism, the altar as a place of sacrifice by fire, and the Eucharist as cannabalism. She also claims that the 'shouting' which is still characteristic of black Christian worship was a survival of the 'African possession by the Gods' (*S. Ch.*, p. 91). As such, she writes in a letter to Langston Hughes, *'they [the whites] have a nerve to laugh at conjure'* (quoted in *ZNH*, p. 192). Hurston claims that these relics of African religious practice had been forced to exist in tandem with the Puritanic abhorrence of the flesh which the enslaved Africans had been made to accept. Pearson's African heritage is powerfully described in the evening of dancing and music, that reminds his mother of her girlhood in slavery: 'So they danced. They called for the instrument they had brought to America in their skins – the drum – and they played upon it' (*JGV*, p. 59). This passage is redolent with the connotations of ancient religious practice as the rhythm is beaten out on a drum 'made by priests' and which 'sits in majesty in the ju-ju house'. The music is described as 'Congo drums talking in Alabama'. African roots are emphasised in the description of Pearson's funeral service, where 'the heavens wailed with a feeling of terrible loss. They beat upon the o-go-doe, the ancient drum. O-go-goe, O-go-doe! . . . the voice of Death' (*JGV*, p. 311).

Through the story of Pearson Hurston interrogates the power and influence of Christianity on black lives, and explores her belief that 'The negro is not a Christian really'. She also examines how an internalisation of the American myth of success can provoke the envy of the folk for those of their number who rise in the social hierarchy. John Pearson is born the bastard son of an ex-slave and her white master. Stigmatised by bastardy and miscegenation, he is abused by a stepfather who cannot bear the sight of his 'yaller' stepson: 'Amy, ah'm tellin' yuh, git dat punkin-colored bastard outa dis house. He don't belong wid us nohow' (*JGV*, p. 23). *Jonah's Gourd Vine* illustrates the destructiveness of internal racial pettiness arising from negative attitudes toward Pearson's mixed blood and the personal success of someone deemed a 'no-hoper'. Despite his disadvantaged background, Pearson, as did Hurston's father, rises to a position of influence within his community, disproving the expectations attached to his humble beginnings. The novel stands as Hurston's tribute to and justification of her father, fictionalised in her tale of a man's battle against his own profligacy, which reaches a lyrical crescendo in the final sermon delivered by Pearson. Based upon the wounds of Jesus, it illustrates the cultural clash in a man who genuinely believes that every sin we commit is a further wound, 'The blues we play in our homes is a club to beat up Jesus, and these social card parties' (p. 271). Yet at the same time, those very 'blues', the 'jooks' and parties castigated are manifestations of the black culture of which he was part. However, powerful and lyrical as this sermon is, Hurston was not the creator. It was collected from C. C. Lovelace, at Eau Gallie in Florida on 3 May 1929, during one of her anthropological expeditions. The criticism of such blatant incorporation of folk-material into fiction has already been noted. Folksy and lyrical as her writing is, the question raised is whether or not she merely creates characters as vehicles for the folklore. She can be defended against this accusation in *Mules and Men* where she preserves the living flesh of her contributors, as well as their stories. The same criticism if levelled at *Jonah's Gourd Vine* can only be refuted if the characterisation of John Pearson is unconvincing. In my opinion, to deny him credibility would involve an act of critical blindness to the conflicts he embodies. Above all, Hurston's depiction of this father/preacher is a plea for his recognition as a man: 'He wuz a man, and nobody knowed him but God' (p. 271). This is her last pronouncement on John Pearson in the novel, and it reinforces the aim she expresses in her letter to James Weldon Johnson in 1934:

Just a word about my novel . . . I have tried to present a Negro preacher who is neither funny nor an imitation Puritan ram-rod in pants. Just the human being and poet that he must be to succeed in a Negro pulpit . . . I see a preacher as a man outside of his pulpit and so far as I am concerned he should be free to follow his bent as other men.[26]

If we judge this novel in the light of Hurston's purpose, then it succeeds. If we try to judge it for what it is not, it cannot help but fail.

John Pearson is a flesh-and-blood man moved by the Spirit, who takes on folk-hero proportions without losing his humanity and epitomises the archetypal patriarchal figure who holds a great attraction for Hurston. He foreshadows her re-creation of the Biblical Moses in her novel *Moses: Man of the Mountain*[27] in which she reclaims this Old Testament figure as an African folklore hero and conjure man. Her stated aim was to explore the roots of myth-making in pagan and Christian tradition, in both of which Moses figures. She presents Moses as a 'two-headed' Hoodoo man of the sort she had met in Haiti, but one of remarkable power, renowned for his magic throughout Africa: 'And this worship of Moses as the greatest one of magic is not confined to Africa. Wherever the children of Africa have been scattered by slavery, there is the acceptance of Moses as the fountain of mystic power' (*Moses*, p. xxii). Moreover, her Moses is not an Israelite, but a mulatto. She suggests that the story of Moses' adoption by Pharoah's sister could have begun as a pacifying, self-protective lie by Miriam to her mother.

Although she adheres rigidly to the narrative sequence of the Old Testament story, her use of black folk idiom and custom establishes Moses as a larger version of John Pearson. Moses' personal magnetism makes him the object of envy and backbiting. When Moses is entranced by the beauty of Zipporah, it is at a 'shindig', which is described as an up-market version of the pay-day jook parties described in *Mules and Men*: 'Moses, tomorrow night there is going to be a big clothes-putting-on and eating down the road a piece here and these two biggest girls have been harassing me and their mamma to go' (p. 128).

Like Pearson, he marries for love. Like Pearson, he discovers he has powers to 'move' people. But whereas Pearson's power comes from his magic with words, Moses' comes from Hoodoo. Even in his final sermon Pearson's words have the power to bring his audience under his sway, whilst Moses uses his extraordinary magic to govern and curb the greed and malice of the Hebrews. Pearson's source of his power is language, Moses' is his African magic.

Hurston emphasises her belief that the Moses story is an incorporation of African history into orthodox Christian tradition: 'In Haiti, the highest God in the pantheon is Damballa Ouedo Ouedo Tocan Freda Dahomey and he is identified as Moses the serpent God' (*Moses*, p. lxxii). Ellease Southerland's illuminating article on Hurston in *Black World*[28] draws several significant parallels between Hurston's Moses and Damballa. She points out that Damballa's recognised sign is the snake, just as is Moses' serpent/stick; that Damballa's 'day' is Wednesday which is why Moses only negotiates with Pharaoh on that day; that in formal meetings Moses bows to each cardinal point as do Hoodoo priests; that Moses possesses the black cat-bone of Hoodoo rituals. Hoodoo man, Moses quite clearly is, yet in his fulfilling of God's wishes for the Hebrews, he embodies the fusion of paganism and Christianity that characterises Afro-American worship explored in *Jonah's Gourd Vine*. In Hurston's depiction of Moses he is presented with less mysticism than the Old Testament figure, but with more mystery. He is less of a patriarch and more of a priest, a wise tactician who becomes a great if reluctant leader of an enslaved nation. He claims no kinship with Hebrews, but is tempted to put his magic to their service by Jethro, who asks: 'How about them Israelites? They're down there in Egypt without no God of their own and no more protection than a bare-headed mule' (p. 156). Hurston challenges the Judaean-Christian proprietorship of Moses and retells the bible story in terms of her own people's suffering in slavery. She re-creates the painful suffering of an enslaved people in her description of the women who choked and stifled their screams in childbirth to keep secret their children's birth, and stresses the impotent rage and hatred experienced by their menfolk. Pharaoh's questioning of the necessity to free his slaves, echoes the patriarchal assumptions which had been expressed by Southern slave-holders: 'What would slaves want to be free for anyway? They are being fed and taken care of. What more could they want?' (p. 183). The infantilising of the blacks under white paternalism is implicit in Pharaoh's question. However, to see this novel simply as an allegory, as Blyden Johnson does in his introduction to the 1981 edition, denies Hurston's stated aim in her introduction, and the allegorical identity cannot be fully sustained. There was no identifiable Moses for Hurston except Marcus Garvey, whose designation as the 'Black

Moses' had not in fact been realised. Moreover, whereas the Old
Testament story is one of deliverance through a leader, Hurston's
Moses harbours thoughts that suggested such a deliverance is illusory:

> He had found out that no man may make another free. Freedom was
> something internal. The outside signs were just sign and symbols of
> the man inside. All you could do was give the opportunity for freedom
> and the man himself must make his own emancipation. (p. 344)

Those looking to find protest against enslavement can find it in this
novel, but they also find a resistance to the idea that freedom is gained
by political action.

An allegorical interpretation of *Moses* is a limited one, and is often
undercut by Hurston's satire. Hemenway amongst other commentators identifies Miriam and Aaron with the black bourgeoisie as objects
of Hurston's satire. As Moses' lieutenants they seek identification
with his power by asking for official posts as symbols of their status.
In their desire for upward mobility they also expose their colorism.
They object to Moses' wife's dark complexion:

> 'It's her color, Moses. She's too dark to be around here.'
> 'Why?'
> 'Well, you see the people, that is, the ladyfolks, don't want her ruling
> over them, dark as she is.' (p. 298)

To Moses, they begin to look like their former Egyptian oppressors:
'He looked at Aaron's face and he noticed the way he walked. His
face looked like Ta-Phar's . . . and he walked like he was conscious
of the envy of men' (p. 250).

Hurston's dislike of blacks who aped whites is documented in *Their
Eyes Were Watching God*[29] in the character of Mrs Turner who along
with Miriam and Aaron are the upstarts of society, representing a
black mentality Hurston despised. Yet despite her contempt for
political self-seekers, Hurston was nevertheless a celebrant of the self-
starter, and offered little comfort to those of her people who were too
lazy to move along the road to the Promised Land: '"Good Gracious!"
somebody grumbled, "I was figuring on going fishing tomorrow
morning. I don't want to be bothered with no packing up today. It's
too much like work and I just got free this morning"' (*Moses*, p. 224).

There is an uneasy tension between the sympathetic rendering of
the Israelites when enslaved and this reaction to their freedom.
Instances like this reduce the perceived allegorical force of the novel,

for she often resorts to humour when it seems inappropriate. The depicted inhumanity of a slave-holding system is undercut when the oppressors issue a decree stating: '2. Babies take notice. Positively no more baby boys allowed among Hebrews. Infants denying the law shall be drowned in the Nile' (p. 12). This somewhat laboured satire reduces any serious allegorical purpose. The novel is more comfortably defined as a satire on the pursuit and handling of power, and the notions of freedom, than an allegory on slavery.

It is also a statement about the personal responsibility of an individual in a social group. Hurston had made her position quite clear in her article 'How it feels to be colored me': 'I do not belong to the sobbing school of Negrohood who hold that nature somehow has given them a lowdown dirty deal and whose feelings are all hurt about it'.[30] Her message to her people is that real freedom lies within the grasp of each individual if only each has the courage and industry to grasp it. The use of the Bible story provides a framework for Hurston's Africanisation of Moses, and as such is an ambitious transference. The 'two-headed' Moses is not fully reconciled with the Biblical character, as Hurston never decides where his power originates. Sometimes it comes from sympathetic magic, sometimes the hand of God. In spite of the allegorical overtones, the humorous depiction of the quarrelling Israelites and the sometimes lyrical beauty of the language, the novel does not cohere into a convincing whole.

Although the novel began as a serious attempt to present a portrayal of Moses as African man of magic, Hurston allowed herself to be diverted by her own inventiveness. As the novel progresses she resorts increasingly to folk dialect and humour for its own sake, so that Moses' utterances vacillate between standard and black English. There are too many conflicting modes of expression to deny Hemenway's evaluation of it as a 'noble failure'. Perhaps this novel marks a movement in Hurston's own spiritual awareness to a pre-Christian perception of God as nature. In her autobiography she expresses her belief that on death she will return to the indestructibility of a natural universe. She had abandoned the religious teachings of her father: 'So I do not pray. I accept the means at my disposal for working out my destiny. It seems to me that I have been given a mind and a will-power for that purpose' (*Dust Tracks*, p. 298). She wrote this a few years after her Moses novel, but her uncertainty about Western religion can be found in *Jonah's Gourd Vine* and *Moses*.

Both novels explore duality of the flesh and the spirit and Hurston suggests that rigid division of these is a denial of humanity: 'Everybody is two beings: one lives and flourishes in the daylight and stands guard. The other being walks and howls at night' (*Moses*, p. 82). Her stance in these novels is less ambiguous on religion than it is on gender, for Pearson and Moses are examples of a socially constructed notion of masculinity. Both are depicted as stereotypical 'real' men: strong, authoritative, protective and invested with irresistible sexual attractiveness. As patriarchal figures their phallo-centric power is treated by Hurston with respect and envy. Much of her fiction reveals that she found masculine power and sexuality compelling forces. Perhaps this comes from her awareness that in a patriarchal society, preacher-poets exercised a power that she as a woman could never emulate. This is borne out by the hostile reception towards Hurston the writer by male critics whose own gender influenced their assessment of her work. Although she had published more books than any other Afro-American woman of her time, the eminent critic Darwin T. Turner's comments in his *In a Minor Chord*,[31] are suspect because of unconscious male chauvinism. In his book Turner places Hurston alongside two other writers of the Harlem Renaissance, Jean Toomer and Countee Culleen, but she alone is judged as an artist in terms of her life – 'a study of Zora Neale Hurston, writer, properly begins with Zora Neale Hurston, wanderer'. Turner's criticism is founded on his distaste for a woman whose life-style, as depicted in her autobiography, epitomises a struggle for self-definement *across* the bounds of gender and colour. He dismisses her works as 'artful, coy, irrational, superficial and shallow', all of which are gendered terms. Perhaps this is because her writing does not fit comfortably into the mainstream of black male protest literature. Such critical assessment does not focus on what she achieved, but on what she, apparently, ignored. Naturally, judged by these standards, she fails. She was black, but *female* and should be judged as such. As Lorraine Bethel points out about the writing of black women:

> We have a distinct Black woman-identified folk-culture based upon our experiences in this society: symbols language and modes of expression that specifically reflect the realities of our lives in a dominant white/male culture. Because Black women rarely gained access to literary expression, this Black woman-identified bonding and folk-culture has often gone unrecorded except through our individual lives and memories.[32]

Nevertheless, although Turner praises her two male-centred novels, *Moses* and *Jonah's Gourd Vine*, he is less happy with the woman-centred *Their Eyes Were Watching God*. The technique of multiple narrative interpolation and manipulation of fictive time long recognised by critics as serving to increase suspense and reader involvement in Emily Brontë's *Wuthering Heights*, he notes in Hurston's novel as a technical weakness. He fails to give credit to Hurston who, by locating her fiction in a culture which included music, song, a female 'best-friend' to confide in, achieves an holistic representation of black life. Nor does he acknowledge that while she uses white middle-class narrative forms, she challenges stereotypical literary presentations of the black female. Her persistent refusal to see her people simply as victims led to a misunderstanding of her writing even by fellow writers like Arna Bontemps.[33] Her ability to manipulate and survive in white male society, often interpreted as betrayal and capitulation, led to an intellectual lynching of Hurston the writer. Undeniably there is an irritating ambivalence in her attitude towards racism in those of her works aimed at a white audience, such as her autobiography, but the race question is not ignored by Hurston. In *Their Eyes Were Watching God* there is a scathing reference to the Jim Crow laws that allow Teacake to be press-ganged into burying hurricane victims – blacks in ditches, whites in coffins. The ludicrous task of differentiating between drowned corpses is emphasised: 'Look at they hair when you cain't tell no other way. And don't lemmee ketch none uh y'all dumpin' white folks, and don't be wastin' no boxes on colored' (*Eyes*, p. 253). Her weapon here is derision, but is no less effective for that. Moreover she made direct attacks upon the Jim Crow laws in articles written for the black press. She was, however, aware that because she did not toe the accepted line on the question of race, her political comments did not meet with consistent approval. With typical courage (or perhaps 'insouciance'), she said, 'whether you like it or not it is no concern of mine' ('How it feels . . .', *I Love Myself* (see n. 20), p. 162).

In her refusal to be blinkered into a hatred of all whites and a eulogising of all blacks, she touched on raw nerves. Just as she had attacked the new black bourgeoisie for losing touch with black roots, so she exposed the colorist attitudes amongst her people. Turner takes her to task on the one hand for 'ignoring' the race question in *Their Eyes Were Watching God* and on the other condemns her for devoting so much attention to the 'color-struck' Mrs Turner. He does not recognise the significance of this character within the novel as a whole. In Janie's search for self-fulfilment she has to learn to love herself as a black woman, and is confronted with Mrs Turner's desire for whiteness: 'Youse different from me. Ah can't blame white folks for hatin' 'em cause Ah can't stand 'em mahself. 'Nother thing, Ah hates tuh see folks lak me and you mixed up wid 'em. Us oughta class off' (*Eyes*, p. 210). Janie's rejection of Mrs Turner's self-hatred is a measure of her own new-found self-love. Moreover, it allows Hurston to examine her people's class-consciousness which she attacks in her fiction and articles. By employing derision as she does in *Their Eyes Were Watching God*, she expresses her contempt for a social organisation she found deplorable in its divisiveness.

The significance and value of her work can only be fully measured if it is examined as part of a black female literary tradition with a history before the Harlem Renaissance, for although a critical response to Hurston's writing was that she was only concerned with herself, my reading of her works persuades me that her main preoccupation was with gender. The black feminist critic, Mary Helen Washington, said:

> One of the main pre-occupations of the Black woman writer has been the Black woman herself – her aspirations, her conflicts, her relationships to her men and to her children (and to other black women, we might add), her creativity.[34]

With this comment in mind I offer an interpretation of Hurston's short stories collected in *Spunk*,[35] and her novel *Their Eyes Were Watching God*.

In her autobiography, Hurston presents an image of herself as a child singled out amongst her peers by a creativity and imagination focused on the idea of travelling a road to new horizons. In 'How it feels to be colored me', she said her favourite place was 'atop the gate post' (*I Love Myself* (see n. 20), p. 152). It is tempting and not unrealistic to say she utilised this experience in her fiction. 'Isis', first published as 'Drenched in Light' in 1924, is a fictionalised remembrance. Isis lives with Grandma Potts (Hurston's mother's maiden name) and is scolded for sitting on the gatepost to wave to, and sometimes briefly accompany, passing travellers. Like the young Hurston of the autobiography, Isis is a dreamer in search of beauty, adventure and freedom. Wearing her grandmother's table-cloth as shawl and with a 'long stemmed daisy' behind her ear, she follows and dances to fairground music. Poor and motherless, Isis is frustrated in her desires by the limiting constraints of class and gender: 'Being the only girl in the family, of course she must wash the dishes, which she did in intervals between frolics with the dogs' (*Spunk*, p. 11). Female readers recognise in Isis both the quintessential female condition in this gender socialisation of the young girl, and also her unquenchable thirst for experience. There is perhaps a significant connection between Hurston's dependance as an aspiring writer upon white patronage, and Isis' perception that white people, the road and freedom went together. Hurston's short story, 'Spunk', first brought her to the attention of the successful white writer of popular fiction, Fannie Hurst, who employed her as a secretary. Told in dialogue, and based upon the store-porch community Hurston knew as a child, 'Spunk' explores the unquestioning belief of the folk in the supernatural, which she had documented in *Tell My Horse*. Everyone accepts in Spunk's account of his fatal accident that the black cat which had distracted him is the reincarnation of his wife's first husband. Interesting as the folkloric elements are, I find the story's most illuminating feature to be in the treatment of heterosexual relationships. The protagonist Lena is without currency: she is simply a desirable object who goes eventually to the cockerel who struts and crows most loudly: 'Then Spunk reaches out an' takes hold of her arm an' says "Lena, youse mine from now on Ah worries for you an' fights for you"' (p. 3). On Spunk's death, the men on the porch ponder upon who would be Lena's next 'owner', and 'whisper coarse conjectures between guzzles of whisky' (p. 8).

Hurston's awareness of the sexual exploitation of women and their evaluation as sex objects is also the theme of 'Muttsy', in which an Eatonville innocent, Pinkie, goes to Harlem in search of work and finds lodgings with 'Ma', nicknamed 'Forty-Dollar Kate'. The sexual implications in Ma's name are fulfilled when she allows the besotted Muttsy into Pinkie's bedroom where she lies intoxicated. Muttsy decides to marry rather than ravish the unconscious girl and slipping his ring on her finger he gloats, '"She's mine . . . all mine"' (p. 32). Like Lena in 'Spunk', Pinkie is seen as something to be purchased. Muttsy intends to 'treat her white' (an interesting aspiration also explored in *Their Eyes Were Watching God*) but once married he returns to his former ways. This critique of heterosexual love and marriage is the theme of 'The Gilded Six Bits' where Missie May and husband Joe play out a fantasy of possession. On each pay-day Joe 'pays' Missie with nine silver dollars thrown onto the porch. He is the stereotypical 'provider', she the devoted housewife: 'Ah'm a real wife, not no dress and breath. Ah might look lak one, but if you burn me you won't get a thing but wife ashes' (*Spunk*, p. 57). This domestic fantasy is shattered when Joe discovers Missie in bed with the swaggering Otis, from whose watch-chain dangles six gold bits. In Otis' panicked flight the six bits become detached, and are pocketed by Joe who realises they are gilded. Months later when Joe makes love to Missy again, he pays her by leaving the spurious coins beneath her pillow. He has bought her 'as if she were any woman in the long house' (*Spunk*, p. 65). Like the money, Missie has been proven counterfeit. Yet no insight into the motivation for her infidelity is given. The underlying assumption is that being a woman, she would automatically go to the highest bidder, as her enslaved foremothers would. Only when he sees his own resemblance in the child Missie bears does Joe resume his former regular payments on pay-days. He pays for her services and resumes his infantilising of mother and child by the teasing gift of candy-kisses. What is playful behaviour at the beginning of the story takes on sinister overtones by the end. This marriage is not so very different for the woman as slavery had been.

Although Hurston never dismisses heterosexual love, there is a persistent exposure of the inadequacies of the institution of marriage. This is powerfully expressed in 'Sweat', where Delia's marriage to Sykes brings her physical and emotional pain, as well as the sweat of unremitting toil. Unlike Hurston's other stories, 'Sweat' owes little to identifiable folklore, but gives a convincing portrait of a marriage in eternal strife. As Sykes squanders his money on other women, Delia sweats over the laundry she does for whites. Spitefully scattering the laundry which reminds him of his own economic inadequacy and knowing of Delia's fear of snakes, Sykes plans to frighten her to death with a rattlesnake. In the event, it is he who dies of snake bite. The image of the snake, with its Edenic and phallic connotations, is an omen of evil identified with the evil in Sykes and the potential for evil in his wife. The effect on Delia of a fifteen-year marriage which brought her only financial and emotional privation arouses pity and admiration in the reader. Delia exhibits the indomitable spirit of her foremothers in her determination to perpetuate beauty in her garden and to pay for her house with her own sweat, fortified only with regular and devoted attendance at her church. By the end of the story she has learned to hate, and as the snake venom begins to work on Sykes she makes no attempt to offer him comfort. The marriage had resulted in a mutual destruction which was physical for Sykes and spiritual for Delia. So exploited and abused had she been by her husband that sympathetic neighbours had likened her to a cane-chew:

> There's plenty men dat takes a wife lak dey do a joint uh sugar-cane.
> It's round, juicy an' sweet when dey gits it. But dey squeeze an' grind
> . . . when dey's satisfied dat dey is wrung dry, dey treats 'em jus' lak
> dey do a cane-chew. Dey throws 'em away. ('Sweat', in *Spunk*, p. 65)

This was the fate planned for Delia, as Sykes intended to bring his new, fat mistress into her house. This is a powerful story in which marriage is seen as a trap sprung by love.

That romantic love could entrap a woman into a life of hard labour, is a recurring motif in Hurston's fiction. In *Their Eyes Were Watching God* Janie is warned by her nanny, that love is: 'de very prong all us black women gits hung on. Dis love! Dats just what's got uh pullin: und uh haullin' and sweatin' and doin' from can't see in de mornin' till can't see at night' (*Eyes*, p. 41). In this novel Hurston begins to explore woman's right to sexual fulfilment as well as to deconstruct affixed gender roles within marriage, marking her engagement with a debate which is still in progress. Hurston takes up where Nella Larsen had left off ten years earlier in her novel *Quicksand*,[36] which ends with the reduction of the heroine Helga Crane to the status of domestic drudge: 'And hardly had she left her bed and become able to walk again without pain, hardly had the children returned from the homes of the neighbours, when she began to have her fifth child' (p. 134).

Although Larsen's novel ends with the coffining of Helga's life within a narrow religious and maternal framework, the issue foregrounded in this, as it is in *Passing*,[37] was not gender itself so much as the tragic consequences of being a mulatta. Hurston does not accord tragic-victim status to her mulatta heroine Janie Crawford, and the resultant novel can be read as a remarkable statement about sexism. *Their Eyes Were Watching God* is a woman-centred novel not simply because it has a female protagonist but because, through Janie, Hurston interrogates gender restrictions as they affect a woman who is also black. In Janie's constant willingness to look forward, Hurston celebrates the female will to survive witnessed in the slave narratives: 'Now women forget all the things they don't want to remember, and remember everything they don't want to forget. The dream is the truth, then they act and do things accordingly' (*Eyes*, p. 9).

Like her enslaved grandmother, the more Janie Crawford is threatened, the more resourceful she becomes in her search for strategies for survival. In this depiction Hurston engages with the problems of class and gender much more than she does with race. Although Janie's early childhood is spent with a grandmother who lives and works with white people, her struggle for identity as an adult is set in all-black Eatonville. Painfully she moves from a position of passivity to an active awareness of a self that she lacked as a child. Shown a photograph of herself with a white family Janie eagerly searches for a self she does not recognise. She is unaware of her colour. She had no name: 'Dey useter call me Alphabet 'cause so many people had done named me different names' (p. 21). Nevertheless her developing consciousness is fashioned by a grandmother who leaves her in no doubt about her assigned role as a black: 'Honey, de white man is de ruler of everything as far as Ah been able tuh find out' (p. 29).

Within black literature there is nothing surprising in this sentiment. What is more insightful, however, is Nanny's comment on gender divisions amongst the blacks themselves. Talking of the burden of labour imposed by the whites on the blacks, this ex-slave says: 'He pick it up because he have to, but he don't tote it. He hand it to his womenfolks. De nigger woman is de mule uh de world so fur as Ah can see' (p. 29). This is an apt inclusion of the sentiment expressed in more than one of the folk-tales Hurston had collected, and is given added force because Nanny is a former slave. Nanny's interpolated slave narrative testifying to the exploitation of black women by white men echoes that described in actual slave narratives. Moreover, Nanny explains that women were the victims also of black men who had abused their positions of authority. Not surprisingly, Nanny wants to protect Janie from having to work as she herself had, as a 'work-ox and a brood-sow' and her ardent wish is that no man 'white or black' would ever make a 'spit-cup' out of Janie. Believing Janie's protection from abuse would lie in a financially secure marriage, Nanny accepts the old widower Killicks' offer of marriage for her granddaughter. Nanny would have been even happier had she lived to see Janie's second alliance with Jody Starks, with whom Janie enjoys a 'white' life-style which includes her very own flower-painted spit-cup. Jody also gives Janie the 'high-stool of do nothin' seen by blacks as the place occupied by married white women. In this aping of white life Janie learns that the 'high-stool', so attractive to her Nanny, is not only uncomfortable, but lonely and silent. In the process through which Janie is eventually to come to terms with her 'blackness' she lives in a simulation of the white 'big-house', painted a 'gloaty, sparkly white', beside which the other houses looked like 'servants' quarters'.

Jody's social aspiration to be a 'big-voice' in Eatonville gradually isolates Janie from the rest of the townspeople. Perched on the high stool she becomes a living symbol of her husband's success, and is told 'You oughta be glad, 'cause dat makes a big woman outa you' (p. 74). Janie's feelings of 'coldness and fear' at Jody's assertion testify to Hurston's rejection of the stereotypical gender role allotted to women in which their fulfilment or otherwise was determined by a man. As nothing more than a reflection of Jody's status, Janie is silenced and removed from social intercourse by a husband whose class-consciousness excludes her from a communal 'mule-dragging' he organises, because he doesn't want her 'talking after such trashy people'. White gender and class divisions with all their duplicity, encapsulated in this comment, are firmly rejected by Hurston who despaired of what she saw as contemptible in a black's wish to emulate the mores of a white society. Jody's desire, like Muttsy's, to 'treat his woman white', might bring self-satisfaction to the man but not happiness to the black woman. Janie's supposed 'elevation' is accompanied by a stifling of her voice as well as her capacity for the laughing and dancing Hurston saw as a positive factor in the lives of her people. Hurston wanted the blacks to perpetuate, not suppress, their joy in living. When Janie is freed to enjoy what living 'black' in the swamplands offered, she hears Mrs Turner's denigration of that life: 'And dey makes me tired. Always laughin'! Dey laughs too much and dey laughs too loud. Always singin' ol' nigger songs!' (p. 210), and scorns it for what it is: a white view of black life.

As Mrs Jody Starks, Janie is as enslaved as Nanny had been. Perhaps the remembrance of her grandmother's definition of the black woman as a mule exacerbates Janie's distress at the treatment of Lum's mule, as her growing dissatisfaction is expressed in 'a little war for helpless things'. The helplessness of dumb animals and women becomes identified when Jody tells her: 'Somebody got to think for woman and chillun and chickens and cows' (p. 110). Once again, as in slavery, women are joined with domestic animals that can be bought and sold. This juxtaposition of farmyard animals and women festers silently in Janie's consciousness, to erupt in an outburst against sexism:

> Sometimes God gits familiar wid us women folks too and talks after his inside business . . . how surprised y'all is goin' tuh be if you ever find out you don't know half as much 'bout us as you think you do. It's so easy to make you' self out God almighty when you ain't got nothin' tuh strain against but women and chickens. (p. 117)

Here Hurston questions the assumption underpinning all patriarchal institutions: that the male is superior to the female, and that it is divinely ordained. Janie's claim to be as cognisant as Jody of God's 'inside business', shatters his smugness and clarifies her feeling that whilst Jody wanted her 'outside', he wilfully repressed her 'inside'.

Like Pinkie, Missie May and Lena, Janie has been bought by a man who can pay for a sex object desired by his peers. Her 'outside' is what attracted male attention: 'The men noticed her firm buttocks like she had grape fruits in her hip pockets, the great rope of black hair swinging to her waist and unravelling in the wind like a plume' (p. 11). Jealously determined to keep Janie's beauty for his eyes only, Jody orders her to wear a head-rag in public, and palliates the visible signs of ageing in his own body with constant reminders of Janie's maturity, disparagingly referring to her as an 'ole' woman and pointing to her sagging behind. Insulated by gender, the 50-year-old Jody expects no retaliation when he publicly reminds Janie that, at 40, her body is ageing. This pornographic debasement of the female is felt by Janie to be like 'somebody snatched off part of a woman's clothes while she wasn't looking' in a crowded street. The sexism which causes the marriage to founder is neatly turned against Jody when Janie silences Jody in public, by describing him in terms commonly used in a derogatory way to females. She tells him that when his pants are down, he looks like 'de change of life'.

Darwin T. Turner sees this as a 'vicious' attack upon Jody, which was 'out of character'. His sympathies, all with Jody, make him see Janie as 'cruel and vindictive'. Missing the sexism Hurston is exposing, he attributes this episode in the novel simply to 'Miss Hurston's continual emphasis upon intraracial and intrafamilial hatred'. The import of this novel as a plea for female self-hood is misread by Turner as an attack upon black family life, when in fact the attack is on male chauvinism. Hurston does not deny the value of family life but deplores the emptiness that unequal gender status can generate within that life. The three 'marriages' of Janie are a narrative strategy which allows an exploration of female fulfilment within heterosexual relationships by a questioning of a number of marital assumptions. Each relationship involves an examination and rejection of fixed attitudes as Janie realises the limitations for herself inherent in all three. Janie's marriage to the elderly Killicks reveals the emptiness of a marriage in which the woman does not love the man and which is entered as an economic haven. In this loveless state Janie determines to keep the domestic bargain she has struck by keeping her work sphere rigidly separate from her husband's; hers was in the kitchen, his in the fields. 'You don't need mah help out dere, Logan. Youse in yo' place and ah'm in mine' (p. 52). It is when Logan threatens to disrupt this arrangement by the purchase of another mule so that she too can work in the field, that Jody Starks makes his opportune appearance on the road outside her house. He talks of far horizons and a life of pampered ease for Janie as his wife. But he, too, has fixed ideas about her place in this scheme. When she is invited to partake in a meeting he quickly interposes: 'but mah wife don't know nothin' 'bout speech-makin'. Ah never married her for nothin' lak dat. She's uh woman and her place is in de home' (p. 69). As Mrs Starks, Janie need never fear being yoked to a ploughing mule, but Jody's materialistic attitude merely places her at the forefront of all domestic animals, in which role she is expected to look upon herself as the 'bell-cow', and the other women as her 'gang'. Jody wears her as an ornament, but constantly belittles her intellect. As he lies dying he is forced to listen to Janie's stored articulation of years of non-communication, when she talks of her mind being 'squeezed' and 'crowded' to make room for her husband's.

There is a sense in which Janie's first two marriages are analogous to two stages in Afro-American history. Nanny's memory of slavery meant that she wanted Janie safely married. Nanny's slave mentality has been shaped by notions of ownership, and Janie reflects bitterly that Nanny had put her 'in the market place to sell'. Moreover, Nanny knows that although marriage to Killicks offers economic protection, it exacts a possible price in domestic 'violence' and pregnancy. I interpret this as a reflection of the post-bellum years, when black women, freed from sexual molestation by owners, sought the imagined haven of settled marriage. The ensuing migrations of rural blacks to the North in search of a 'white' life-style I think are reflected in Janie's second marriage. Jody represents the new black bourgeoisie intent upon minimising their cultural distinctiveness from whites. This novel rejects this second stage in Afro-American realisation, and offers in the third marriage a black alternative that was perhaps too revolutionary for Hurston's male critics. On Starks' death, Janie's 'outside' rigidly observes the formalities of mourning, but 'inside the expensive black folds were resurrection and life'. Freed from economic need, Janie reassesses her life and comes to the conclusion that she hates the grandmother who had died on her knees, praying. Our shock at this confession recedes, however, when we realise that what Janie hates, as did Hurston herself, was the mentality that slavery had produced in Nanny. Janie's failed marriages represent Hurston's rejection of the taint of white influence, and the third marriage her vision of a black alternative. Only with the drifting, guitar-playing Teacake does Janie blossom into self-hood. His gift to Janie is a love that frees her from the prison of imposed assumptions. Teacake invites her to join him in the hitherto male preserves of playing checkers, shooting and night fishing. Janie rejoices that at last 'someone wanted her to play'. Her 'inside' as well as her 'outside' was wanted. Their marriage is a life of shared experience, and so her soul 'crawled out from its hiding place', and Janie's female identity is given space to grow. Her 'Alphabet' name of childhood had been replaced in turn by Killicks, Starks and Woods, names significantly allied to the marriages offered. Janie's life with Killicks effectively 'kills' her youthful search for joy and love, whilst marriage to Starks diminishes her because of Jody's conceptualising of life as one of stark immutable contrasts: black and white; husband and wife; possessor and possessed. As Mrs Woods, Teacake offers her a natural 'black' life in which she can flourish and grow without restraint. An essential feature of this naturalness is delight in 'playing' which gives free expression to a sense of fun and pleasure emphatically denied by the Puritan ethic which had been foisted onto the Afro-American. What is seen by white society as evidence of the indolent, irresponsible nature of laughter-loving blacks, Hurston celebrates as proof of her people's spirit.

When Jody, in his desire to make Janie conform to white concepts of behaviour, slaps her, 'she wasn't petal open' to him anymore, whereas she recognises Teacake as a 'bee to a blossom'. This is consistent with the framework in the novel established when, in the garden away from the narrow confines of Nanny's kitchen, Janie dreams:

Oh to be a pear-tree – *Any* tree in bloom! With kissing bees singing of the beginning of the world! She was sixteen. She had glossy leaves and bursting buds, she wanted to struggle with life but it seemed to elude her. (p. 25)

Her visionary pear-tree withers when her hopeful spring is joined to Killicks' winter, to re-surface as sterile in her marriage to Starks: 'She had no more blossomy openings dusting pollen over her man, neither any glistening young fruit where the petals used to be' (p. 112). Her visionary pear-tree becomes a reality only when Teacake comes as a fertilising agent. He is associated with the joyous stream of living, whereas Jody's metaphor is the 'road' of aspiration, a metaphor used by Hurston of herself. The conflict between the rooted growth of a tree and the rootless pursuit of a road points to a paradox in Hurston herself. She claims to have written this novel to commemorate a love affair whilst on anthropological fieldwork. If this is true, the road of ambition had led her away from sustaining this relationship. The 'road' involves effort and pain, even for Janie who saw herself as a 'rut in the road' becoming ceaselessly worn down by her husband Jody. Only in Teacake are the two metaphors resolved: 'He seemed to be crushing scent out of the world with his footsteps. Crushing aromatic herbs with every step he took' (p. 161). This metaphorical underlining of Janie's gradual awakening to life is further emphasised by the symbolic significance of clothes. Marriage to Killicks is symbolised by the apron which she throws away on the road when she elopes with Starks. The discarded apron signals her escape from a life which threatens to perpetuate Janie as a 'mule of de world', but it is replaced by another symbol of enslavement in the head-rag, significantly discarded in widowhood, when she luxuriates in her freedom: 'This freedom feeling was fine. These men didn't represent a thing she wanted to know about' (p. 139). Under none of the constraints she had endured in her other marriage choices, she chooses to marry Teacake freely. The completeness of their shared experience is symbolised in the overalls – a unisex garment, which she dons willingly to work with him.

On Janie's return to Eatonville after Teacake's death, her self-hood is signalled by her freely swinging hair and the overalls. Her appearance results in a ferment of questioning by the townspeople: 'What she doin' coming back here in dem overalls? Can't she find no dress to put on? . . . What dat forty year ole 'oman doin' wid her hair swingin' down her back like some gal?' (p. 10). These questions are posed at the beginning of Janie's history and are resolved in narrative shifts and techniques which enrich the novel. The reader is invited to share Phoebe's role of confidante and is led convincingly into a narrative that shifts easily from first person to omniscient narrator. Moreover, Hurston operates with ease within the already established black female literary tradition which embraces slave narratives like Nanny's. Yet despite the undisputed femaleness of the structure, imagery and attitudes in this text, to claim it as 'feminist' in the light of recent feminist politics would be inaccurate. Objections can be made to the limitation of Janie's liberation, which is realised through the agency of a man and is within a heterosexual relationship. Although Hurston knew that heterosexual politics often involved violence against women, and even the adoring Teacake beats Janie, she appears unwilling to surrender the cherished notion of romantic love. Curiously, however, while she subscribes to this notion, she is prepared to challenge the stereotypical roles of ownership and oppression that heterosexual love often implied for women.

In his article on *Their Eyes Were Watching God*, S. Jay Walker claims that Janie's return to Eatonville brought women's liberation to the town.[38] He quotes Phoebe's response as evidence: '"Lawd," Phoebe breathed out heavily, "Ah done growed ten feet higher from jus' listenin' tuh you, Janie. Ah ain't satisfied wid mahself no mo'. Ah means tuh make Sam take me fishin' wid him after this"' (p. 285). However, Phoebe's response is not a completely liberated one, as it is still dependent upon a man. True liberation comes when women can take *themselves* off fishing. So I cannot agree with Walker's contention that women's liberation had arrived in the black town. Janie's story is a step on the road towards that goal, but the road still stretched ahead. On the other hand, a feminist reading of the novel's subtext might see Janie's marriages as a preparedness for self-sufficiency. It is true that her growth is at the expense of men. She makes Logan feel impotent, she publicly announces Jody's impotence, and she shoots and kills Teacake when he is made mad by the bite of a rabid dog. Such a reading might be attractive to feminists. If accepted, however, it must be seen as further evidence of the conflict in Hurston herself, for she was unable to rid herself of a faith in heterosexual love as a fulfilling experience, although her own life had been a refutation of this.

I think that her antipathy to be judged as a member of a group would negate any allegiance to a women's liberation movement. In heterosexual as well as racial politics, she stresses the responsibility of the individual. When S. Jay Walker imagines that women's liberation arrived in Eatonville with Janie, he ignores Janie's response to Phoebe's reaction to her story: 'Two things everybody's got tuh do fuh themselves. They got to go tuh God, and they got tuh find about livin' fuh themselves' (p. 285). God, in this novel, is the experience of love that Janie finds with Teacake. He is paradoxically also the overwhelming power of natural forces unleashed in the hurricane. In this, I see something prophetic in Hurston's gropings for a closeness to a God not associated with an institutionalised Church. She anticipates Alice Walker's replacement of Christian belief by a pantheistic faith: 'I don't believe there is a God beyond nature. The world is God. Man is God.'[39] At the same time, Janie's eventual contentment as Teacake's widow is a pointer to the possibilities of the female capacity to live alone, albeit sustained by memories of love. What is interesting in this novel is that Hurston reconstructs the idea of female fulfilment in that Janie's is not dependent upon motherhood or a lasting relationship with a man. Teacake's madness and his shooting by Janie are used to show that a woman *can* live happily without a man, and this resolution is a refutation of the happy ending which typified the popular romantic novel.

It seems strange that when Alice Walker visited Eatonville she encountered little enthusiasm for the memory of Zora Neale Hurston. Even Mathilda Moseley, a named contributor to *Mules and Men*, exhibited suspicion and hostility under Walker's questioning (*In Search of*, p. 97). Had Mathilda genuinely forgotten, or did she not wish to be reminded of her acquaintance with Hurston, who had been an extraordinarily outrageous product of Eatonville? Hurston's early reputation as scholar and writer had been sullied by an allegation that she had sexually corrupted a juvenile. Did the respectable octogenarian wish to disassociate herself from Hurston for this reason? Or did she resent being immortalised alongside the knife-wielding Big Sweet or the sexual free-wheeler Ella Wall? Or did she suspect her own role in the drama of Lucy Hurston's death when young Zora was unable to obey her mother's wishes about the observation of the rituals of dying, for in *Jonah's Gourd Vine* the neighbour who prevented this is named as 'Mathilda Moseley'? Whatever the reason for Mrs Moseley's reluctance to remember, the fact is that by 1963 she disclaims memory and most of Hurston's works were out of print.

We can assume that this publishing vacuum resulted from the lack of critical approval from those who give shape to the canon, and not because her writing lacked appeal. Her work, so full of wit and humour, captures the musical vitality of black language and idiom and is certainly a treasure-house of black culture. Her verbal register is wide and her tone could be angry, satirical, mocking, or powerfully lyrical. The rich lyricism of the black sermons is matched at times in her own descriptions:

> Polk County. Black men laughing and singing. They go down in the phosphate mines and bring up the wet dust of the bones of pre-historic monsters, . . . Huge ribs, twenty feet from belly to backbone three feet high, bearing witness to the mighty monster of the deep when the painted land rose up and did her first dance with the morning sun. (*Dust Tracks*, p. 180)

Black experience was translated into her fiction, where it was certainly a source of strength, although it could be vitiated by over-use. Having read all her published material, I have noticed that the same folk-phrases, idioms and customs are employed repetitively in her various writings, and lose their freshness. I do not agree, however, with Darwin T. Turner's criticism of what he considered was an extraneous inclusion of a chapter on storytelling in *Their Eyes Were Watching God*. I see that particular chapter's importance in its emphasis on the folk-experience from which Janie was being excluded. What may well be a valid criticism, however, is that when Hurston attempts to write outside her black experience she is less convincing. Her one 'white' novel is her last, *Seraph on the Suwanee*,[40] which Toni Cade Bambara describes as a 'dropped stitch' in the total fabric of Hurston's writing.

In one respect, this novel represents Hurston's wish to be recognised as a novelist whose work could have a universal appeal. In a letter to Carl Van Vechten she talks of hopes of 'breaking that silly old rule about Negroes not writing about white people' (*ZNH*, p. 308). The protagonists in *Seraph on the Suwanee* are white, and it is from their perspective that non-whites are viewed. Initially only the husband, Jim Meserve, has cordial contact with blacks, and this enables Hurston to make a point about her people's capacity for pleasure. Joe says to Jim:

> I speck youse right about that Saturday night business, mister Jim. Fact of the matter is, I knows youse dead right. But if you even was to be a Negro just *one* Saturday night, you'd never want to be white no more. (*Seraph*, p. 40)

Jim's wife, Arvay, the product of a narrow religious upbringing which had fostered in her the desire to be a missionary, only gradually learns to recognise the humanity of her husband's non-white friends. However, racial tension is not the mainspring of the novel, which focuses on the theme of love and marriage. In her portrayal of Arvay, Hurston was clearly influenced by Freudian psychology, for she offers the reader an in-depth analysis of a guilt-ridden woman who associates carnal love with guilt: she is 'too nice' to be 'natural' in her husband's estimation. In some ways her situation is a development of Janie Crawford's, and in others the opposite. Perhaps because she *is* white, she is depicted as an hysterical neurotic, overwhelmed by a sense of inferiority. As Mrs Jim Meserve she has Janie's promised 'high stool' *and* an ever-loving husband. Yet her behaviour undermines the marital relationship because she despises herself for her own sexuality: 'She hated the man violently and she hated him because he had so much power over her' (*Seraph*, p. 137). Nor can she be assured of her own worth: 'She didn't belong where she was, that was it. Jim was a Meserve. Angeline was a Meserve, but so far as they were concerned she was still a Henson. Sort of a handmaiden around the home' (*Seraph*, p. 174).

Arvay is a woman in search of self-hood, like Janie, but unlike Janie she is never presented as being capable of independent development. Guilt-ridden because her first-born son is mentally defective, she progresses towards middle age exhibiting total commitment to her children, but never to her husband. With one child dead, and two married, she faces an imagined sense of uselessness: 'She felt like a dammed up creek. Green scum covering her over' (*Seraph*, p. 221). The solution to Arvay's problem is provided in complete immersion in the marital embrace. Having convincingly explored the entrapment that marriage afforded, Hurston then suggests that happiness lies in its acceptance and enjoyment. Arvay's hysteria disappears when she learns this. The justification Hurston offers for this reconciliation is that a good union will include compatibility of the mind *and* the body. This is convincingly resolved in *Their Eyes Were Watching God*, because Janie and Teacake exercise a mutual power over each other. In Arvay's case, the marriage is cemented only when she bows to Jim's mastery of her, at whose command she strips naked, and with whom even consensual intercourse is seen as sado-masochistic rape. This rather distasteful element could be there as a titillating attraction to the reader, or it could be an expression of Hurston's personal, unfulfilled search for a lasting sexual relationship. In the final outcome, I think the novel fails because there is an unresolved tension between Hurston's psychological probing of Arvay and the overly simple conclusion that psychic ills can be cured in bed.

I suspect that this novel emanates as much from Hurston's own unresolved attitudes towards love and marriage, as a desire to broaden her fictional range. Much as Hurston had striven for the elusive goal of perfect love, she did not find it in life: 'Who had canceled the well-advertised tour of the moon? Somebody had turned a hose on the sun. What I had taken for eternity turned out to be a moment walking in its sleep' (*Dust Tracks*, p. 251). Like Arvay, Hurston constantly searched for reassurance and security. She had not found it in actual marriage, so she tries to create her wished-for union in fiction. Part of Hurston wanted to believe in Jim Meserve's male chauvinism:

> Women folks don't have no mind to make up nohow. They wasn't made for that. Lady folks were just made to laugh and act loving and kind and have a good man to do for them all he's able . . . (*Seraph*, p. 23)

The older that Hurston became, and the more poverty loomed – as it did when she was writing this novel – the more attractive must have seemed Jim Meserve's idea of what women were 'made for'. Marriage to a Jim Meserve would have insulated any woman from the humiliating experience of having to beg, as Hurston did, for an advance from her publishers, to 'buy necessities'. The ever-present threat of poverty, to which she fell finally and sadly a victim, perhaps explains why Hurston had wished she had been in less of a hurry as a writer: 'In fact, I regret all of my books. It is one of the tragedies of life that one cannot have all the wisdom one is ever to possess in the beginning' (*Dust Tracks*, p. 212).

The haste she exhibited in her expressed determination to 'wrassle' up a future or die in the attempt might also explain her readiness to play up to her white patrons and readers. Her autobiography was severely edited when first published, and passages critical of American foreign policy were excised. This, and a reading of articles she wrote for the black press, show that she was only able to speak directly when not dependent upon white publishers. I cannot accept, however, the opinion of those critics who said she never addressed herself to the problem of race. As a black woman, everything she wrote concerned the problems associated with race, *and* gender.

My research into Hurston's writings has convinced me that they contain much to give delight and cause for thought. I feel that much criticism of her work has been based upon misconceptions of her position as a black woman whose life defies categorisation. Toni Cade Bambara delights in this particular characteristic, seeing it as an example of Hurston's unwillingness to 'behave' in an acceptable (conventional) way. I interpret this somewhat differently. Hurston possessed a chameleon quality enabling her to project a self suited to the occasion, for, like the chameleon, her various personae were defensive camouflage. As the two dates given for Hurston's birth indicate, she would add or subtract years as the purpose suited her. No wonder she is an enigma. Photographs of her reveal a woman who could appear stunningly gay and sophisticated, eagerly innocent, thoughtful and even homely. It is not surprising that Mary Helen Washington, in her introduction to *I Love Myself*, quotes descriptions of Hurston given by friends who remembered her as 'big-boned . . . handsome and light yellow', as 'rather short and squat and black as coal', and of 'a reddish light brown'. No doubt, Hurston was able to convince her fellows that all three descriptions were true. She could be bizarre, exotic, arrogantly black, or a servile opportunist playing the darkie. These were her chosen strategies of survival. In the end, she was a woman, and perhaps the outcome of any 'search' for that woman is encapsulated in the words she uses to describe Arvay:

> All that had happened to her, good or bad, was a part of her own self and had come out of her. Within her own flesh were many mysteries.
> (*Seraph*, p. 309)

Hurston's flesh was unquestionably female and her femaleness echoes over the years, striking sympathetic chords in women readers of today. Being black and female in the America of the first half of the twentieth century were in themselves causes of constraint. When to these is added her ambition to be a writer it is not surprising that, given the circumstances of her life, all she achieved was by a process of negotiation, in which the strategies of survival she used have sometimes obscured her achievements as a writer.

Her lifetime encompassing the rural poverty of the South, engagement with the Harlem Renaissance and eventual obscurity, coincided with America's involvement in two world wars, in which black men fought and died for an America which still denied them full human and civil rights. The ebullient optimism of the Harlem Renaissance disappeared as the frustration of a generation of war veterans erupted in racial disturbances, giving way to a black determinism expressed in the retreat into Naturalism of writers such as Richard Wright and Ann Petry.[41] The interwar years had shown Marcus Garvey's inability to fulfil his people's dream of him as a second Moses to lead them to a Promised Land. Nevertheless his 'back to Africa' movement was potently realised in the writing of Hurston, in whose retrieval and incorporation into her own writing of the unrecorded black oral culture, an Afro-American identity was found. Hurston, however, like Angelou, was to discover that African roots did not negate the fact that black Americans are American, and that problems of race have to be confronted and solved within, and not outside, America. Hurston died in 1961, at the very beginning of the decade which was to see a 'Second Renaissance' in black literature with a burgeoning of talented writers. In Paule Marshall, Audre Lorde, Maya Angelou, Toni Morrison and Alice Walker are some of the women whose writing gives further definition to the issues of race, class and gender with which Hurston had engaged.

—— 4 ——

Paule Marshall (b. 1929)
and Audre Lorde (b. 1934)
A celebration of infinite variety

Paule Marshall was born in 1929 in Brooklyn, where she grew into adolescence during the years of the Great Depression. Not far away from Brooklyn, in Harlem in 1934, Audre Lorde was born and reared. Both spent time at Hunter College in New York, and both were first-generation Americans born of parents who had migrated to the United States from the Caribbean. They shared an experience of a city childhood in areas of New York that are now synonymous with the social disadvantages which are the lot of the black and the poor. Their own experience of being black and female in their particular environments provided the material which as writers they used in startlingly different ways. Marshall emerged as a writer of short stories and novels, Lorde as a writer of poetry, essays and feminist theory, and to date a 'bio-mythography' in *Zami*.[1] Their writing gives proof of Hurston's comment about American black women in her autobiography that: 'Our lives are so diversified, internal attitudes so varied, appearances and capabilities so different, that there is no possible classification so catholic that it will cover us all' (*Dust Tracks*, p. 237).

Here Hurston was commenting on the fatuous impossibility of categorising the black American simply on the basis of skin colour, not only because the variety of skin tones is infinite, but because such a definition also ignores the complexity of the cultural, tribal and racial elements that constitute the individual. In *Tell My Horse* Hurston records in particular her sense of feeling different when she went to the Caribbean: 'It is a curious thing to be a woman in the Caribbean after you have been a woman in these United States' (p. 57). She argues that life for the black American woman was less harsh than that of the Caribbean woman, who lived under the continuing influence of British imperialism. While her opinions might not have been accurate, they nonetheless illustrate her sense that in spite of a common African ancestry, Caribbean women had been shaped by a different social construct. Hurston's claim that individual uniqueness is a celebration and manifestation of humanity, is clearly met in the awareness of cultural and sexual difference, inscribed in the works of Marshall and Lorde. As the children of West Indian parents who had emigrated to New York in search of an imagined improvement in their economic prospects, their familial backgrounds and expectations marked them off from their black sisters in the South. Marshall and Lorde came from a line of black mothers whose experience of diaspora was not focused on separation from their children, as was that of the Afro-American woman in the South, but in self-imposed economic exile from their Caribbean homeland. They came to the United States with a hungry determination to pursue the American dream. If Hurston's literary grandmother was the racially oppressed Harriet Wilson of *Our Nig*, then Mrs Seacole, the entrepreneurial product of Western imperialism in the West Indies, was the literary foremother of Lorde and Marshall. Although they would share with all American women of colour in a white-dominated society the burden of racial prejudice, Marshall and Lorde have – and project – their awareness of their distinct and separate West Indian identity. Despite their common ancestral heritage in slavery, differing political and economic circumstances had allowed the Afro-Caribbean culture and language to develop along lines which had separated them from the consciousness of the rural black Southern heartland. They write from a black experience founded in a different cultural heritage, and it is in their celebration of difference that their work strengthens the developing tradition of black women's writing in America. That this was an unconscious adding of voice to an established but unrecognised tradition, is underlined by Marshall's comment that: 'I didn't know that Zora Neale Hurston existed and was busy writing and being published during those years.'[2] Her unawareness of Hurston's writing points to an undervaluing and muffling of black women's experience, and the cultural invisibility of blacks in a society which blindly believes itself to be homogenously white. Marshall and Lorde write out of their black female selves, and so speak with the clarity, freshness and sincerity that come from listening to their own community, using the language met there, rather than that of the dominant culture.

The foregrounding of dominant white culture left black writers largely unaware of the literature of the Harlem Renaissance. This is attested to by their recollection of an introduction to literature through the works of Shakespeare, the Romantic poets and nineteenth century English novelists. Perhaps because of the remoteness of this cultural expression from another time and place, their own spontaneous creativity was less contaminated, less fettered by the forbidding weight of the English literary canon. Certainly Marshall remembers that, although she devoured the English texts with pleasure, she was conscious of a sense of something missing. Her awareness of black literary voices which would fill that void filtered through to her in the snatches of Paul Lawrence Dunbar's poetry, leading her to ask the white librarian diffidently for books by black writers, 'at first with a feeling of shame – the shame I and many others used to experience in those days whenever "Negro" or "colored" came up' (from 'The Poets in the kitchen', 1983, in *Merle*, p. 11). Marshall's sense of black inferiority was displaced when she herself began to write, and to capture so accurately the musical cadences and linguistic flexibility of the West Indian community in New York. The vividness of ordinary speech, as Marshall renders it in dialogue, gives to her writing a special beauty. In the kitchen of her Brooklyn brownstone where her mother gossiped with other West Indian women, Marshall listened to their discussion of topics belying the myth that women talked only of men, babies and domestic issues, as 'they talked – endlessly, passionately, poetically, and with impressive range' (*Merle*, p. 5). In *Browngirl, Brownstones*,[3] Marshall re-creates the seriousness of the female conversations she had heard as a child, when the kitchen functioned as the source of physical and mental nourishment, as it did for Claudia in Morrison's *The Bluest Eye*. It is in the kitchen of the old brownstone where Silla Boyce supplements the family income by the preparation for sale of Barbadian delicacies, to the accompaniment of discussion of sexual and world politics. In this, Silla's comments on the impact of political decisions on the lives of women are perceptive: 'It's the poor people got to suffer and mothers with their sons' (p. 69). Despite their exclusion from the written culture of America, these immigrant women were fully aware of economic and political oppression, which they assessed with perception and understanding.

The dialogue in Marshall's fiction shows that the West Indian manipulation of the language of their imperialist masters signalled their successful preservation of their own cultural identity. The syntactical changes made in West Indian use of English, like those demonstrated in Hurston's study of Southern black language, are not to be seen as corruption born of ignorance, but examples of imaginative verbal versatility. The West Indians had adapted the imposed language of colonialism to suit their own needs, transforming it 'into an idiom, an instrument that more adequately described them' ('Poets in the kitchen', in *Merle*, p. 8). They incorporated Africanisms like to 'yam' for 'eat', vividly described pregnancy as 'tumbling big', and graphically referred to any woman who gave sexual favours freely as a 'thoroughfare' or a 'free-bee'. The adjectival intensification produced by repetition, as in 'full-full', 'hard-hard', 'bright-bright', is peculiar to West Indian language, as is the juxtaposition of opposites in 'beautiful-ugly'. Marshall ponders this last usage and suggests that it comes from the African sense of the duality of existence that, whilst acknowledged, was never allowed to harden into separates. The idea that the African sees with the soul as well as the eyes, is a dominant one in Marshall's work, as it is in Toni Morrison's. Marshall values this as a faculty to be preserved rather than denied, just as she recognises that her ancestors' enslavement had been resisted in a language that should also be preserved. The English reader is conscious of Marshall's rendering of that language as a musical experience. The lilting cadences are produced by syntactical changes such as the rejection of the adjectival pronoun 'our' in favour of 'we', the unusual placing of a preposition as in 'so much of money', the favouring of the first over the third personal pronoun, and the creation of a past tense by the prefix 'did' rather than the suffix '-ed'. When her characters address each other as 'soul-gel' or 'C'dear', Marshall succeeds in following the advice of another displaced cultural alien, Joseph Conrad, who said a writer had 'to make you hear, to make you feel, to make you see'.

In Marshall's West Indian dialogue we can hear the voice of her people, and through her writing we can grasp something of her experience as a black woman. The double-bind of gender and race became for Marshall a triple-bind with the added awareness of her family's immigrant status. Describing her mother and her friends, she says: 'Indeed, you might say, they suffered a triple invisibility, being black, being female and foreigners' ('Poets in the kitchen', *Merle*, p. 7). The struggle for visibility and the price exacted for it is the subject-matter of *Browngirl, Brownstones*, published in 1959. This is a neglected but significant novel, addressing issues which rose to dominance in the 1960s, when civil rights were demanded simultaneously with the social emancipation of all women. Although the Women's Movement gathered strength in the 1960s, it did not suddenly emerge from a vacuum. Circumstances were propitious for the explosion of demands women made, some of which were met, but none of which was new. Marshall's short story 'The Valley Between'[4] had appeared in 1954, and prefigures the emerging consciousness of women in the 1960s. The theme, of the emotional conflict suffered by women whose marital responsibilities are perceived as obstacles to a personal fulfilment sought through education, is now commonplace, but was not so when Marshall wrote the story. Perhaps a deliberate authorial distancing device, in a story admitted to be disguised autobiography, is that the protagonists are white. Like Alice Walker's *Meridian*, Marshall's Cassie resents the personal bondage and the repetitious preparation of milk feeds to meet the constant demand 'Mommy-milk, Mommy-milk' brought by young motherhood. The metaphor of imprisonment in the rituals of food preparation and domestic chores emphasises Cassie as the feeder, who goes herself intellectually unnourished. The reality of domestic isolation and incessant demands of house and childcare are a refutation of Cassie's innocent girlhood dreams. Nevertheless her negative socialisation into accepting motherhood as the summation of female aspiration, is being passed on to her own child whom she repeatedly tells to go and play with her dolls. Cassie's unfocused sense of non-fulfilment and disappointment is imaged in the broken doll she is trying to mend, 'trying unconsciously to fix its broken head back into the socket of the neck' (*Merle*, p. 17). Like the doll, Cassie is out of joint, uncomfortable within the domestic role allotted to her, fearfully contemplating a lifetime spent in 'one compressed limited space' (*Merle*, p. 20). Matrimonial strife grows when she resumes her interrupted education and is brought to crisis point when her child falls ill. Maternal duty is the emotional weapon with which the husband bludgeons the guilt-ridden mother back into her 'proper' place. Reluctantly Cassie stays at home, with the conscious weight of desperate generations of unfulfilled women in 'her mother's footsteps on the floor above'. Within this marriage in the 1950s, Cassie has no choice.

That the price exacted for economic security can be spiritual imprisonment is tangential in 'The Valley Between', but is the dichotomy at the root of the woman-centred novel *Browngirl, Brownstones*. The tragic consequences of a denial of African spirituality for materialism is enacted through the awareness of the girl-child Selina, whose maturation and recognition of familial and community ties are charted in the four-part structure of the novel. Selina's painful growth is the focus of the novel, but is widened to embrace Marshall's concern for the spiritual health of a community of West Indians who had flooded into Brooklyn 'like a dark sea nudging its way onto a white beach and staining the sand' (*Browngirl*, p. 4). The Barbadians were seeking a future built on belief in the 'Allmighty Dollar', for which they were prepared to work hard, and with which they would 'buy house'. With diligence and enterprise these landless people strive to become the owners of the once-splendid brownstone houses which they rented out for multiple occupancy, and in so doing they run the risk of losing their souls to commercialism. Marshall situates Selina Boyce in such a heavy, ornate brownstone house still bearing the imprint of previous affluent, white owners and a history of exploitation, the remnants of which live on in the figures of the ageing white servant and her illegitimate daughter who rent rooms there. The old woman is the disabled debris of a past in which she had been sexually exploited by her employers' son. Selina feels the weight of the brownstone's white past, but envies the imagined grace and gentility of the original white owner. Here Selina feels trapped. She feels an intruder, capitalising on the faded splendour of an alien culture and perpetuating an exploitation which was no part of her own.

Even as a 10 year-old, Selina resents – although cannot analyse – the lack of grace in her own life. The immediate cause of discontent is the conflict of interests between her parents. Her charming, fun-loving father is depicted as bringing the Caribbean sunshine into the coldness of Brooklyn, where he sprawls at ease in the sun parlour, dreaming of the house he would build someday on his land in Barbados. His indulged youth, spent in sunshine and 'spreeing', had ill equipped him for the cold reality of the capitalist heart of America. Conversely, the mother, Silla, is associated with the colours and sensations of a Northern winter and 'brought the theme of winter into the park with her dark dress amid the summer green' (p. 16). Where Deighton, the husband, is carefree, she is resolute; where he is resigned to defeat, she is determined to succeed; where he seeks pleasure as an end in itself, she embraces work as a means to an end.

Silla's intransigence is initially repellent, until Marshall explains what lies behind her single devotion to property. Unlike Deighton, Silla had not been indulged in her youth, spent as a member of the 'Third Class' – 'a set of little children picking grass in a cane-field from the time God sun rise in his heaven till it set' (p. 45). The child Selina does not fully appreciate the mother's experience, and enjoys a fierce love/hate relationship with a mother who is both awesome and beautiful.

In Book I, Marshall swiftly establishes the character of the new brownstone community, composed of individuals who each represent an aspect of an old order passing to make way for a new. Her concern is that the 'New York' children of West Indian parents should not lose contact with their Caribbean heritage, although she recognises that progress brings change. The old servant and her daughter living in a single upper room are the remnants of a decadent white order and as such are rootless amongst the West Indian immigrants, while Suggie, the 'free-bee' who clings to her West Indian homeland with nips of rum and sexual encounters, is doomed in the American economic jungle, as is Deighton Boyce. Only Deighton's wife Silla seems capable of manipulating for survival. She is felt as a brooding presence in the house, a sense reinforced by Marshall's introduction of each resident with Silla's opinion of their characters. Silla sees Suggie as a 'concubine don know shame' (p. 17), Deighton as a man who is 'always looking for something big and praying hard not to find it' (p. 21), Miss Thompson as guilty of self-neglect in her efforts to care for someone else's neglected children, and the white tenants as better off dead. Her harsh but pragmatic judgements are in accord with the capitalist ethos of the society she wants to join. In this, Marshall recognises spiritual danger. In her pursuit of the American dream of monetary success, Silla risks losing contact with the real sun of her West Indian heritage. In contrast to generations of Southern blacks born into an inhospitable society, Silla had *chosen* to live in America. The difference in attitude between Southern black and West Indian is exemplified in the difference between Silla and Miss Thompson, who had been crippled by sexual exploitation in the South. Silla, whose relentless pursuit of money is fuelled by memories of an economic exploitation from which she is determined she will save her own children, despises Miss Thompson's generosity to those who are not her kin. Pity for others is a luxury Silla cannot afford. Yet she is not presented without sympathy, as Marshall gradually reveals the complexity of Silla's motivation to Selina and the reader simultaneously. When Silla speaks of her West Indian childhood she does not think of lazy sunshine, but economic oppression in a class-ridden society where gender differences are particularly rigid. Hurston says of the Caribbean islands: 'Women get no bonus for being female down there. She can do the same labors as a man or a mule and nobody thinks anything about it' (*Tell My Horse*, p. 59). In *Browngirl* Silla becomes 'the collective voice of all the Bajan women, the vehicle through which the former suffering found utterance' (*Browngirl*, p. 45).

The themes established in Book I are strengthened in Book II, a bitter-sweet evocation of the pre-pubescent Selina as she trembles on the brink of menstrual initiation into her mother's community of women. Having listened in disbelief to a friend's account of sexuality, Selina is both attracted and repelled by it: attracted by the mysterious activity of young lovers, repelled by an adult womanhood represented by the mother, who is imaged in the kitchen, sitting 'cool, alert, caged in sunlight from the barred window' (p. 52). When Selina sees the caged animals in the zoo, this image returns and destroys her pleasure. She realises that freedom is a transient myth, that the brief respite of childhood will give way to the entrapment of womanhood. Selina's initiation into the female adult world is accomplished in Book III in the ritualistic scene in the kitchen, where she threateningly offers to Silla's friends the shards of a broken glass as a rejection of inclusion in an increasingly materialistic world. The metaphor for Selina's emotional struggle to retain integrity is the Second World War in which the territorial battles between European nations are echoed in the struggle between her parents for control over Deighton's land in Barbados. Familial battle-lines are drawn, with Silla and daughter Ina in one camp, Deighton and Selina in the other. In Silla's eyes Deighton is an economic fool, idly dreaming of a house he would never build, whilst she schemed to 'buy house'. For him the land was a dream, for Silla the land was the means to make a dream come true. She would use the land-sale money as investment capital. In this deadly battle, Selina supports her father, although she recognises that her mother is the family's real bedrock. When war breaks out it is the mother, as the reliable oracular element in their lives, who explains the significance of the conflict; it is the mother who sees the church as a weapon of social control: 'the rum shops and the church join together to keep we pacify and in ignorance' (p. 70). Acutely aware of the economic exploitation of the many by the few, Silla is determined to redress the balance in her personal life, by becoming one of the few. Selina sits listening in admiration at her mother's fluency and power with words into which the mother pours her forceful personality and intelligence, recognising that 'The words were living things to her. She sensed them bestriding the air and charging the room with strong colors' (p. 70).

In Book IV Selina's blossoming womanhood brings an understanding of her mother, herself and the West Indian community. The repetition and passing on of female experience explored in 'The Valley Between' becomes a point of crisis for Selina, who knows that her mother will stop at nothing to become a property owner, but is horrified when her lover points out that she, too, is prepared to be ruthless in pursuit of a desire. Shocked by the recognition, she disclaims it – 'that's the way my mother is, not me' (p. 248). Yet she determines to abuse the newly formed Barbadian Association's scholarship money to fund a new life for herself and her lover. Selina, too, is in moral danger as an exploiter. That she eventually rejects the scholarship and decides to go to Barbados in search of herself is a sign of her possible survival. She pulls back from the moral abyss at the same time as she becomes aware of a racism from which her parents had protected her. As adulthood takes her deeper into the larger world of American society, her race-consciousness becomes stronger. She learns from her disillusioned lover, who seems resigned to the 'victim' status so strongly resisted in Hurston's life and writing. Quoting James Baldwin, Clive says: 'Maybe our own dark faces remind them of all that is dark and unknown and terrifying within themselves' (p. 253). Theory becomes experience in Selina's encounter with a white friend's mother, whose patronising interrogation and smiling questions are framed to remind Selina of her inferior position as a black. With references to the usefulness of West Indian women as house servants, she asks Selina to 'perform' by saying something in West Indian dialect. Confronted with the stereotypical assumptions about her people, Selina is made sadder, but wiser about her mother's driving motivation.

Marshall's view of the West Indian in America is projected through an intense mother/daughter relationship in which Selina's understanding of the mother develops simultaneously with her awareness of her own cultural heritage. Her narrative position is both within and without, as she adopts an omniscient narrative stance yet focuses reader attention through the filter of Selina, who from the beginning is a watcher. Selina's childhood is marked by isolation, from a sister distanced from her by adolescence and a mother she both loved and hated. In her turn, Silla is exasperated by Selina's fantasy of Barbadian life, and views her with 'enraged love', waving a hand that 'dismissed' yet 'embraced' her. This emotional vacillation colours the relationship in which each can recognise themselves in the other. Even as a child, Selina senses that self-knowledge depended upon an understanding of Silla. Only when she confronts racism does she appreciate Silla's strength and resilience and is overwhelmed with admiration for her mother's survival, and ponders her father's defection by suicide: 'How had the mother survived? She who had not chosen death by water?' (p. 293). Silla had been prepared to sacrifice herself completely to provide economic security for her children, whilst Deighton had chosen death rather than face the reality of his economic failure.

Selina never stops loving her father, but evaluates his acceptance of 'victim' status as his lack of self-discipline and application. He attempts accountancy, then music – 'Besides you does get peoples' respect when you's a musician' (p. 84) – but is never truly committed to the pursuit of money. The machinery of capitalism defeats him, metaphorically and literally, when he is caught and permanently crippled in the 'hungry maw' of the machine he ineptly operates, leaving Selina to wonder why the machinery bothers to destroy a father 'already crushed inside'. Deighton's relationship with things mechanical defines his incompatibility with American life, in contrast with Silla who 'worked at an old fashioned lathe which resembled an over-size cook-stove' (p. 99). This analogy points to Silla's perception of both of these machines as a means to an end. With both, she can make money. She pursues financial goals with the relentlessness of a machine: 'only the mother's formidable force could match that of the machines' (p. 100). When Selina cites Gatha Steed's daughter's loveless marriage as an example of how materialism can destroy fine feeling, Silla's response – that she would prefer a dollar in the hand to love – is a defiant cry which is belied by her own sexual attraction towards her husband. Silla learns to stifle and suppress feelings of love that are obstacles to financial goals. When she is seduced into surrendering the land-money cheque to Deighton, she knows she has relented in a foolish way. Deighton spends every penny of the money that was legally his anyway, on presents. As Silla picks up and smashes his new trumpet in rage, Marshall sees her in terms of toil and machinery. She is like 'a cane-cutter wielding a golden machette through ripened corn, or a piston rising and plunging in its cylinder' (p. 131). Deighton's splendidly irresponsible gesture is seen as a denial of Silla's work and striving. Where Silla had succumbed to the lure of materialism, Deighton found eventual solace in a religious movement presided over by the self-proclaimed God, Father Peace, whose sect's denial of the concept of fatherhood relieves Deighton of the responsibility of economic provision for his family. This episode reflects Marshall's personal experience of her own father's defection from his family to work with Father Divine, and in the telling of her father's religious mania there is the conviction of witnessed experience (p. 100).

The Boyce marriage founders on the rocks of different values, aspirations and experience. Deighton's American life began with a whimsical jumping of his ship, whilst Silla's was fired by West Indian immigrant determination to succeed. She scrubbed 'Jew floor', doubled up on jobs, sold her cooked wares, worked in a factory, and studied nursing with the single purpose of buying a house and living 'white'. She has no desire to *be* white, but like Hurston's Jody Starks she wants the life-style enjoyed by whites. Marshall admires the diligence of Silla, Virgil Farnum and Gatha Steed, who 'study the dollar', but warns of the danger to their humanity that materialism brings. The Steed wedding provides the setting for the climactic events which signal Deighton's absolute destruction. Mocked by fellow Barbadians for his fecklessness, Deighton does not accompany his family to the celebrations, which are in full swing when he arrives. Silla is dancing with an old Barbadian who comments on the undeniable pull of the past: 'How can you forget the past, mahn? You does try, but it's here today and there waiting for you tomorrow' (p. 145). His remarks, about dancing, could apply to the choice Silla faces on Deighton's appearance at the wedding – between the Barbadian sunshine and pleasure-loving of her husband, and communal contempt for his economic ineptitude. The latter wins, but is the result of a communal rather than a single consciousness, as the wedding guests in a wheeling, ritualistic dance turn their backs on Deighton, whilst singing, 'Small island, go back where you belong'.

This communal rejection is a visible manifestation of communal tyranny as well as succour, which disorientates Selina, for although pained by her father's public humiliation, she plays a part in it as one in the dancing network likened to 'a giant amoeba which changed shape yet always remained in one piece' (p. 148). The dance reminds her of the communal identity she felt on a family visit to Coney Island, and affirms her need to belong to her community which offers security within an alien host culture. At the same time, Marshall shows that ghettoised living, whilst self-protective, can be dangerously exclusive. Exploitative rents charged to black Americans by West Indian landlords produce one response, 'Even though they ain Bajans they's still our color' (p. 223), contrasted with, 'You got to be hard and sometimes misuse others, even your own' (p. 224). The misuse and abuse of others is the inevitable by-product of capitalism, as destructive as the machine that crippled Deighton. In betraying and defrauding Deighton, Silla had opted to join a system that was the despoiling agent of her own childhood. She had been infected by the capitalist disease.

Marshall depicts her West Indian people, like Mrs Seacole, as determined to make the system work for their benefit. She shows us a community, unlike that in Ann Petry's *The Street*, where unemployment is not a factor in existence. Indeed Marshall does not dodge the issue that West Indians and black Americans have different aspirations: 'West Indian peoples are sure peculiar, but you got to hand it to them, they knows how to get ahead' (p. 215), a fact Marshall states with a mixture of pride and alarm. The spiritual loss inherent in an absolute embracing of capitalism is shown in Silla, and Selina's hope for safety lies in her return to Barbados in search of a meaningful past. Selina's subsequent self-examination is left to the reader's hopeful imagination in this novel, but the Islands are explored in detail in Marshall's collection of novellas, *Soul Clap Hands and Sing*, published in 1961.[5] Except for 'Brooklyn', in these fictions Marshall replaces the urban setting dominated by crowded houses, office blocks and factories where nature is confined to artificial parks, with the landscapes of the Caribbean. The protagonists in this quartet of stories are old men whom Marshal explains 'share a common predicament' in that 'their lives have been essentially empty' (*Merle*, p. 51). In each, the man's encounter with a younger woman confronts him with self-truth. Each is located in a place where the effects of imperialism or enforced migration, are evident: 'Brooklyn', 'Barbados', 'British Guiana' and 'Brazil'. In this collection Marshall explores racial as well as sexual politics with varying degrees of success. The envisaged encounter in 'Brooklyn', between a white

Jewish teacher and a black female student who has to suffer his sexual harassment, Marshall claims is a re-creation of her own experience as a student when, 'If propositioned, you either co-operated, and were sometimes rewarded with an "A", whether your work deserved it or not, or you refused and ran the risk of getting a "C" or worse, or you dropped the course' (*Merle*, p. 27).

By focusing on the abuse of a power relationship which lies, as it does in racist or economic exploitation, at the base of the whole spectrum of sexual harassment, Marshall uses fiction to make political statements. The female student, who needs the academic expertise of the sexually aggressive male, has to negotiate the minefield of sexual, as well as racial, politics. The phallic significance of Berman's cigarette smoking is emphasised when Marshall probes his mind while he is shown fingering a cigarette: 'For some time he fondled it, his fingers shaping soft, voluptuous gestures, his warped old man's hands looking strangely abandoned on the bare desk and limp as if the bones had been crushed' (*Merle*, p. 28). The limpness of his hands emphasises his fear of impotency, his cigarette being a substitute for the power about which he can only dream. The pornographic attention he pays to the cigarette is linked with his private fantasies about copulation with a Rubens or a Gauguin nude. The notion of pornography as the projection of the sexual fantasy of the watching male is seen in his dream of a nude in a boudoir where 'the sun like a voyeur at the half-closed shutters', peeps. The pornographic pleasure of the power-abuser is demonstrated in Berman's reaction to the girl's responses to his menacing sexuality. Her shrinking fear makes him feel powerful, 'Her slight apprehensiveness pleased him in its suggestion of a submissiveness which gave him, as she arose uncertainly, a feeling of certainty and command' (*Merle*, p. 56). Eventually the girl is the victor in this relationship, which might be attributed more to revengeful wish-fulfilment on Marshall's part than fact. The girl student asserts herself with: 'You're so old you're like a cup I could break in my hand' (*Merle*, p. 47), as she leaves him to the darkness of his empty life.

Sexual exploitation is the aim of the old man in 'Barbados', who like the teacher in 'Brooklyn' is seeking succour and compensation for his own inadequacy, in the body of a young woman. A Barbadian returned from America where he spent his working life as a hospital boiler-man, Mr Watford's lonely retirement is lived out on a small farm where he has planted dwarf coconuts because 'with their stunted trunks, they always appeared young' (*Merle*, p. 56). He apes the white life he had seen in America as he sits visibly on his porch, wearing a hospital doctor's uniform, and reading a Boston newspaper. The anger engendered by the American racism he had encountered had been internalised by him into a hatred for his fellow blacks, to whom he affected superiority, and prevents his taking real pleasure in his island home. The empty ritual of his existence is disturbed by his neighbour, the aptly named Mr Goodman, who literally smells of living. This corpulent father of fourteen children, whose Barbadian life had been fulfilling, introduces a boy and a girl to him as workers, pointing out:

> Things is different to before. I mean to say, the young people nowadays is different to how we was. They not just sitting back and taking things no more. They not so frighten for the white people as we was. (*Merle*, p. 58)

Watford's jealous contact with the young Barbadian male revives memories of his own youth, when he had felt pride in his people's capacity for life, and when 'he had always found something unutterably graceful and free in their gestures' (*Merle*, p. 56), despite his sense of shame at their 'easy ways'. The political slogan sported by the young man – 'And the old order shall pass' – sums up the eventual demise of those like Mr Watford, and the hope for a better future. Clearly, as in *Browngirl*, Marshall is emphasising the sterility of a life spent in denial of one's own cultural roots. Watford's embrace of the American life had drained him of vitality and rendered him meaningless to the young Barbadian man, and an object of contempt for the girl after whom he lusted. She eventually does to Watford what the girl in 'Brooklyn' did to Berman. Emphasising his lack of appeal, she says: 'You aint people, Mr Watford'. The appurtenances of a 'white' life are left in disarray as the heart he had so long denied, falters and stops, but not before he realises the waste of his life, as he 'gazed mutely upon the waste and pretence which had spanned his years' (*Merle*, p. 67).

A life wasted is the subject of 'British Guiana' in the person of a man who, having missed an offered chance to discover his identity by going into the island Bush, had subsequently squandered his talents. This is an interesting reworking of the tragic mulatta story in the black literary tradition, taking as subject the mulatto Gerald Motley, whose name reflects his uncertain status as one of mixed blood. Lonely, old, fat and alcoholic, he works as the 'puppet' controller of a radio station governed still by British interests. His affiliation with white society has destroyed his identity, as it had Mr Watford's, and disillusionment as a 'token black' in the media has left him wearing the motley of the tragic clown. To his club mates, he says: 'The name, gentlemen? Gerald Ramsdeen Motley. My title sirs? B. S. W. C: Bastard Spawned of the World's Commingling' (*Soul*, p. 70). As a 'colored', Motley is not a member of the ruling white class; as a well-paid employee, he is separated from the blacks. His own chance for self-realisation when the Bush had 'closed around him, becoming another dimension of himself, the self he had sought' (*Soul*, p. 74) he had ignored in favour of his mistress. His opportunity to become attuned once more to the vital natural world with which his black ancestors had been in communion, was lost for ever. Meeting that ex-mistress after a separation of thirty years reveals the emptiness of a life decision made in favour of a woman he probably never really liked. A possible latent homosexual love is hinted at in his promotion of his young male protégé, Parrish, and his realisation about his ex-mistress that 'he could have confessed that although he had not known it then, he had found her woman's form distasteful' (*Soul*, p. 123). His death in a car accident brings a sense of relief rather than tragedy, perhaps because Marshall only hints at his homosexuality and glances at his lost contact with the natural in the island. She does not give enough insight into his early potential to suggest that his life *had* been a tragic waste. There is nothing in Motley to suggest either strength or struggle; he is, and was, nothing more than a victim of accident.

Still exploring the loss of identity in those who adopt an alien persona in search of material success, her complex story 'Brazil' can be read as an interrogation of the tyranny of gender construction. Caliban (Hector Guimares) is an ageing artiste who retires to discover that his real identity had been obliterated by his stage character of a comic Caliban. In his stage routine the tiny 'Caliban' appears as a boxer, accompanied by a long-legged 'Miranda'. In reality Hector is no monster, but a man in search of his lost youth, and his wife 'Miranda' is no innocent pastoral virgin, but an ex-mistress who surrounds herself with ostentatious, material artefacts. Caliban is in reality a small, sad man, whose personality had been gradually annexed by the monster of his stage creation. His uncertain identity is emphasised in the references to mirrors. When quarrelling with Miranda, a slammed door jars his 'mirror on his dressing table so that his reflection wavered out of shape within its somber, mottled depth' (*Soul*, p. 138). His personal identity, erased by the stage image created for him by Miranda, has no substance. When he realises his inner emptiness – the void left when his life had been drained in the stage parody of the war between the sexes – he embarks upon a destructive rampage in Miranda's flat, smashing 'the mirrors and his reflection there'. Only when his reflection is destroyed are his despair and confusion dispelled. Although the story focuses on the hollowness of the artificially constructed gender identity of a man, it resonates with the frustrated rage of women, whose social construction as wife and mother can lead to middle-aged confusion and lack of self-identity.

This issue is specifically and with more conviction addressed in 'Reena',[6] a short story published in 1962 which locates the problem of identity where Marshall had experienced it, among 'the comparatively small group of young black women I knew best' (*Merle*, p. 71). Narrated in the first person, the story is a confessional retelling of a meeting with a girlhood friend, at the funeral of Reena's Aunt Vi, who had spent her life facelessly serving whites. The funeral allows the women to confront the continuance of the black woman's social definition in a white society, 'that definition of me, of her and millions like us, formulated by others to serve out their fantasies' (*Merle*, p. 73). In their youth they had believed they could reject white labels and redefine themselves. Reena's first step towards self-definition had been taken when she put an extra 'e' into her name. Forcing all to acknowledge her act of self-naming, Reena would 'imprint those "e"s on your mind with the indelible black of her eyes and a threatening finger that was like a quill' (*Merle*, p. 14). This image neatly joins the power of naming with language as instruments of social control which the women begin to examine. Discussing the tyranny of a white concept of female beauty, Reena, like Maya Angelou and Morrison's Pecola Breedlove, confesses: 'I had my share of waking up to find myself with long, blonde curls, blue eyes and skin like milk' (*Merle*, pp. 18–19). As the two examine and reject the labels of 'victim' and 'sex object', they realise they still have a political responsibility to struggle for a self-definition which would give meaning to the sacrificial toil of all the ancestral women like Aunt Vi. Marshall concludes this story with the thought that this duty will be fulfilled only if the succeeding generations of black women reclaim the history of their Afro-American mothers.

The need to embrace and celebrate the values and lives of their enslaved mothers becomes a strengthening preoccupation in Marshall's writing, poignantly explored in 'To Da-Duh, in Memorian',[7] which commemorates a childhood visit to her grandmother, Da-Duh, in Barbados. Like Toni Morrison's Pilate, Alice Walker's Lissy and her own character Aunt Cuney in *Praisesong for the Widow*,[8] Da-Duh is an ancestor figure, symbolic of 'the long line of black women and men – African and New World – who made my [Marshall's] being possible' (*Merle*, p. 95). In this story Marshall holds the American and Barbadian worlds in productive contrast as she re-creates her grandmother's attempts to pass on to her granddaughter her own accumulated knowledge of the natural virtues of Barbados, which were constantly rebutted by childish tales of a North perpetually covered in snow. Having absorbed the alien artificiality of white culture, Da-Duh's granddaughter entertains her with performances of slick dances to the music of tin-pan alley, causing the old woman 'to stare at me as if I were a creature from Mars' (*Merle*, p. 102). The conflict in culture was such that the child might well have been from another planet. Ever anxious not to be outdone, Da-Duh leads the girl deeper into the island, pointing to the magnificence of an especially tall palm-tree, only to be topped by the child's reference to the Empire State Building. Da-Duh's offerings from the natural world are out-rivalled by her granddaughter's boasts of industrialised society's wonders. Da-Duh died in 1937, on a day when the Barbadian sky echoed to the ultimate manifestation of destructive technological progress in the thundering of threatening British planes. Da-Duh's 'American' grandchild salvaged precious wisdom from this memory of her grandmother, which is amplified in her later writing.

The formidable Da-Duh, who rightly suspects that to worship the machine is to follow a false God, re-emerges in *The Chosen Place, The Timeless People*,[9] published in 1971, in the figure of Leesy, whose life had been spent on the fictional Bourne Island. When Leesy's great-nephew dies driving a car he had restored, she knows that her innate distrust of machinery is justified. This is not to suggest a hankering in Marshall for a pre-industrial pastoral idyll, and Leesy's stubborn refusal to transport her sugar-cane by motor in favour of a donkey is not seen as wise, but understandable. Like Da-Duh, Leesy embodies a wisdom brought from Africa which it is peril to ignore. She had retained the African faculty of seeing beyond and through reality, described by Hurston in *Tell My Horse*, which persuaded her, as it did the Western-educated Merle, of the life of seemingly inanimate objects. When Leesy and Merle abandon a journey because of a landslide the road is described as having 'run off' in the night. Merle 'goads' and then 'rests' her battered car as if it were living, and accepts Leesy's interpretation of a dream visit from the dead. Marshall's concern is that African spiritual wisdom such as Leesy's is preserved and allowed to coexist with Western science on equal terms. The novel, now sadly out of print, exists in a shortened story – 'Merle' – in a Virago edition, which excludes the in-depth portraits of many characters in the novel. Marshall claims that Merle is her own favourite amongst her fictional characters, but in a reading of the novel she is a vehicle for, rather than the essence of, the subject matter. Capitalistic exploitation, already explored in the lives of West Indian migrants to Brooklyn, is shown in *Chosen Place* as the reason for that migration. Taking up where *Browngirl* ends, it offers a penetrating vision of the Barbados Selina Boyce would have found. Selina, like Merle, would have been disappointed.

Marshall allows the reader, like the visiting Americans Saul and Harriet, to see Bourne Island initially from the air, where it appears as a tiny green speck in the blue Caribbean. Gradually, the reader is taken deeper into the physical and spiritual life of the island, which itself seems to expand with acquaintance. The small island is a microcosm of West Indian community life, still exploited by imperialist interests, and under threat from an alien culture which can only be resisted by a cleaving to an African cultural heritage. Merle's retelling of African spider stories to the island children is an instance of this, but the message of the novel, as well as an explanation of Marshall's narrative method, is formulated by the visitor, Saul: 'But sometimes it is necessary to go back before you can go forward, really forward. And that's not only true for people – individuals – but nations as well' (p. 359).

Marshall does not offer a romantic or sentimentalised vision of an island paradise, but an exploration of imperialist rape. The economic and political history of Bourne Island is one of exploitation with deep historical roots, and resounding consequences. The initial despoli-ation began with the planting of sugar-cane to please the palates of white Europeans, and continued with the enslavement of Africans to work the crops. Economic, social and sexual exploitation are concentrated in an island so small that Merle's white forefather had populated the island with his offspring. He had sired, at 75, 'the last of his forty children he had from the black women who worked on his estate' (p. 69). Illegitimacy and miscegenation had produced a society as surely shaped by racism as that of America, although the resultant social structure in the island differed to that in the South, where *all* with black blood were relegated to the same underclass. In the Bourne Island social hierarchy the agents of the controlling imperialist interests are at the top, and at the bottom are the 'Little Fellas', descendants of slaves. In the middle and belonging nowhere are those of mixed blood like Merle and Gerald Motley in 'British Guiana'. The pernicious consequences of slavery are at the forefront of this novel, whose four-part structure begins with 'Heirs and descendants'. The islanders of slave ancestry, Leesy and Vere, are the 'Little Fellas', Harriet Amron and Sir John are imperialist exploiters, Merle and her friend Lyle Hutson are the displaced coloured. Lyle, a barrister, who has succumbed to Savile Row suits and fat fees, allies himself to a ruling class which still holds him at arm's length. Merle, on the other hand, is equally ineffectual as a middle-aged revolutionary, whose compulsive, nagging talk simply disguises her despair. Her confused identity is apparent in her wearing of clothes of multi-coloured African cloth, and her driving of an old Bentley which had belonged to the island's British governor. Emotionally she is allied to the 'Little Fella', yet when bureaucratic and exploitative interests defeat them, she retreats into ineffectual cataleptic depression. Like Lyle, Merle had been educated in England, where it is suggested that she fell prey to the sexual attentions of a white Englishwoman, whose gifts of money she had accepted. Merle's enslaved state is symbolised by her wearing of that woman's gift of 'Pendant silver ear-rings carved in the form of those saints to be found on certain European churches' (p. 4). Only when making love does Merle ever remove these symbols of European culture and oppression, and her eventual abandonment of these, along with skin-whitening and hair-straightening, are marks of her eventual freedom.

The island represents 'every place that has been wantonly used, its substance stripped away and then abandoned' (p. 100). Yet despite its economic despoliation, Bourne Island has a resilient beauty which flashes out in the zinnias that Merle breathes in, the wild flowers Harriet picks, and the Cassia tree which blooms briefly once a year. The island has a power and beauty which can heal the spiritual wounds of those who respond to it, as Saul Amron does when he and Harriet confront the Bush which Motley in 'British Guiana' had turned his back on, and the experience pushes them apart. As Saul becomes committed to the 'Little Fellas', his wife Harriet's faith rests in the organising, paternalistic power of the Almighty Dollar. Imperceptibly their allegiances separate them, as surely as their beds begin to slide apart until 'there was a thin gulf which reached to the floor between them' (p. 147). Saul strives to find economic solutions that recognise the Islanders' own resources, whilst the ever-cool, neatly groomed Harriet unconsciously plays the charitable lady bountiful of Victorian philanthropy. Hers is a distant ministering, 'She appeared immunised to all' (p. 175). As she dispenses drinks, bandages and hospitality she preserves intact her air of aloof superiority. She is symbolic of the old colonial order. In a position of control, she feels no shared humanity with the Bournehills poor, and anticipates her return to America and 'the life and people we know' (p. 230). When relaxing on a beach in the white residential area she is irritated by the intrusion of poor black children. Implicit in this is her feeling that these poor are acceptable in Bournehills, where they *belonged*, but not where they are visible to the rich.

The moment of revelation for Selina in *Browngirl* comes within Afro-Caribbean folk ritual, as it does for Avey when in *Praisesong for the Widow* she joins in the African dancing on Carriacou. The importance of ritual as a reminder of a cultural history is also emphasised in the carnival in *Chosen Place*, when celebration of the Island's history acts as an agent of purgation. Masks are dropped and hidden truths are forced into the open: Saul and Merle share and confront past mistakes; Harriet's racism is inescapable when, swept into the carnival by young revellers, she thinks they should be 'bathed, their mouths scrubbed clean of the tobacco and rum smell, and put to bed' (p. 295). Harriet Amron's provision of funds for research into a possible project for economic recovery had seemed like benevolent philanthropy. Yet Harriet's wealth was produced by the economic sins of a female ancestor who 'had launched the family's modest wealth by her small-scale specialisation in the West Indian trade' (p. 37) – a trade which involved providing, and providing for, slave labour. In truth Harriet's inheritance included a belief in the superiority of the whites, and a racist dislike of people of colour. The reader, and Merle, make the inevitable connection between Harriet and the 'someone' of whom she had reminded Merle. She is like the Englishwoman who thought she had bought Merle.

The carnival is dominated by the Bournehills' dramatic rendering of Ned Cuffee's slave rebellion, when imperialist rule was overturned and for a short time the Islanders lived free and proved their self-sufficiency: 'For food there had been the yam, cassava and sweet potato grown in the fields. Breadfruit and mango had been plentiful on the trees. They had fished the Bournehills sea' (p. 263). The imaginative re-enactment of that historical moment is full of pride, and Marshall's belief in the power of Afro-Caribbean history to revitalise the community is affirmed. Yet no easy solutions are offered. Fiction cannot provide easy answers to a heritage of rape and enslavement which Saul describes as a 'whole goddam inhuman system . . . [which] got started in this part of the world long before you were born' (p. 358). The only hope offered by Marshall is that in remembering the past Saul and Merle might make individual contributions to a less-encumbered future. Merle has to rid herself of all the memorabilia in her private room that had 'expressed her struggle for identity' and her 'desire for reconciliation'. In dispensing with the confused jumble of her emotional luggage, Merle is able to put the past into perspective and steps into a future – minus her ear-rings.

In her latest novel, *Praisesong for the Widow* (1983), Marshall deepens her exploration of a materialistic burdening which is also the subject-matter of Morrison's *Song of Solomon*. Marshall, like Morrison, takes her title from a particular element in African myth and ritual, and utilises the African slaves' mythical ability to leave their physical enslavement to return to their spiritual homeland. *Praisesong* is an harmonious blending of the narrative themes of her earlier writing encompassed in an increasingly metaphorical style, in which metaphorical structure and meaning are inseparable. It opens with the affluent widow, Avey Johnson, desperately trying to cram her many clothes into suitcases as she plans to abandon a Caribbean cruise ship. Immediate questions are raised: why is the widow leaving the cruise midway? Why stealthily? What is she running from or to? The answers lie in the past, as the corseted and brogued Avey is suddenly overwhelmed by memories of barefoot dancing in her early married life. Avey Johnson is what Silla Boyce of *Browngirl* would become – affluent but empty. As Marshall moves away from the brownstone setting of her first novel, to a West Indian island setting, so she strengthens her political affirmation of the need to reclaim the past. *Praisesong* reveals her confident grip on her material and a greater clarity of vision, being less diffuse than *Browngirl*, less accusatory than *Chosen Place* and, because less obviously dominated by linear time, more pervasive. Chronology is replaced by a circulatory interdependence of past and present, as Avey Johnson's past crowds her present with clamorous memories, pressing for attention. Long-suppressed denial of her roots appears in dreams of Aunt Cuney, who had been the repository of Ibo myths about their landing in America, when, struck by a vision of their enslaved future, they turned in a body and 'walked' back across the ocean to Africa. Aunt Cuney had wanted to pass this knowledge on to her female descendant, Avatara. Rational materialism had dimmed this memory in Avey and, with it, her spiritual heritage from those pure-born Africans who, Cuney's grandmother had said, 'could see in more ways than one' (*Praisesong*, p. 37).

In *Praisesong*, Avey's neglect of Aunt Cuney's teaching precipitates a crisis signalled by her inability to recognise her own mirrored reflection. Thirty years of absorption into a middle-class life-style have transformed her into a stranger: 'she could not place the woman in beige crepe de chine and pearls' (p. 48). She is lost amongst the gloves and corsets which symbolise the unnatural constraints of a life spent in pursuit of money success. Predominantly the action in this novel takes place in the tortured consciousness of Avey as she struggles to accommodate the significance of a past in which, in spite of affluence, she had lost more than she had gained. In their embracing of white values and in their neglect of ancestral history, Avey and her husband had denied that which had defined them. Having gorged herself in the consumer paradise of affluence, when Avey sits at the sumptuously laden dinner table, she feels uncomfortably bloated with the accumulated years of an undigested self. The cruise food causes nausea and the 'long line girdle she had on with its bones and heavy latex was beginning to chafe her' (p. 71). An impending time of reckoning is at hand which cannot be dispelled by antacid tablets. The symptoms of her spiritual disorder multiply as she is assailed by flooding memories of her life with her now-dead husband Jay, who had married a hopeful Avatara to see her transformed into 'Avey'. From Avatara, to Avey, then to Avey Johnson, was how she had defined herself, and now 'the woman to whom these names belonged had gone away' (p. 141). Her identities had been shaped by circumstances in which her beloved Jay had become the accountant, Jerome Johnson. With sharpening clarity she realises her husband had lost himself in his pursuit of a career, and had died spiritually years before physical death claimed his exhausted body. Grieving for a love which had been vibrant with mutual joy, she recalls their enjoyment of the jazz and Blues music that had been their contact with their African past: 'The Jay who emerged from the music of an evening, the self that would never be seen down at the store, was open, witty, playful, even outrageous at times' (p. 95). Jay's spontaneous joy died in years of work and study as he climbed out of the ghetto onto the financial ladder, where he gradually disappeared, 'went into eclipse' as his sunshine was extinguished in material acquisition.

Marshall does not criticise Jerome Johnson for doing his best, but laments that the 'best' was perceived as living 'white'. With successful pursuit of the materialist dream, his colour faded on his 'strange pallid face'. He even talked 'white', and thought 'white'. His separation from the black roots which had nourished him are in his dismissal of less successful black men: 'That's the trouble with half these Negroes you see out here. Always working for the white man instead of getting out and doing for themselves' (p. 131). He distances himself from those he considers – as would a white – lazy and shiftless. His spiritual death causes him to reject the black music and dancing which he and Avey had rejoiced in. Watching friends dancing, he fulminates at their pleasure, saying: 'If it was left to me I'd close down every dancehall in Harlem and burn every drum! That's the only way these Negroes out here'll be making any progress' (p. 132). He had turned his back on his people and his heritage from which he sought physical as well as spiritual distance. Progress from the slums had placed himself and Avey in a black middle-class ghetto, ironically named North White Plains, where they insulated themselves from the reality of black disadvantage and the violence of 'Watts and Selina and the tanks and stoner guns in the streets of Detroit' (p. 140). Jealously guarding their new found status, they refused to be identified with the civil rights struggle.

Afraid of their own blackness the Johnsons had surrounded themselves with images of whiteness which Avey carries into widowhood. The cruise ship from which she flees is significantly named 'Bianca Pride', epitomising white values, with its white name, white colour, its iceberg appearance in the blue of the Caribbean. In the 'Versailles' dining-room Avey had enjoyed food created to please over-indulged palates. She begins to find the food cloying and nauseating, and her fellow passengers look to her like living corpses.

Her prized mink wrap becomes an obscene reality – the skins of living animals – and her envisaged home like a museum crammed with the artefacts of a dead civilisation. The futility of a life spent in pursuit of white success is brought home to her when her light-skinned cruise companion Thomasina says of Avey's defection, 'it . . . don't . . . pay . . . to . . . go . . . no . . . place . . . with . . . *niggers*' (p. 27). Acceptance of white values was an implicit acceptance of white racism from which these black women could not hide, any more than Avey could from nightmares in which she and her Aunt Cuney are physically fighting. Psychically disturbed by these dreams of her dead Aunt, as Jadine was by dreams of ancestor women in Morrison's *Tar Baby*, Avey waits on Grenada for a flight home. In a few short hours she unconsciously begins a rebirth as she sheds her clothes in a hotel bedroom. The unlayering of her body, that she does as if she were a child learning to undress, symbolises a rejection of the materialism which was choking her. Her watch, which only measured time in the present, is discarded, her dress unironed, her hair uncombed and her face unpowdered. Images of birth abound, 'the caul' over her mind is lifted as her resistance to her ancestral past crumbles. Wandering on the beach where she meets Lebert Joseph, she experiences a child-like stubbornness and makes a face at Lebert's back. Persuaded by Lebert to join the annual trip to Carriacou to witness the ancient dances of the African nations, she recaptures the sense of confraternity experienced on her Coney Island excursions as a child. The passage to Carriacou is one of birth trauma for Avey, and the metaphor of rebirth is skilfully presented. The narrow, stormy channel through which the small craft passes is like the birth canal, the 'gaping hole' through which it goes leads to the bright waters of a life's beginning. The accumulated sickness of her adult years are vomited and defecated out of her newly purged body, in convulsive abdominal contractions. Finally, like a baby who had soiled itself, she is bathed, baptised anew, in readiness for the dancing. With the help of the old Joseph, Avey had given birth to herself. Like Aunt Cuney, Joseph is 'someone who possessed ways of seeing that went beyond sight' (p. 172). When Avey had strayed into his rum shop he had looked inside her, seen the emptiness, and strives to save her soul. When Avey joins in the tribal dancing of the 'Pardon Me', an African placation of the spirits of their ancestral dead, he is described as feeling like a proud father. Cleansed and purified, Avey returns to America resolved to take her grandchildren to the Ibo landing-place, and pass on Aunt Cuney's heritage.

Praisesong, like Hurston's *Their Eyes Were Watching God*, is a love story in which the death of the male partner leaves the female protagonist alone to evaluate meaning. Janie Crawford's happiness is found in memories of a shared 'black' life with Teacake; Avey's sadness is that she and Jerome had turned their backs upon that life. *Praisesong* is a compelling and tightly constructed novel in which form and meaning fuse into a poetic whole, marking a unified resolution of the thematic concerns explored singly in Marshall's earlier fiction. It expresses the culmination of Marshall's search for meaning, which had begun with narrative exploration of oppression, and ends to date with a coherent vision of a possible future built upon a cherished past. Ancestral heritage had been found in Carriacou, the island from which Audre Lorde's mother had emigrated to America. It is the legendary way in which Carriacou women love each other that Lorde sees as her own heritage in *Zami*. She shares with Marshall a West Indian culture celebrated with pride: 'I am proud to be of stock from the country that mounted the first Black English speaking People's Revolution in this hemisphere. Much has been lost in Grenada, but not all – not the spirit of her people' ('Grenada Revisited', in *Sister Outsider*, p. 189).[10]

Lorde reported a Grenadian visit which verifies Marshall's fictional depiction in *Chosen Place* of the Westminster low road's disintegration. Lorde records seeing men and women mending 'the road ahead of us with hoes and rock hammers, wheelbarrows and other hand tools' (*Sister*, p. 178). In this punchy essay she records the legacy of colonialism in a society riddled with classism and colorism. Like Marshall, Lorde applauds West Indians' rejection of superficial solutions imposed from the outside as evidence of the islanders' spirit of resistance and independence. These are qualities placed high on Lorde's list of human values, and are expressed in her prose and poetry.

The compass of this present work does not allow for a protracted study of her poetry, but its emotional source is clearly defined in her essays. In 'Poetry is not a luxury' Lorde stresses the need for black women to 'respect those hidden sources of our power from where true knowledge and therefore lasting action comes' (*Sister*, p. 37). It is in Lorde's connection between emotion and action, between poetry and rhetoric, between the personal and the political, that we can discern the cutting edge of her feminist consciousness. With clarity and courage she articulates some of women's fiercest and long-hidden dreams. She urges women to verbalise their instinctive wisdom and so express selves that have been hitherto suppressed. She argues that to hide a self-truth is to bow to oppression, and as a lesbian mother she claims the right to express her own sexuality without the burden of society's opprobrium. It is Lorde's belief that to maintain silence in the face of oppression is to give that oppression tacit acceptance. In 'The transformation of Silence into Language and action' (*Sister*, p. 40), she articulates her very real fear of being silenced for ever because of the breast cancer she had developed. The possibility of a premature death gives urgency to her appeal to all women to speak up before it is too late. She recognises the courage needed in a self-expression which involves a painful exposure of an inner self, and admits that her own courage was strengthened by her knowledge of her African heritage. She describes how the Afro-American harvest festival 'Kwanga' embodies a message of encouragement to all women: 'Kujichagulia – self-determination – the decision to define ourselves, name ourselves, and speak for ourselves, instead of being defined and spoken for by others' (*Sister*, p. 43).

Self-definition must be preceded by self-knowledge – a process which Lorde admits is painful but necessary if the uniqueness of each individual is to be celebrated. She argues that human energy becomes a dynamic press for progress when, and only when, human differences are recognised. In 'Scratching the Surface' (*Sister*, p. 45) she says that within a patriarchal society any departure from heterosexuality is considered deviant and produces homophobia. This she says springs from a fear of difference which she identifies as being at the root of oppression wherever it occurs in human relationships. The failure of the imagination to encompass the notion of difference as a powerful and regenerative source for good, has in turn led to the ascribing of false power to that which is perceived as different: 'To the racist, Black people are so powerful that the presence of one can contaminate a whole lineage; to the heterosexist, lesbians are so powerful that the presence of one can contaminate a whole sex' (*Sister*, p. 51). She insists that black men and women should unite against racism and that *all* women, irrespective of colour, should unite against sexism, in the belief that human progress is possible only if the individual is freed from any societal categorisation which gives hierarchical power to a race, class, gender or one definition of sexuality.

In the essay 'Erotic as Power' Lorde's thesis is that the erotic is a natural, female resource which has been perverted, suppressed and controlled under patriarchal order, wherein it has been misnamed or confused with pornography. She recalls that the root of 'erotic' is the Greek word 'eros' meaning love, which she further defines as a desire to share rather than to use. Pornography she defines as 'sensation without feeling': an absence of sharing; an exploitation she identifies with sexism. In words addressed to those black men who equate a rejection of sexism by their women with a racial betrayal, she warns that sexism is a white disease with which they could become infected. She could well have had in mind the supposed response of Stokely Carmichael in 1965 to a question about what position black women should take in the struggle for civil rights. The answer he gave was 'Prone'. As Marshall's fiction depicts the spiritual disabling of those people who too readily accept capitalist goals and gods, so Lorde's essays warn that sexism and racism are no different in kind: 'It is not the destiny of Black Americans to repeat white America's mistakes. But we will if we mistake the trappings of success in a sick society for the signs of a meaningful life' (*Sister*, p. 63).

Her vision of a society freed from the restrictive concepts of class, race and gender is embodied in all she writes. She also tries to make the personal political in her role as a mother. Her wish for the son she has reared is that he will develop into the sort of person *he*, not she or society, prescribes. She constantly reiterates the message that the personal *is* political, and that the female psyche can only be unlocked in the process of rigorous self-examination. Nevertheless, just as she warns black men not to repeat the strategies of oppression they had learned from whites in the course of their own oppression, so she warns all those who care to listen that a new social structure will need new tools of analysis. In 'The Master's tools will not dismantle the Master's House' she emphasises her belief that contemporary society is built upon an idea of human conformity which denies diversity. She demands more than a tokenism towards difference: 'Difference must be not merely tolerated, but seen as a fund of necessary polarities between which our creativity can spark like a dialectic' (*Sister*, p. 111). Lorde warns that social repression of difference produces a corrosive loathing born of fear.

Many of Lorde's ideas have become absorbed into current feminist thinking, but even in this she advises caution. Women's voices are, and should remain, diverse – 'some problems we share as women, some we do not' (*Sister*, p. 119). The fierceness of feminist debate illustrates the truth of this observation, which Lorde in her celebration of difference would surely commend, for she warns that feminists should not replace masculine orthodoxy with a feminine one. She insists that the intensity of discussion should not give way to division, and that diversity should produce strength. In 'Learning from the 60's' she observes that any movement towards liberation is a complex one, and that anger should be directed towards the forces of repression and not dissipated in internal wrangling. At a time when the black community regarded the struggle against racism and sexism as mutually exclusive, this warning was pertinent. Yet her warning is equally true of the Women's Movement which, to survive and grow, has to acknowledge a diversity of opinion within its ranks. She talks of the danger inherent in assuming that 'Blackness' (and here we might substitute 'femaleness') is a totality; that unity means uniformity. She echoes Hurston's claim that black people 'are not some standard digestible quantity' (*Sister*, p. 136), and nor are women, black or white. Above all else Lorde stresses that self-love is vital to human health and happiness, a lesson reiterated by Angelou, Toni Morrison and Alice Walker. In 'Eye to Eye' she points out that this self-love must be for blacks deeper than 'Black is Beautiful' and must begin with a reclamation of self. It is not surprising that much of what Lorde says is applicable and attractive to white as well as black women.

Lorde's advocation of a positive appreciation of difference which transcends mere tolerance, is a unifying one. Her philosophy is certainly women-loving but it is not destructively men-hating. Sexual and racial oppression is the product of the disease of unloving; wholeness, as Alice Walker demonstrates in *The Color Purple*, is the loving acceptance of difference. Lorde foregrounds women in the belief that if they can reclaim a life-force which society has sought to stifle, then everyone will benefit. This life-force in black women had suffered particular attack in America, yet these women can still lay claim to a 'history of use and sharing of power, from the Amazon legions of Dahomey, thro' the Ashanti Warrior Queen Yaa Asantewaa and the freedom fighter Harriet Tubman' (*Sister*, p. 151). To this list can be added those black American women writers whose fiction springs from a reclamation of their African culture, and in whose writing fictional stereotyping of black women has been destroyed. Along with Morrison, Walker, Angelou and Marshall, Lorde recognises the communal succouring of the individual, no matter how the community is defined. In Lorde's case, where her colour and her lesbianism rendered her an outsider in society, her nourishment comes from the loving support of other women. These she tenderly names in her poetry and in *The Cancer Journals*.[11] In this she shares the horror, pain and fear of radical mastectomy as she had experienced and confided it to her private diary. As a message of compassionate hope to all women who suffer the same disease and surgery, *The Cancer Journals* is outstandingly direct and honest. Pain and despair are not minimised but Lorde focuses on living, not dying. Her decision not to 'lie' about her absent breast, by refusing to wear a prosthesis, illustrates her determination to live positively; not cautiously, but deliberately. In this journal she offers her own courage to fellow cancer sufferers. In facing up to, *naming* and so controlling her illness, she shows that it can be survived – whole.

In this journal she expresses her will to carry on working. The result of that work is *Zami*:

> *1/2/80*
> The novel is finished at last. It has been a lifeline. I do not have to win in order to know my dreams are valid, I only have to believe in a process of which I am a part. My work kept me alive this past year, my work and my love of women. (*Journals*, p. 5)

During her illness she fully engaged in the emotions of anger, pain and love which make up that process which is life. In all her writing she explores her own self, but no more so than in *Zami*, which she described in an interview as a 'biomythography'.[12] In this invented description she creates a new name for the 'autobiography' which recognises the mythical, historical and subjective constituents of that genre. *Zami*, she said, is 'a fiction built from many stories'.

One source of *Zami* is her West Indian consciousness which allows her to comment that Grenadians walk like Africans and Trinidadians do not. Her perception of Grenada had been shaped by a mother who was one of a long line of 'Black island women who defined themselves by what they did' (*Zami*, p. 9). Autobiography is a self-definition which takes account of the shaping of the individual self-awareness by familial and social forces. Lorde's early awareness came from a mother who talked of Carriacou as 'home'. An emigrant islander, she felt an alien stranger in America, homesick and uprooted – 'Most of all she missed the Sunday-long boat trips that took her to Aunt Anni's at Carriacou' (p. 11). Like Marshall's grandmother Da-Duh, Lorde's mother had tried to pass on to her children her own inherited culture. They soon became conversant with the medicinal properties of plants which they had never seen growing. When as an adult Lorde scalded herself she immediately applied cocoa butter to the scalded area, *knowing* that this would heal the scars. Lorde knew too that family hair and nail clippings had to be meticulously burned, presumably to prevent those who wished them evil from using them in Hoodoo ritual. In *Zami* the mother is presented as caring but constrained, powerful yet powerless – a 'Black dyke' – in that she was woman-oriented, but would have rejected that description of herself in any sexual sense. The mother/daughter relationship Lorde describes is one of deep longing on her part to love and be loved by a mother who increasingly held her at arm's length. Lorde's memories are of a childhood seen in a myopic daze of extreme short-sightedness, but coloured by an emotional distancing from parents she longed to touch. Her love of her mother was mixed with awe at her power within the family and the West Indian community. Her greatest desire was to please this woman in whose eyes she felt imperfect:

> My mother had two faces and a frying pot
> where she cooked up her daughters
> into girls
> before she fixed our dinner.
> My mother had two faces
> and a broken pot
> where she hid out a perfect daughter
> who was not me
> I am the sun and moon forever hungry
> for her eyes.
> From 'From the House of Yemanja'[13]

The fierce love/hate relationship which has the intensity of Marshall's Selina and Silla Boyce, is neither completely delineated nor reconciled in *Zami*, perhaps because Marshall's was fictional and Lorde's was based on reality, and resolution is easier in fiction than in life. The rebellious adolescence Lorde describes does seem to indicate a deep and unbridgable rift between daughter and parents. It is likely, though never explicitly stated, that the mother recognised Lorde's ambiguous sexuality and feared for her survival in a hostile society, where to be black and female were disadvantages enough. To have admitted to lesbian sexuality in the 1930s and 1940s, as Lorde was to discover in the 1950s, was a perilous act. Moreover, West Indian survival in America depended upon strategies of negation – 'Self preservation starts very early in West Indian families' (p. 22). Such protectiveness meant that her parents would studiously ignore a racism against which they felt powerless. When Lorde and her mother were spat upon in the street, the mother cleaned off the spittle, complaining that 'people spat in the wind' and took no heed of where the spittle landed. The mother's pain was controlled in public but would erupt occasionally in the violence of the powerless to the abused. When Lorde complains to her mother that at school her colour meant that her intellectual brightness was not rewarded, her mother erupts with pent-up fury. The mother had known all along that this would be Lorde's experience at school and admonishes her never to expect fairness. But her pain, her contempt is directed not only at the whites but also at her child: 'What kind of a ninny raise up here to think those good-for-nothing white piss-jets would pass over some little jacabat girl to elect you anything' (p. 60).

Although recognised by the parents, racism was never discussed or named in front of the children, in the vain hope that a silent refusal to define it would offer protection. On the occasion of the graduation-present outing to Washington on the 4th of July, they have to confront reality. On a day symbolising democracy and freedom, the family are refused service in an ice-cream parlour. Lorde's memory of this is dominated by a 'whiteness' which had set her family apart. The waitress, the ice-cream, the heat, the pavement and the monuments were all white. The painful, humiliating 'recognition' scene laid the seeds for Lorde's fervour to see political change. Although Lorde learned 'diversionary defences' against racism from her mother, she sadly accepted that although such defences enabled survival, it was not a survival 'whole'.

In Lorde's view passive refusal to confront racism is a form of spiritual suicide. Moreover, parental protectiveness of this kind is double-edged, in that the shock of awareness is greater for children who enter the larger society of school unprepared for it. When the Lordes were the first black family to live in the previously white Washington Heights, the suicide of their Jewish landlord was attributed to their arrival. Lorde was questioned about this at the Catholic school where she was also the first ever black pupil. There, despite its government by the Sisters of Charity, she encountered blatant racial discrimination: 'Their racism was unadorned, unexcused and particularly painful because I was unprepared for it' (p. 59).

Racism was inscribed in the education system, from the division of children into 'fairies' and 'brownies' to the storybooks 'about people who were different from us. They were blond and white and lived in houses with trees around them and had dogs named Spot' (p. 18). Lorde's experience of such schooling is a reality fictionalised in Morrison's *The Bluest Eye*. The fictional Pecola Breedlove could not survive the experience; happily Lorde did, and her growing curiosity about what the word 'colored' meant gradually sharpened into a positive determination to love her blackness. 'I grew Black as my need for life, for affirmation, for love, for sharing – copying from my mother what was in her unfulfilled' (p. 58).

Yet in spite of Lorde's growing armour of self-love she was not immune to the pain of racist or sexist abuse. She re-creates the squirming discomfort of a child who is defenceless against the sexual molestation of a comic-book vendor, and the painful memory of the suicide of her teenaged friend Gennie, who had been subject to parental abuse of a physical and probably sexual nature. Gennie's death, about which Lorde cannot talk to her parents, serves to increase her sense of adolescent isolation. Feeling an 'outsider' because of her colour, her near-blindness, her sexuality, she decides to leave school to join the adult world of work, where racial discrimination is again a factor. She discovers that some employers regularly hired and fired black workers after the three weeks they were allowed to work before they were eligible to join the union. She worked with women in a process that caused liver and kidney cancer, about which no warning had been given. To the sexual and racial exploitation of women with which she had grown up, was added economic exploitation. Unlike her mother, who refuses to give oppression credibility by naming it, Lorde feels she has to name oppression wherever she meets it:

> So it is better to speak
> remembering
> We were never meant to survive
> From 'A Litany for Survival'[14]

Although this poem is about the need for non-heterosexuals to resist oppression, the message has a wider application.

In the exploration of her own sexuality, she uncovers and confronts racism within lesbian groups, for being lesbian did not give black women 'insider' status within a minority group oppressed because of sexuality rather than race. Blackness still made them 'outsiders'. Lorde notices the difference in the attitudes of heterosexuals towards herself and a white lover. She knew that bouncers at gay clubs hesitated to admit black women. Within the lesbian community there was silence about the reality of race. Never at ease with deceitful silence, Lorde acknowledges and confronts this discrimination. At the gay clubs she frequented she 'saw no reflection in any of the faces' and knew that 'being an outsider at the Bagatelle had everything to do with being black' (p. 220). The emotional loneliness of those individual black lesbians who in the 1950s admitted their sexuality, as did Lorde, was exacerbated by the racism they met. Lorde's admission of racist oppression within a sexually oppressed group is honest and frank. She loves women, but does not see them as uncontaminated by the social diseases of classism, racism and, strangely enough, sexism. In her description of the iconography of the lesbian community she comments upon the 'butch' and the 'femme': a role-playing which she describes as a reflection of the worst aspect of heterosexual relationships, in which sharing is replaced by power and submission. Such lesbian pairings had nothing to do with the 'erotic' defined in her essay on that subject.

Although Lorde criticises aspects of lesbian groups which she saw as wrong, she nevertheless celebrates her inclusion through them in a sisterhood: 'Lesbians were probably the only Black and White women in New York City in the fifties who were making any real attempt to communicate with each other' (p. 179). Where such communications were successful, as between Lorde and her white lover Eudora, it is remembered with tenderness and joy. Explicit descriptions of love-making project a passion which is not destructive, and a delight that is never distasteful. She remembers Afrekete, 'who came out of a dream to me being always hard and real as the fine hairs along the underedge of my navel' (p. 249). The mutual physical delight of a caring relationship between two women is powerfully depicted in language which is poetic. She evokes the same lyricism as found in Hurston's description of Polk County, or Angelou's of Africa, whether she is describing love-making or the sights and sounds of a Manhattan Sunday. The pickle-vendor is seen as presiding 'over wooden vats of assorted sizes and shades of green and succulent submarines, each one denoting a different stage of flavour of picklement' (p. 130). Sensual images bring to life a scene in which the reader can taste those pickles. Her language has the power to

create the erotic in the task of pounding garlic – a task forever linked
for her with her first menstruation. The downward thrust of the pestle
rotates in an hypnotic rhythm: 'Back and forth, round, up and down,
back, forth, round, round, up and down . . . There was a heavy
fulness at the root of me that was exciting and dangerous' (p. 78).
Sensuality and physical pleasure combine in this powerful memory
of her awakening sexuality.

In *Zami* Lorde writes from and about her body in a way that would
delight Hélène Cixous.[15] With delight she reclaims language to
describe the female experiences of sexuality and backstreet abortions
with equal poetic conviction. Her writing is the product of lived
experience which she had recorded in journal jottings. She attributes
her delight in language to her West Indian mother who, like Paule
Marshall's, had filled her childhood with stories of her West Indian
home where Lorde grew up with the acquaintance of different
'languages'. There was the Grenadian poly-language of her parents,
who secretly discussed serious matters in their patois; the idioms of
her mother tongue wherein a back massage is described as 'raising
your zandalee'; and the language she learned at school. Perhaps this
cultural richness aroused Lorde's awareness of the potential of
language to express the hitherto incommunicable.

Lorde's writing reveals to the reader that there is a triple-bind: that
of being female, black and gay; perhaps even a quadruple-bind if
West Indian is added to it. She and Marshall in their own ways explore
and celebrate differences arising from their shared West Indian
cultural heritage, and the difficulty of being the first-generation
American (Silla Boyce's 'New York' children) or first-generation
(admitted) non-heterosexual. Yet their work, despite a shared
cultural background, illustrates the rich diversity of a creativity
which, although nurtured in the same environment, is expressed in
excitingly different ways. It is such diversity in experience as well as
articulation which gives strength and vibrancy to the fabric of black
women's writing in America.

— 5 —

Maya Angelou (b. 1928)
Autobiography: The creation of a
positive black female self

When Claudia Tate asked Angelou if her writings are novels or autobiographies, the emphatic reply was 'autobiography'.[1] Implicit in this definition is recognition of a clear generic difference between the novel and autobiography: the former is a fiction in which the author employs narrative techniques to disguise authorial control, the latter where the author is subject. Nevertheless, it is a nonsense to assume that autobiographical writing is the truth, the whole truth, and nothing but the truth, nor should the reader expect it to be. Not only does memory play us all false, but autobiography is an intensely subjective reconstruction of past events and past selves, wherein the desire to be honest is mitigated by the desire to protect the self. Image protection involves the autobiographer in a process of selection and retrospective ordering of a past experience in which the adult offers a reconstruction of that remembered self. As such it gives the reader an image of the author's self which is self-reflective, the eye is the 'I'. When the adult Angelou tries to reconstruct the self who had been raped as a child, she insists 'But that happened . . . '. She is aware that the process of memory is a constant re-creation of experience in which disguise and distortion are protective strategies: a process which is enlarged in any sustained autobiographical restructuring of the author's past. Angelou's is truly life-writing, in that it is ongoing and, as yet, after five volumes, unfinished. These autobiographical volumes are an instance of a propitious historical conjuncture in the 1970s. Stephanie M. Demetrakspoulos, in Jelinek's *Women's Autobiography in America: Essays in Criticism*,[2] points the connection:

> Certain kinds of autobiographies have flourished and clustered around specific historical events. The large number of American female autobiographies recently published can be connected to a new

self-consciousness in women, attributable to the latest feminist
movement, which centres in the United States. (p. 181)

The 'self-consciousness' described might well have been new for
white American women, but was certainly not so for black women.
The 'specific historical' event of enslavement was one that black, not
white, women had endured. Angelou's autobiographical writing must
be seen as an adding to the clamorous voices of her ancestors who had
survived to bear witness to that experience, and which testify to their
claims for attention as oppressed women possessed of colossal will.

Although there is no evidence that Angelou actively embraced the
feminist movement, she pays tribute to the encouragement received
from fellow women writers in the Harlem Writers' Guild, which
supported blacks in their early apprenticeship as writers. A
chronological reading of her autobiographical writing, beginning with
her own joyful hymn of survival in *I Know Why the Caged Bird Sings*,[3]
published in 1969, gradually reveals the painful, growing politicisation
of her awareness of the particular problems of being a black American
female:

> The Black female is assaulted in her tender years by all those common
> forces of nature at the same time that she is caught in the tripartite
> crossfire of masculine prejudices, white illogical hate and Black lack of
> power. (p. 265)

The slave narratives of her female ancestors had testified to these
forces, and stand as stark witnesses to the powerlessness of the
enslaved African in the face of the consequent unleashing of
humanity's potential for inhumanity. That Angelou, a century and a
half later, can still take racial oppression as her subject, says much
about the placing of her people in white American society, and
reinforces the particular importance of autobiographical statement in
the tradition of black writing, as inspirational and political. However,
it is a tradition which has not remained static. The accounts of barely
literate slaves, some of whose stories were transcribed by others or
ghosted by sympathetic whites, are primitive ancestors to Angelou's
sustained and sophisticated narratives. Moreover, the tone has
changed from that of the rendered pain characterising slave
narratives, to the joyous celebration of survival found in Angelou's
writing.

In his account of black autobiographical writing, Stephen
Butterfield distinguishes between the male and female autobiographic

traditions which evolved from the slave narratives. In this he describes the male accounts as 'testimonials' to the inhumanity of slavery, arguing that the frustrated rage inscribed in these narratives survives to find later expression in the black male 'protest' novels such as Wright's *Native Son*. In contrast to the black man's desire to speak for a whole race, Butterfield sees the impetus in black women's narratives and their subsequent literature as being personal rather than social.[4] Onto the slave narratives writers like Hurston and Angelou have grafted the single voice of the Blues, so that the life-road travelled is described and offered as a personal rather than a social record. The obstacles presented by class, race and gender as they are described in the slave narratives still exist, but in Angelou's handling they can be surmounted and overcome. Like Hurston before her, Angelou undoubtedly celebrates her own self, charting the road she has travelled, but unlike Hurston, she is not politically ambivalent. The reader of Angelou's works is left in no doubt that she sees her own experience as a part of her people's.

In her work on autobiography, Jelinek postulates that a distinguishing pattern in male autobiographical writing is that it 'not only focuses on its author, but also reveals his connectedness to the rest of society: it is representative of his times, a mirror of his era' (Jelinek, p. 7). Moreover, she identifies the characteristic quality of male autobiographies as the confident tone with which they tell how encountered difficulties were overcome. This assertion is exemplified in Booker T. Washington's *Up From Slavery*, first published in 1901, which maps a life from slave cabin to at least a dinner in the White House. Washington's slow progress from ignorance and poverty gives way to the records of highly applauded public speeches for national consumption and testimonials from the mighty to the success of his projects. In no way does Washington suggest that his progress was easy, but he does postulate that it was possible. On the other hand Richard Wright's autobiography *Black Boy*, published in 1945, is full of undisguised rage against a white oppression; a rage which is absent in Booker T. Washington's own life account. Like Washington, Wright believed that his own life could be ameliorated through education, not necessarily for self-advancement, but as a weapon in his constant struggle against racism. Both of these men were re-creating their past selves in terms of success against enormous odds, Wright with obvious, Washington perhaps with disguised, rage, but both with the advancement of coloured people in mind. Seen in the context of these two male autobiographies as exemplars, Angelou's works seem to me to be a unique blending of the male and female qualities identified by Jelinek, and have an extra, special ingredient. Stephen Butterfield, in his account of black American autobiography, identifies the further dimension added by Angelou to the male 'success' story: 'She also speaks of the special problems encountered by black women and affirms life in a way that no male author could duplicate.' Angelou writes within an established black autobiographic tradition, which she employs to give a positive female image. She also feminises what had been an immensely popular white male tradition in late nineteenth-century American writing, of the braggart heroes created by Horatio Alger.[5] His output of over 150 publications of tales for and about poor boys who make good, provided male role models for the aspiring working-class boy. Angelou adapts this tradition to show that girls too can have their share of adventure and success, and, what is more, it can happen to a black girl. Sexism, racism and classism are all ingredients in Angelou's life, and she beats them all. This is one good reason why white women also enjoy her autobiographies.

Now that autobiographical writing has been accorded the 'respectability' of critical analysis, and is no longer seen simply as useful source material for scholars, the literary skills which shape Angelou's writing are afforded serious attention. One significant feature of her craftwork is in her selection and patterning of her life experiences, which she then weaves into an inspirational fabric of survival:

> All my work, my life, everything is about survival. All my work is meant to say 'You may encounter many defeats, but you must never be defeated'. In fact, the encountering might be the very experience which creates the vitality and the power to endure.[6]

Her autobiographies illustrate her personal survival, as well as presenting her as an exemplar of the possibilities open to all who nourish the indomitable spirit of their African ancestors. Her insistence upon the potential for personal, as well as conscious collective, action against the social cage within which black Americans had been constrained, must be seen within the political context of white power. Within a multi-ethnic society where whites are politically dominant, a white citizen's social origins might be given significance in an hierarchical class system, but her skin colour is irrelevant. For blacks in such a society, colour is the dimension marking them off as 'The Other'. Regina Blackburn writes in an essay:

> Most African women autobiographies confess to one incident in their early lives that awakened them to their color; this recognition scene evoked an awareness of their blackness and its significance, and it had a lasting influence in their lives.[7]

Richard Wright's *Black Boy* demonstrates how such a 'recognition scene' as a young man aroused in him an all-consuming rage, and a determination to smash and destroy the cage of entrapment. In the recognition scene in *I Know Why the Caged Bird Sings*, when Angelou's grandmother is vilified and taunted by the obscenity of white children, Angelou claims that the experienced humiliation gave way to a feeling of triumph. In her reconstruction of that event, Angelou rejoices in a victory as Momma Henderson retains her dignity. Angelou seems to be less preoccupied than her black male counterparts with smashing angrily at the bars of the racial cage. Her concern is to explore the cage in order to salvage the means to transcend and escape. Like Wright's Bigger Thomas in *Native Son* Angelou wants to fly, but recognises that a caged bird could batter itself to death on the bars in impotent rage:

> But a bird that stalks
> down his narrow cage
> can seldom see through
> his bars of rage
> his wings are clipped and
> his feet are tied
> so he opens his throat to sing.[8]

This poem crystallises the essential difference between Angelou's personal search for self-definition and that of many black male writers, whose anger had hardened into a single-minded determination to shake white men into recognition of their own institutionalised inhumanity. The rage against the illogicality of white racism is no less apparent in Angelou's writing than it is in black male writing, but its effectiveness is amplified for the reader because it is inscribed in the remembered experience of a joyous survivor.

Although now a university teacher herself, circumstances had not enabled Angelou to pursue the education which Booker T. Washington had advocated as essential to success. Yet, like him, she too has been welcomed into the corridors of white power in

Washington. She did more than just survive. Her poem of address to the nation when she stood in front of President Clinton during his inauguration was heard and seen by millions of people. She has certainly come a long way from the childhood in Arkansas she reconstructs in *Caged Bird*, when she was inexplicably rejected by her parents and sent to live with her grandmother in the rural South. The traumas associated with being young, female and black are exacerbated by her rape by her mother's boyfriend on a visit North. *Caged Bird* ends with her search for sexual identity in an experimental sexual encounter, and the birth of a son to the 16-year-old Angelou. The second volume, *Gather Together in my Name*,[9] describes Angelou as a young mother, bent upon survival for herself and her child. Marriage provides this for a while as shown in volume 3, *Singin' and Swingin' and Gettin' Merry Like Christmas*.[10] In this she also charts her developing career in show business and her maturing awareness of both black sexism and white racism. The widening of her horizons resulting from European travel as a singer and dancer sharpened her political awareness, and also caused her to suffer the agonies of guilt experienced by all women who have to combine career with mothering. She is assaulted by the constant conflict of choices as she struggles to be both a good mother and an economic provider. Volume 4, *Heart of a Woman*,[11] reflects her growth in maturity in that it is less concerned with her own development, focusing as it does on her active involvement in black politics. It describes her association with the Civil Rights Movement, her marriage to an African freedom-fighter and her life with him in Africa. Her last volume, *All God's Children Need Travelling Shoes*,[12] gives the reader a much more 'public' Angelou, one who is fully politicised and whose self-definition had been changed by life in Ghana where she confronts the reality of her black Americanism. Significantly her son, whose growth into manhood had been described alongside his mother's growth into self-recognition, stays in Africa whilst she returns to the United States with a fully realised identity as a black American woman who, despite her African ancestry, is fully American.

The substance of her autobiographies is provided by Angelou's search for her black female self. The narrative pattern established is one of growth through movement from ignorance to awareness, from the identity imposed on her as Momma Henderson's granddaughter, or as Viv Baxter's daughter, to the adult Angelou as she perceived herself. The process involved is painful, as one by one she faces and has to overcome the constraints imposed upon her by her race and gender. From each encounter with the realities inscribed in these social constructs, she salvages strength and beauty to emerge as an Amazonian woman. Throughout, her survival tactic is the same: to view each set-back as an opportunity for growth and victory. This formidable adult identity has its roots in her early consciousness of the power of naming. In slavery the right to self-naming was denied to blacks, and Booker T. Washington tells how one of the first acts of the newly freed slaves was to rename themselves and discard the name of the slaveholder. Many, we are told, took the names of prominent statesmen, Presidents in particular, and most added a single initial before their surnames, in the belief that this brought them in line with 'a white man's entitlements'. The new name was the first step towards self-definition. Touchiness about being 'called out of his name' is emphasised by Angelou in *Caged Bird*: 'It was a dangerous practice to call a Negro anything that could be loosely construed as insulting because of the centuries of their having been called niggers, jigs, dinges, blackbirds, crows, boots and spooks' (p. 106).

Like Hurston's Janie Crawford, Angelou stresses that individual recognition is denied by misnaming, and this damages self-esteem. Hence her given name Marguerite is transformed to 'Maya', her brother's name for her, and her surname Johnston into the show-business corruption of her first married name, 'Angelos', to 'Angelou'. In this sense, she named herself. However, identity is more complex than familial naming, and is shaped by an awareness of social identity – of how the individual is perceived within a community. This is brought home to Angelou when living in West Africa. Her stay there was seen initially as a return to her ancestral homeland. Allying herself with a group of expatriate black Americans she had anticipated immediate, open-armed acceptance, only to find this was a presumptuous expectation. Despite her African descent, Angelou becomes conscious that she is regarded by the Africans as alien. Speaking of the black American, she said: 'Which one of us could know that the years of bondage, brutalities, the mixture of other bloods, customs and languages had transformed us into an unrecognisable tribe' (*AGC*, p. 20).

It seems that she arrives at full political awareness and identity simultaneously. When hurt by African hostility to American politics, she accepts that despite the enslavement of her ancestors, she is still an American. In a psychic experience that reminds one of Hurston's prophetic visions in her own autobiography, Angelou is convinced that in the Ewe people of Keta, she finds her tribal origins. Startled by her precognition of this place she had never before visited, the six-foot Angelou is addressed with recognition by an 'unusually tall' woman with whom she feels kinship. She has found the source of her racial identity.

Her struggle for self-definition as a female begins in childhood when she confronts society's evaluation of the female as an object of beauty. Dreaming of looking like a movie star, like Pecola and her mother Pauline Breedlove in Morrison's *The Bluest Eye*, she equates blue eyes with social acceptance – 'My light blue eyes were going to hypnotise them' (*Caged Bird*, p. 4). She dreamed of waking up one day as a little white girl. Regina Blackburn associates Angelou's then self-loathing with her hatred of her colour:

> Of all these here encountered, Maya Angelou expressed the most severe self-hatred derived from her appearance. Beaten down by massive self-loathing and self shame, she felt her appearance was too offensive to merit any kind of true affection from others.' (Jelinek, p. 103)

Blackburn suggests that Angelou hated being black. Sondra O'Neal[13] argues differently, that Angelou's dissatisfaction with her appearance was a natural response to early self-examination and feelings of guilt. The fact was that the gawky, skinny 'shit colored' Angelou was not a pretty child. Blackness itself was no disbarment in Angelou's eyes to beauty. Her brother Bailey was lauded for his velvet black skin. However, as a black girl she had to accommodate dominant white aesthetic values governing the concept of female beauty, so was constantly dismayed by her kinky hair and stringy frame. In his book on black American autobiography Stephen Butterfield describes this obsession with the physical self as a peculiarly female bondage. What he does not say, however, is that this anxiety about physical self is a product of male dominance and the consequential definition of the female through the eyes of the observing male who evaluates the female as 'object'. Angelou's self-evaluation as ugly was enlarged by self-comparison with the dazzling beauty of a mother who did look like a film star, and was further reinforced by the reiteration of white beauty in the media. Michelle Wallace discusses this in her book *Black Macho and the Myth of Superwoman*,[14] and perhaps accounts for Viv Baxter's accepted beauty:

America had room among its beauty contestants for the buxom Mae West, the bug eyes of Bette Davis, the masculinity of Joan Crawford, but the black woman was only allowed entry if her hair was straight, her skin light, and her features European; in other words, if she was as nearly indistinguishable from a white woman as possible.' (p. 158)

Viv Baxter more nearly approached the ideal of white beauty than did her daughter, who admits that 'I was too tall and raw-skinny' (*S&S*, p. 7). Only in maturity with the knowledge of success is the devaluation of self as a 'body' displaced.

Although she retrospectively minimises the psychological damage suffered when she and Bailey are posted like parcels to their paternal grandmother, Angelou admits that her bewilderment was mixed with feelings of guilt. She and Bailey searched themselves for their culpability for this parental rejection. Not surprisingly, Angelou's search for reassurance, her measure of self-worth, depended upon how much she felt loved. Her need to be loved, warmed and held by a loving parent accounts for her bewildered reaction to her sexual molestation by Mr Freeman. His initial embraces had given her pleasure as expressions of affection from a trusted adult. After the horror of her rape, the trial and subsequent murder of Mr Freeman heightened her sense of guilt. She decides not to speak. Only through Mrs Flowers' tender encouragement does the 8-year-old Angelou gradually recover from the trauma of her experience. She begins to speak again when she begins to feel liked, and 'respected not as Mrs Henderson's grandchild or Bailey's sister, but for just being Marguerite Johnston' (*Caged Bird*, p. 98).

Momma Henderson's friend, Mrs Flowers, is projected as a 'lady', 'refined as Whitefolks'. She is remembered as intelligent, well-read, genteel and beautiful: an obvious denial of the stereotypical rural black woman. In her portrait of Mrs Flowers Angelou destroys a literary stereotype of black women as ill-educated and empty-headed, as effectively as she and Bailey had torn to pieces a white doll sent by their mother as a Christmas present. Sondra O'Neal sees Angelou's challenging and refutation of stereotypes of black women as her most positive achievement, which 'provides seldom seen role models for cultural criteria'.[15] Angelou certainly mocks the cinematic stereotypes of the eye-rolling, loose-lipped black chauffeur and his female counterpart, the squawking, ineffectual ladies' maid. The limited social expectations of blacks are reinforced by their representation in the media, and begin, Angelou tells us, in an educational system that envisages black male success in sport and black female success in domestic service. Each individual black woman depicted by Angelou is a denial of this literary and media stereotyping. Refusal to be categorised is exemplified in the portraits of her family in which she recasts the ancestral mother figure met in Walker, Morrison, Lorde and Marshall by having them function in a comtemporary setting. Her grandmothers have the wisdom of the female ancestor which affords spiritual succouring, but they also have the practical ability to operate successfully in twentieth-century America. Momma Henderson is no bandanna'd Mammy. She is a resourceful entrepreneur, God-fearing, dignified and astute: the living refutation of the stereotypical Mammy, traditionally relegated to the kitchen of white employers. Momma Henderson's kitchen and her stove are her own: her home a place of safety for her people. When Angelou describes her own flight from a possible police action over a brothel she owned, she fled to Momma for security, who 'was, as ever, the matriarch' (*GT*, p. 76). It is, in fact, matriarchal support and influence that Angelou describes in her autobiographies. Circumstances had left Momma Henderson, Viv Baxter and Angelou to make their own way in life when husbands died or disappeared. Grandmother Baxter, although married still, is depicted as a Northern matriarch who, like her Southern rural counterpart, had employed her skills and resources to manipulate her environment. Presiding over a household of sons, she is presented as forceful enough to control the police and subdue tough criminals. There is no suggestion that she is ever in less than full control of her life and family.

In the writing and creation of a past self, Angelou suggests that her own self-esteem was nurtured into growth by older black women, and it is in her presentation of these female friends and family that she makes her strongest statements. Whether in Stamps, San Francisco, Europe or Africa, she celebrates the support they gave her, even when the reader questions the actuality of this, particularly when faced with the portrayal of Angelou's dynamic mother. Perhaps the most challenging of Angelou's anti-stereotypical female portraits is that of her mother, the dazzling Viv Baxter. Like the grandmothers, she is shown as strong, but at times the reader feels that she is strong at the expense of maternal nurturing. It is difficult to be convinced that Angelou never harboured feelings of resentment against a mother whose determination to pursue her own life overrode the needs of the children she had borne. As is typical of autobiographical writing involving the depiction of a person still living, the sensitive autobiographer is intent upon offering no damage to a loved one's portrait. I feel that Angelou's sensitivity, and genuine love of her mother, produces a picture which is not fully convincing. The vivacious Viv was much married, loved dancing, gambling and life, and believed that 'sympathy' was next to 'shit' in the dictionary. Angelou passes this off as an encouraging dictum, a spur to self-realisation. Yet there were times when the young Johnston children needed that sympathy, when 'can't do means don't care' was not a suitable response to their situation. Viv Baxter had 'a store of aphorisms which she dished out as the occasion demanded' (*Caged Bird*, p. 261), and in a peculiar way these aphorisms, all pointing to the need for self-reliance, sum up our fullest knowledge of Viv Baxter. Certain facts are glossed over deliberately, like Mr Freeman's solitary care of the children when Viv had not returned home from a night out. As a teenage mother, Angelou knew that she could expect snappy advice but little else from her mother, who told her: 'you're a woman. You make up your own mind' (*Caged Bird*, p. 30). Sometimes her mother proferred money, as she did when Angelou had to pay her own fare home from the European tour of 'Porgy and Bess', but the trip was only necessary because Viv Baxter had abdicated from the responsibility she had undertaken for Angelou's son. The cause of the disruption between Bailey and his mother is never revealed, but its finality is stamped when Bailey says, 'how can I fear a woman when the baddest one I've ever heard of is my mother?' (*GT*, p. 195). This could of course mean that his mother's reputation belied the reality, but it could also mean that Bailey had lost the devotional reverence with which he had formerly regarded her. Angelou wants us to admire a mother who can shoot a business partner, stab a lover (and seemingly go unpunished for both assaults), is determined to be the first ever black woman in the US Marines, and who deliberately runs the gauntlet of racist hostility in a recently de-segregated Fresco hotel. Viv Baxter is portrayed as beautiful, battling and breathtaking, but there is an understated anguish in Angelou's comment that 'Under and after the high spirits was my aching knowledge that she had spent years not needing us' (*HOAW*, p. 35). Of course, it could be argued that in this portrait of her own mother, Angelou was deliberately exploding another stereotypical myth: that motherhood in itself is completely fulfilling, that mothering is a biological rather than a social function. However, her own life and love of her son deny this. Perhaps the insecurity experienced because of parental rejection founded in Angelou a determination to protect her own child from similar suffering. In fact one of the most rewarding of the relationships Angelou describes is that between herself and the son she raised to manhood. Guy is the other half of the equation of herself in Angelou's life. Her shielding of her baby as she sleeps is symbolic of an instinctive mothering which becomes a conscious and tigerish protection of the child as he grows. Angelou tells how Viv Baxter taught her to 'row my own boat, paddle my own canoe, hoist my own sail. She warned, in fact "If you want something done, do it yourself"' (*S&S*, p. 14). Fine words; but they can be seen as an abrogation of parental responsibility. Conversely, Angelou confesses to being guilt-ridden at any imputation that she herself was falling short in the caring of her own child.

Gather Together in my Name, in spite of its enlivenment by Angelou's sense of humour, is a stark volume, delineating the sleazy environment in which the young Angelou took menial jobs to maintain her child and herself. Driven by the need to earn enough to provide for them both, Angelou was forced to leave Guy daily with various child-minders, by one of whom he was kidnapped for a month. Her agonised despair gives way to relief when she finds him, but her joy is tempered by the return of a guilt which had characterised her childhood: 'My sobs broke free on the waves of my first guilt' (*GT*, p. 192). Guilt is the common lot of women torn between the conflicting responsibilities of childcare and economic need to earn money. The intensity of her guilt reflects the 'life-long' paranoia she describes in *Caged Bird*, which is exacerbated by the distress of her child whenever she leaves for work. When she marries the white Greek Angelos, she believes she has found an economic haven, only to discover that his patriarchal attitudes entailed a subjugation completely alien to her nature, and a denial of the familial role models she claims to have had. On the failure of that marriage, Angelou confronts a demanding test of loyalties when offered the opportunity to tour with a show in Europe. The choice between a developing career and her desire to be with her son proves a difficult one to make, but Europe wins in spite of an anxiety heightened by memories of her own feelings when separated as a child from her mother. It is refreshing and reassuring for women readers who have faced the same situation, that although constantly assailed by guilt, partially assuaged by the sending of money home, Angelou admits to very mixed feelings with which they can identify. Her own self-fulfilment had to be balanced against her child's needs. Many women will recognise this internalised debate:

> No matter what it cost in loneliness, I was doing the good mother thing to leave my son at home. Thus had I soothed my guilt, never admitting that I was revelling in the freedom from the nuisance of a small child's chatter. (*S&S*, p. 246)

Superadded to these feelings recognised by women of any colour, is the especial fear of black American mothers for their sons, who were the ready prey of white racists. Momma Henderson had to hide her crippled son in the vegetable store when trigger-happy Klansmen (those whom Booker T. Washington had claimed had disappeared!) were abroad in the South, and Angelou's fears for her son in the Northern cities are equally valid. She claims to have taken a pistol to a gang of black youths who threatened Guy, though in her retrospective explanation of this violence she sees these youths as the inevitable product of an inequitable society, which opinion might have been prompted by her awareness of later sociological reports. She might also have been influenced by Malcolm X's powerful autobiography[16] which was published in 1965, in which he argues that the high incidence of serious juvenile crime amongst young blacks was the inevitable product of their social deprivation in the urban ghettos. In spite of the rationalisation of the violence in black communities, we are nevertheless quite certain that if necessary she would have used that pistol against her son's would-be attackers. Nevertheless she argues that the real threat to all black sons comes from whites; that the black American mother knows that:

> Beyond her door, all authority is in the hands of people who do not look or think or act like her and her children. Teachers, doctors, sales clerks, librarians, policemen, welfare workers are white and exert control over her family's moods, conditions and personality. (*HOAW*, p. 37)

The emotional turmoil Angelou endured as a black mother, as described in *Singin' and Swingin'*, exacts a price. Although in typical fashion she understates her distress – for there is no note of wailing complaint in her writing – her admitted 'life-long' paranoia results in a nervous collapse. She describes her withdrawal from an actual consultation with a white psychiatrist, because she fears being labelled 'another case of Negro paranoia' (*S&S*, p. 261), and sets about healing herself. That process involves her in a continuous struggle to be the economic provider and protector of her son, who in turn engaged in his own search for independence. His groping towards a self-definition as positive as his mother's is signalled by his abandoning of his given name 'Clyde' in favour of 'Guy'. Guy is described as moving inexorably into a life where he is independent of his mother. When he reaches adolescence, the mother–son relationship is subtly altered, as he begins to express concern for her safety and pride in her achievements: 'Maya Angelou is a great singer and she is my mother' (*S&S*, p. 269). In *Heart of a Woman* Guy's independence is realised when he leaves home for university, and is sealed forever in *All God's Children Need Travelling Shoes* by his decision to remain in Ghana on his mother's return to America.

In Ghana, Angelou's son had educational and life-style opportunities denied to the majority of black American boys. There he could develop untouched by the mindless racism recorded in *Caged Bird*, succinctly expressed as a fact that 'The Black Woman in the South who raises sons, grandsons and nephews had her heartstrings tied to be a hanging noose' (*Caged Bird*, p. 110). Nor would he suffer the humiliation Angelou describes was hers as a high-school student, whose intelligence simply sharpened her awareness that her education would be nullified by the racism in her society. In her reconstruction of that time she emphasises the despair of young blacks who confront the enormity of the societal disadvantages of their colour. She recalls feeling empty when listening to the white man's address, delivered on graduation day. As a mature woman, she describes it as 'awful' to 'have no control over my life. It was brutal to be young and already trained to sit quietly and listen to charges brought against my color with no chance of defence' (*Caged Bird*, p. 176). Yet even this 'defeat' she turns into a salvaging. When the children sing the 'Negro' National Anthem, a poem by James Weldon Johnson, she claims in retrospect to have been uplifted in a surge of racial pride.

Whether such convenient patterning of despair and hope is factually correct, whether the hope is in fact a retrospective imposition, is irrelevant. What *is* important is that Angelou imposes this pattern onto her selection of experiences described. Although she left school early, and unlike Hurston did not follow a 'white' pattern of higher education, her personal development seems to have been in no way hampered by her exclusion from this process. Her quick intelligence and facility for learning are seen in her claim that no matter where her travels take her, she endeavours to communicate in the language of that country. She does not, like the British, expect everyone to speak *her* language. What she minimises about the process of second-language acquisition is the diligence needed to succeed. She turns a difficulty into a possibility with the same assurance which she exhibited in facing various set-backs in her life.

Angelou's evaluation of her life encounters is a positive one in that she seizes upon negative experiences as learning opportunities. Life, in her evocation of it, is something to be surmounted, and racism something to be recognised and resisted. The burden of racial disadvantage experienced at school was a preparation for what she would encounter in the adult world of work. In show business she was acutely aware that white dancers had more job opportunities than black. The entertainment club, 'The Garden of Allah', described in *Singin' and Swingin'* was a 1950s version of Harlem's Cotton Club, where whites 'slummed'. The tentacles of racist attitudes are inescapable in the life described by Angelou. *Heart of a Woman* opens with a graphic illustration of institutionalised racism when she determines to live in a white neighbourhood in San Francisco, and can rent only through the helpful subterfuge of a white Jew, who is himself subjected to racist abuse. Nor was racism mitigated, as Booker T. Washington had envisioned, by black success, as the sad portrait of Billie Holliday reveals. Despite her acclaim as an artist, she was still regarded as a 'nigger'. Hurston had known what the social implications of that term were, and so did Angelou. She illustrates this in an incident where a white dentist said he would rather die than put his hand into her black mouth to extract a painful tooth. Segregation and Jim Crow laws were so rigidly enforced in her childhood environment that she claims never to have encountered whites at all. But she knew 'that they were different, to be dreaded, and in that dread was included the hostility of the powerless against the powerful'. The impotence of the blacks was a measure of their economic disadvantage, they were 'the poor against the rich, the worker against the worked for and the ragged against the well-dressed' (*Caged Bird*, p. 25). She learned as a child that all the negatives were the social inheritance of her people. It is these negatives that her own life disproves, but the pain remains.

As Angelou sets about dismembering the fictional stereotyping of black women, she destroys the 'Magnolia Myth' so conveniently perpetuated in white literature. Early memories of work-worn Southern cotton-pickers, evoked mockingly by Angelou, are at variance with their mythical presentation:

> There is a much loved region in the American fantasy where pale white women float eternally under black magnolia trees, and white men with soft hands brush wisps of wisteria from the creamy shoulders of their lady loves. Harmonious black music drifts (like a perfume) through the precious air, and nothing of a threatening nature intrudes. (*GT*, p. 73)

With economic and graphic detail, using soft sounds and gentle words – 'float', 'soft', 'wisps', 'drifts' – she points to the insubstantiality of that picture of the South. The reality is equally graphic, but starkly, tersely conveyed in the double adjectives identified by Hurston as characteristic of black American idiom: 'The South I returned to, was flesh-real and swollen-belly poor' (*GT*, p. 73). In later years Angelou was to confront the stereotyped picture of gay, song-singing 'cotton pickers' with so much rage that she was told by fellow blacks 'that my paranoia was embarrassing' (*Caged Bird*, p. 10). That self-confessed paranoia, referred to more than once in her work, is not, however, turned inward, as it is in Morrison's Cholly Breedlove, to fester and destroy. Instead it is harnessed to find expression in direct political activity. *Heart of a Woman* and *All God's Children* recount her involvement in the movement for civil rights: a demand for equality which had been fuelled with the disillusionment of black soldiers of the Second World War, and their involvement in Vietnam. Toni Morrison in *Sula* and *Jazz* shows how black soldiers were discarded by an ungrateful nation in 1918, an experience repeated in Angelou's recollection of 1946, when she saw returning soldiers who had 'snatched the remaining Jews from the hell of concentration camps' (*GT*, p. 4). Black war veterans had naively believed that the Jewish holocaust, when laid bare to the world, would kill racial prejudice for ever. Their return to America was to unemployment and life in overcrowded urban ghettos.

Angelou's politicisation dominates her last two autobiographical volumes. Association with Martin Luther King, Ralph Abernathy and Wyatt Walker, from that long line of preachers who became race leaders, introduced Angelou to the complexity of politics. As a young mother her perception of life had been governed by a series of polarities – 'black/white, up/down, life/death, rich/poor, love/hate, happy/sad, and no mitigating areas in between' (*GT*, p. 65) – a simplistic view that she was to modify in later life. She learned that the struggle for civil rights had different faces. One was that of the Black Muslims who offered a solution to black identity in a separatism which displaced the magnolia myth of an infantilised subclass of blacks contentedly serving the whites. In their demand for a separate black nation within America, a new myth of black supremacy was forged, which offered black Americans a new vision of themselves.[17] Compelling role models from the worlds of art and entertainment swelled their ranks: LeRoi Jones renamed himself Imamu Baraka, and on his becoming the world heavyweight boxing champion Cassius Clay rejected his slave name to become Mohammed Ali. Malcolm X was the powerful spokesperson for the Black Muslims until his visit to Mecca caused him to re-evaluate the doctrine of hatred which he had been preaching. The other face of resistance was the passive one preached by the Christian, Dr Martin Luther King, whose doctrine was non-violent. He urged his people to exercise their right to vote and to seek economic improvement and racial equality through the ballot box. Both King and Malcolm X were to die at the hands of assassins within two years of each other.

To find political wisdom, Angelou had to listen to and judge many voices. Politically naive herself, her education was completed by her African husband, Vus. He taught her a valuable lesson (one that when preached by Hurston had engendered hostility), and that was that blacks, like whites, are fallible humans. He told her that: 'Black people are human. No more, no less. Our backgrounds, our history make us act differently' (*HOAW*, p. 175). Vus taught her that black activists were not seeking a society where power did not exist, but one where that power could be exchanged and rest in their hands; that world politics is about who possesses and exercises power. Moreover Vus stressed that for a black American the place to fight for that power was not in Africa, but America. This is the knowledge she acquires and records in *All God's Children*. Distressed by African hostility to American foreign policy, she realises she cannot defile the 'Stars and Stripes', for 'it lifted us up with its promise and broke our hearts with its denial' (*AGC*, p. 127). Angelou witnesses Malcolm X's African visit, when, having defected from the Black Muslim faith, he was shunned by his former friend Mohammed Ali. She saw disunity among her brothers. She learned too that there existed a black hierarchical structure which enabled Shirley DuBois, at will, to arrange a meeting between Malcolm X and Nkrumah. She learned, in effect, that the real world of politics does not operate simply on idealism, and that the will to exploit others is endemic in the human race. She herself was not free of this urge, and her exploitation of the lesbian prostitutes in *Gather Together* does not redound to her credit, despite her attempts to explain it away. Her own exploitation by a pimp, who ensnared her into prostitution for a while, is evidence too that the exploitation of black women is not confined solely to white men.

Angelou's two 'admitted' marriages to men of different cultural backgrounds – one being a Greek, the other an African – founder because of their patriarchal attitudes which defined her in terms of themselves. Both husbands gave unspoken belief to marriage as an institution bearing the inscription of male dominance. Angelou's own expectations of marriage had been shaped by the media's notion of romantic love and marriage, promising a 'June Allyson screen-role life', which Angelou confesses she would have 'done anything to get' (*GT*, p. 189). Struggling as a single parent, Angelou's dreams of the perfect home, complete with rose-framed doorway, were fed by the sentiments expressed in popular songs and the scenarios enacted in popular romantic films. In reality, marriage provided economic security for Angelou, at the price of an intolerable self-subjugation. As the wife of a man who did not wish his wife to work outside the home, she experiences the same sense of imprisonment feared by Alice Walker's bride in 'Roselily', and says 'I made no protest at the bonds that were closing around my existence' (*GT*, p. 33). Angelos assumed that he himself should be everything to his wife, so denied her access to friends of whom he disapproved and belittled the church to which she belonged. She was stifled. In spite of her husband's innate kindness, marriage became a site of struggle and oppression in which Angelou 'lost territory', in a power struggle as real as that between warring nations. When she decides to make a bid for her own share of that power, the marriage collapses. Yet this failure did not discourage the optimistic Angelou in her quest for a fulfilling marriage. She nearly married an entirely unsuitable bail-bondsman, who shared none of her intellectual pursuits, although he was an exciting sexual partner and financially stable. Instead, she married Vus Make, the charismatic African freedom-fighter, whose sexuality is matched by his political fervour, but who offers no financial security whatsoever. Within this marriage, Angelou once again confronts a sexism characteristic of the gender roles constructed within society. Although in financial ruin, Vus can only be persuaded to allow Angelou to work once he has 'vetted' and given his approval to her eventual employers. Angelou was still torn between desire for the media-created ideal of marriage and her refusal to be a handmaid in that relationship: 'I wanted to be a wife and to create a beautiful home to make my man happy, but there was more to life than being a diligent maid with a permanent pussy' (*HOAW*, p. 143). Vus was enough of a Victorian to expect domestic service and sexual loyalty from a wife, but did not feel bound by the same moral code. His double standards made a torment of the marriage, from which Angelou was eventually freed by a ritualistic gathering of their African friends. Like Hurston, Angelou found the gender roles of traditional marriage too restrictive of her own free spirit.

It is interesting to note that the suffocating 'kindness' of her first marriage produces in her a compulsion to seek solace in the church she had known as a child. Feeling physically and emotionally strained gives rise to an overwhelming need for spiritual release. This is not an uncommon reaction to worldly stress, and is Delia's motivating force in Hurston's story 'Sweat'. The embracing of Christianity by enslaved Africans, as Hurston points out in *The Sanctified Church*, in many ways expressed their hopes for freedom. Christian teaching of God's final Judgement Day meant 'that the mean whitefolks was going to get their comeuppance' (*Caged Bird*, p. 123). Angelou, like Alice Walker, can write of flirting and laughing in church, but salvages the communal comfort the gatherings supplied. Although Angelou's sense of the comic enables her to paint an hilarious account of a church-goer's religious fervour, resulting in the accidental knocking out of the preacher's false teeth, she does not laugh at the religious experience itself. Although not given to zealous piety, she admits that her early religious upbringing was something of value that she would never totally reject:

> The fact of my Southern upbringing, the fact of my born blackness meant that I was for the rest of my life a member of that righteous band, and would be whether or not I ever went to church again. (*GT*, p. 46)

That the church acted as a focus for black identity and that the melodious sermons provided a cathartic spiritual release from oppression, is quite clear in the account of the revivalist meeting described in *Caged Bird*. Even Johnny Mae and Frankie, the lesbian prostitutes, whose life-style might be construed as a denial of Christian precepts, regularly attended Sunday service in church.

Although Angelou acknowledges that the Christian God is deemed as white, she says she cannot believe Him to be prejudiced, and is concerned to inculcate Christian teaching into her own son. The need for a spiritual anchorage is a human one, as is the direct relationship between the depth of human desire for this and suffered adversity, and Angelou's own need for the church appears greatest when she is under most social pressure. She may not have liked the concept of the white-bearded, old, white God, dismissed by Shug in Walker's *The Color Purple*, but she needed something. She sought guidance from a Rabbi, being attracted to Judaism because of the recognised parallels between the diaspora and subsequent persecution of the Jews, and that of her own people. Under the influence of a white girl who offered her employment in a record shop, she even tried the Christian Scientist Church, but found it too sterile. She missed the spiritual fervour she had known in the black church and craved for the music, the emotional bonding, the sense of community which characterised black worship. When unhappy with Angelos, she visited black churches in secret, with a furtive hunger: 'The spirituals and gospel songs were sweeter than sugar. I wanted my mouth full of them and the sounds of my people fell like sweet oil in my ears' (*S&S*, p. 33). The language she uses here emphasises that the church was a source of nourishment and balm to her, as it had been to her enslaved ancestors.

Her early dependence upon a religion which promises survival and overcoming through endurance, is diminished in her later volumes, and is replaced by a more active determination for personal and professional success. The Harlem Writers' Guild, where black writers met to discuss their work, involved the daunting process of submitting work for the critical evaluation of fellow artists. Constructive criticism, if heeded, involved rewriting, and Angelou confesses her deflation at the prospect, but says: 'I had to try. If I ended in defeat, at least I would be trying. Trying to overcome was black people's honourable tradition' (*HOAW*, p. 43). With a diminution of her total reliance on the communal succouring of religion, Angelou's self-image attains a new level of dignity. Her expressed wish is to share that dignity with her people. By using her talents she raises the consciousness of her readers, as she had raised awareness of a national self in her rendering of black freedom songs.

Grown from the image of an unhappy, bewildered small girl, obsessed by a need for love and security, emerges the mature, self-confident internationally known woman, whose triumphant survival is celebrated in her writing. The double jeopardy of gender and colour is shown to be surmountable.

What are illuminating in this metamorphosis are the strategies for survival used by Angelou to lessen the impact of racist and gender oppression. One significant strategy is humour. As is seen in the writing of other black women writers, particularly in Hurston and Walker, an irrepressible sense of fun takes the bitter edge off experience, rendering the pain no less real but nevertheless endurable. Angelou's comic range is wide. Within it is her ability to render and sustain the action and dialogue in wildly funny scenes, as in her 'Preach it' memory of church-going; a felicitous use of the terse, gritty one-liner for the underscoring of a serious observation, as in 'Lana Turner and Rita Hayworth get discovered, Black girls get uncovered' (*GT*, p. 73); and an ability to capture the pathos of the self-deprecating naivety in 'would you like to have a sexual intercourse with me?' (*Caged Bird*, p. 274). She incorporates black idioms in her dialogue which are wry illustrations of black Americans' awareness of white power and the linguistic subterfuges of disguise employed by blacks to preserve their privacy. She reminds the reader that when asked by a white where he is going, a black will tell where he had been. She can laugh as an adult at the racism in Stamps in her suggestion that black children were only allowed chocolate ice-cream, or at the resultant baldness of the 'Porgy and Bess' cast members who decided to have their hair straightened whilst in Europe. Behind this laughter at themselves lies the deep pain at the incomprehensible nature of racism, and knowledge that blackness only really matters to whites, because 'the white world has given it [blackness] meaning – political, social, economic, psychological and philosophical'.[18] The need for the black person to wear a protective mask in the face of white hostility, to treat all whites with caution in anticipation of antipathy, are attitudes to which Angelou admits in herself. She is suspicious when white people, like her co-worker in the record store, offer normal friendship. Unaccustomed to kindness from a white source, she has to overcome her surprise at their involvement in the Civil Rights Movement. That this suspicion of any seeming humanity from white people is not peculiar to Angelou is a fact endorsed by Stephen Butterfield, who comments upon the black Americans' need for disguise: 'Never let the white folks know what you really think. If you're sad, laugh. If you're bleeding inside, dance' (Butterfield, *Black Autobiography in America*, p. 102). When growing up, Angelou adopted many masks. Womanhood entails role-playing as lover, mother, wife and entertainer. Her life is presented as a series of accommodations to meet the demands of these roles. When necessary she can be a Creole cook, a diplomatic hostess, a political activist or a gun-toting mother, and is equally convincing in each role.

Her power to persuade the reader into an acceptance of the self-image she creates lies in the flexibility of her language. To express her determination to become a conductress, she uses the capitalised words of a moral sampler: 'I WOULD HAVE THE JOB. I WOULD BE A CONDUCTRESS AND SLING A FULL MONEY CHANGER FROM MY BELT. I WOULD' (*Caged Bird*, p. 260). In the light of such determination it is no surprise to see this particular ambition fulfilled. With equal impact she re-creates the emotional intensity with which the blacks in Stamps crowded into Momma Henderson's store to listen to the radio broadcast of the Joe Louis heavyweight boxing world championship fight. Skilfully interwoven into the boxing commentator's disembodied words are the tense, living reactions of the audience, their groans and joyful exhalations at Louis' progress to victory, and her own interpretation of the significance of the event for her people. She can manipulate language to catch the sights, sounds and smells of an occasion with deftness, economy and vividness. Angelou has a highly developed pictorial perception, which can rival Dickens' ability to evoke a teeming city. There is life and movement in her envisaged urban landscapes thronging with people. Witness Cairo:

> Emaciated men in long tattered robes flailed and ranted at heavily burdened mules. Sleek limousines rode through the droppings of camels that waved their wide behinds casually as they sashayed in the shadow of skyscrapers. Well-dressed women in pairs, or accompanied by men, took no notice of their sisters, covered from head to toe in voluminous heavy wraps. Children ran everywhere, shouting under the wheels of rickety carts, dodging the tires of careering taxis. (*HOAW*, p. 213)

Here no noun is left unqualified; the verbs so vigorous and apt that they do not require adverbial assistance. The writing is tight, precise and controlled, in sentences each of which is in itself a snapshot. The exotic fascination of a city where the ancient and the modern, the natural and technological so strangely co-mingle, is immutably fixed. With equal skill, the brooding tranquillity of Venice is captured:

> The ancient buildings sat closed and remote, holding dead glories within their walls. The canals fanned in every direction from the pavement edge, while red and black gondolas slid along the water's surface like toy boats sailing on ice. The gondoliers whose crafts were empty sang to amuse themselves or to attract customers. They chanted bits of arias and popular music and their voices pranced over the water, young and irresistible. (*S&S*, p. 162)

The elegant splendour of the European Renaissance past is suggested by words 'remote', 'sat', 'dead glories', the ubiquitous water by 'fanned', and the serenity of the scene by sibilance and the simile 'like toy boats sailing on ice'. Romance is in the singing of the gondoliers whose voices 'pranced' in the hope and expectation of youthful manhood. Such landscape painting in words is evidence of Angelou's mastery of language and her craft as a writer. Each word is carefully chosen, each image honed and polished to perfection.

Often her language is heavily sensuous, creating scenes which momentarily evoke a whole way of life. Smell, colour and taste are often the Proustian triggers for buried memories of her childhood:

> In my memory, Stamps is a place of light, shadow, sounds and entrancing odours. The earth smell was pungent, spiced with the odour of cattle manure, the yellowish acid of the ponds and rivers, the deep pots of greens and beans cooking for hours with smoked or cured pork. (*GT*, p. 74)

The uniqueness of that memory is conveyed in a mixture of smells: of the earth, natural processes and cooking food. In the first two volumes of her autobiography in particular, food is a significant indicator of moments of happiness. Remembered childhood high-spots are associated with stolen candy bars, the craving for and gorging of tinned pineapple, and the occasional communal picnic, all of which are particularly appropriate in a re-creation of a child's awareness of the world. Over the two decades in which her life-writing has been produced, there is less emphasis on food as a sensory pleasure. In adult life she associates the cooking and sharing of food as a token of friendship. This aspect of domesticity, where the woman is inevitably concerned with food preparation and house care, is echoed in her imagery. When Uncle Willie is hidden by his mother, he is 'casseroled' between 'layer upon layer' of vegetables, and discarded war veterans are likened to forgotten laundry left to flap on a washing line. The variety and flexibility in her use of language helps sustain a flowing, unimpeded narrative pace. She maintains a balance between descriptive commentary and dramatic scenes in economic dialogue. Although not conveyed in black American language, her dialogue captures the flavour of that speech through her incorporation of idiom and vernacular usage. Like Hurston, she uses words like 'bodacious', 'siddity' and 'sashay' alongside formal register. The rich inventiveness of black language, the ready quip and humour, the beautiful power of the sermon, are celebrations of the linguistic skills of her people. In Angelou's language the characteristics of black American language, previously analysed and praised by Hurston, are manifest. She shows that years of oppression have reduced neither her people's passion to communicate nor their adherence to their own cultural values.

Angelou sees these values as living realities, particularly in the rural South, where Momma Henderson lived by the dicta that cleanliness was next to Godliness, and that Godliness was displayed by loyalty to kin and community: 'Values among Southern rural blacks are not quite the same as those existing elsewhere. Age has more worth than wealth and religious piety more value than beauty' (*GT*, p. 78). If this is so, then clearly the black migration to the Northern industrial cities put these values under extreme pressure. Urban deprivation is recognised as a contributory factor to criminality amongst the economically depressed, no matter what colour they are. Angelou touches on the horrors of hard drug abuse in underprivileged ghettos, and the intra-racial violence of gangs of black youths whose behaviour she interprets as the inevitable expression of any group that feels undervalued. However, there is a sense in which her attempt to explain this social phenomenon is accomplished by a glamorising of aspects of behaviour which not only members of the dominant white groups in society would describe as 'anti-social'. The gambling, prostitution and flouting of the law, the schemes of Daddy Cliddel's confidence-trickster friends, are offered as laudable and justifiable examples of survival. She suggests that in ghettoised living a separate moral code evolves, in which a society's ethics are determined by its needs. The hero of the black American ghetto is hence one 'who is offered only the crumb from the country's table, but by ingenuity and courage is able to take for himself a Lucullan feast' (*Caged Bird*,

p. 218). We cannot imagine that Momma Henderson would have subscribed to this proposition if the 'ingenuity' involved criminality, and perhaps Angelou's anguish at Bailey's imprisonment causes her to attempt this justification. Indeed it is difficult to reconcile the lively, intelligent, quick-witted Bailey of her childhood with the shadowy stranger who leaves home at 16 to fend for himself. Perhaps Angelou is blaming the ghetto for Bailey's eventual fall, but this leaves unresolved tension between the influence of the ghetto and that of matriarchal nurturing.

Angelou presents herself as one of a long line of strong, fighting, female survivors. When she claims that the 'formidable character' of the black American female is 'often met with amazement, distaste, and even belligerence' (*Caged Bird*, p. 265), perhaps she had in mind the Moynihan Report, which recommended a return to the home for working black women, in order to elevate the status of their menfolk. This report identifies matriarchy as the destructive force of discontent within the black community. Such an analysis of the ills of black life was met with hostility from educated black women, and was cogently refuted in Michelle Wallace's *Black Macho and the Myth of Superwoman*. Wallace argues that black matriarchy was a white myth, and that adherence to these mythical constructs of black men and women was the real cause of conflict. She suggests that slavery had produced two distinct female archetypes: one who had been privileged by pre-Civil War emancipation, or was held by dint of sexual or domestic service in special favour; the other a poor, strong but nevertheless rebellious woman, like Sojourner Truth who had laboured like a man. Wallace describes the first as 'Black Lady', the second as 'Amazon'. Mrs Flowers is Angelou's depiction of the first, and Angelou's created self-image is a reflection of the second.

The reader is presented with strong female survivors who also act as protectors of their menfolk. Momma protects the crippled Willie, Grandma Baxter is a dominant force who rules her 'mean sons', and we are told that it is Viv Baxter who arranges for Bailey to be employed by the railway company. Angelou, the teenage mother, will do anything to support and protect her own son. She depicts black women in a positive way, as functioning with immeasurable strength and courage within their familial and communal network. Their menfolk are presented as functioning heroically, if at times criminally, in a more public sphere. Joe Louis' world boxing championship is related to a surge of racial pride, her uncles are applauded because they operate effectively outside the law, Daddy Cliddel's involvement in rackets stands as evidence of his ability to manipulate and survive in a macho society. There is some danger in this. If Michelle Wallace is correct in her argument that there exists between black men and women a profound distrust, partly encouraged by white racism and partly the result of ignorance about the sexual politics of their experience, then Angelou's writing could be seen to collude, albeit unwittingly, in this process. She certainly destroys the literary stereotyping of the black woman as Aunt Jemima or Sapphire, but in so doing she reinforces the archetypal Amazon described by Michelle Wallace.

This 'Amazon' not only possesses physical and emotional indomit-ability, but she is also strictly heterosexual. Although Angelou attempts to justify her callous treatment of the lesbian prostitutes as a natural urge for revenge, she betrays a lack of sympathetic understanding of them in her reference to them as 'thick headed lecherous old hags' and 'nasty things'. Struck in this, as in the reference to Billie Holliday's rumoured lesbianism, is a less than compassionate note for women she seems to consider in some way perverse. This is discordant with the dominant theme in her writing, which is one of love, but could of course be simply an honest re-creation of how she had viewed lesbianism when she was a young woman. Her ignorance and fear of non-heterosexuality, or indeed heterosexuality, had after all occasioned her to offer the experimental sex that had resulted in her pregnancy. Her search for her own sexual identity was part of her search for a self that she could deem worthy of love. The process of self-loving necessary for personal growth moves through familial, communal, racial and, finally, national love.

Her writing is a vivid reflection of the burdens of race, class and gender carried by black American women. That she chooses the autobiographic rather than fictional mode to do this, says much for her courage as well as her skill, for it involves a degree of self-revelation that leaves her, as author, vulnerable to misinterpretative attack. We should not judge the Angelou that exists, but the Angelou created, and the narrative skills and selection that have gone into this creation. Fidelity to the factual truth, she never claims, which explains why she omits any mention of her former husband Paul du Feu. If Angelou has 'edited out' that particular episode in her life, we can assume it was because it could not be accommodated within the narrative framework she had constructed for herself. When necessary she will understate or muffle, as well as heighten, admitting 'I was never loath to exaggerate a tale to make my point' (*GT*, p. 192), and the 'point' she makes about survival in spite of social pressures is one that gives delight. Her message of possible regeneration built upon individual belief in a bright tomorrow, permeates her autobiographies as it does the poem she composed for the Presidential inauguration. In 'On The Pulse Of Morning', she urges the American people to: 'Lift up your eyes upon/ The day breaking for you./ Give birth again/ To the dream.' Her reiteration of the American dream of human possibilities might at first glance appear to be a capitulation to the very dream which had for so long excluded the blacks in America, except that she emphasises the multi-ethnicity of American society:

> Each of you, descendants of some passed
> On Traveller, has been paid for . . .
> You, the Turk, the Arab, the
> Swede, the German, the Eskimo,
> the Scot, You, the Ahanti, the Yoruba, the
> Kru, bought,
> Sold, stolen, arriving on a
> nightmare,
> Praying for a dream

Her poem is designed to remind all watching and listening Americans, black and white, of ancestral struggles and tribulations in America, and to emphasise the need to create unity out of immense ethnic and cultural diversity. The debt to her own people is evident in her deliberate utilisation of the motifs of the rock and the tree found in Negro spirituals, an incorporation which emphasises a contribution to American culture which had gone unnoticed in the past. In this poem she universalises the philosophy for living which her auto-biographies had preached, that: 'History, despite its wrenching pain,/ Cannot be unlived, but if faced/ With courage, need not be lived again'. The message is to look forward without forgetting the past, in the belief that 'Each new hour holds new chances/ For new beginnings'. The dream of national progress is, in Angelou's eyes, one which can – and must – be enacted in each individual's determination to 'Mould it into the shape of your most/ Private need. Sculp it into/ The image of your most public self'. This, I believe is exactly what she herself does in her autobiographical writing.

The appeal of Angelou's writing for women readers who are neither black nor American is in her creation of a positive female role model.

Although Angelou's experience of sexism was exacerbated by its intersection with a racism which white women did not suffer (unless it is in the pain of a self-examination revealing racial attitudes they themselves have been socialised into holding), they respond with recognition to her identification of gender oppression. They delight in her success and seek identification with a woman who takes such delight in femaleness. Above all they are left with the concept of 'phenomenal woman', in Angelou's creation of a positive female self:

> Now you understand
> just why my head's not bowed.
> I don't shout or jump about
> or have to talk real loud.
> When you see me passing
> it ought to make you proud.
>
> I say in the click of my heels
> The bend of my hair,
> The palm of my hand
> The need for my care.
>
> 'Cause I'm a woman
> Phenomenally.
> Phenomenal woman.
> That's me.[19]

I do not believe that Angelou intends this description of women to be exclusive of white women.

— 6 —

Toni Morrison (b. 1931)
The power of the ancestors

I wrote *Sula* and *The Bluest Eye* because they were books I wanted to read. No one had written them yet, so I wrote them.[1]

Although the 1960s, since described as the Second Black Renaissance, brought an explosion of talented black writers to the attention of the American reading public, clearly Toni Morrison perceived a void in the canon where a black female voice should be. A chronological reading of Morrison's work will show that her own voice – heard in *The Bluest Eye* (published in 1970)[2] and *Sula* (1974),[3] where she focuses on the black female – gathers strength in later work as she considers the issues of female friendship, different aspects of love, and the succour afforded by community. The voice is also avowedly black and female. In an interview with the BBC in 1988,[4] she explains her insistence upon being described as a *black woman* writer. She recalls her sense that writers like Richard Wright, Ralph Ellison and James Baldwin, whose published success was a guarantee that the black voice was heard, were not speaking to her. Nor could they speak *for* her. She listened in vain to hear in their work 'that interior life of the female'. Although rejoicing that black writers were being paid serious attention, Morrison was questioning the perpetuation of the masculinisation of the canon, with its implicit assumption that man, black or white, spoke for both genders. Black women, she says, are interested in each other, and so 'write from another place'. That 'other place' is one where their physical and spiritual beauty was denied, and their sexual exploitation and economic displacement suffered. The black male voice, she felt, could articulate the experience of blackness, but not femaleness.

In her six novels to date, Toni Morrison sings her own song. The themes explored are not in themselves new, but her variations are consistent with her own developing vision. Morrison identifies the 'place' where the female voice originates as the site of struggle for a self-definition and self-love whose nourishment comes from a reclamation of ancestry. The need to reclaim the past in order to define the female self in terms of inherited culture, is both a feminist and a racial urge. In the 1960s, when the seeds of Morrison's early novels were germinating, the need of black Americans was for an awareness of an ancestral past *before* their enslaved American experience wherein their supposed inferiority had been inscribed and reinforced. Similarly women, black and white, were demanding that their own contribution to the culture of their society was given recognition. Ellen Moers' *Literary Women*,[5] published in 1963, and Elaine Showalter's *A Literature of Their Own*[6] in 1978, were pioneering efforts to claim a white female European literary tradition, but both drew upon white canonical texts. Only by the efforts of black women academics such as Barbara Christian, whose *Black Women Novelists*[7] in 1980 gave coherence to a black female literary tradition, has the writing of black women been recognised. When Morrison began writing, she was building on and adding to a then-unrecognised tradition. Her concern to reclaim and find her place within black cultural history is translated in her fictions in a foregrounding of that history. What was a muted theme in her early novels, swells to dominance in *Beloved* (1987)[8] where she faces the unspeakable source of her people's oppression: slavery. In the aforementioned interview Morrison admits this was a very difficult thing to do:

> I kept saying I know why nobody ever does this – it's not possible. It is difficult to dwell in areas that are problematic. Black people's press was towards freedom, progress – and so they could not dwell in that area and stay healthy. (BBC Interview)

She recognises this to be a healthy impulse in a moving away from slavery, but suggests that in blocking out the whole experience some things of value might be lost. Courageously she confronts the diaspora of her enslaved ancestors and, without diminishing its enormity, affirms the positives of black life and culture that enabled survival. In her most recent novel *Jazz* (1992),[9] Morrison addresses the Harlem of 1926, where so many dispossessed Southern blacks gathered, and for whom the music they made was a source of healing.

Her need to articulate the uniqueness of female experience is realised in the woman-centred *The Bluest Eye* and *Sula*, which chart the progress of her female protagonists from childhood into womanhood. Both are bleak in their tragic conclusions for the protagonists, whose double burden of race and gender are unmitigated. The deranged Pecola Breedlove in *The Bluest Eye* is doomed to live for ever in a state of perverted childhood, whilst Sula and Nel live into an adulthood ultimately only given coherence by the death of Sula and Nel's belated recognition of an abiding friendship. Moving from the centrality of female experience in *Song of Solomon* (1977),[10] she shows a male protagonist, Milkman Dead, as he is piloted between conflicting values to discover an ancestry which provides him with identity. *Tar Baby* (1981)[11] intensifies the theme of conflicting cultural values, personified in the tug of love between Jadine and Son, whilst *Beloved* delineates an ex-slave mother's struggle with a past which is projected as the haunting of her people. *Jazz* (1992) moves into another important period in the history of blacks in America, and again stresses that dispossession can be overcome if contact with ancestral principles is intact. Her first four novels provide an ever-deepening insight into clashing value systems, embodied in the destructive conflict between the white and black worlds; between black women; between black men; between black men and women. In *Beloved* reconciliation with a mutual past is achieved, allowing the former slaves Sethe and Paul D. to anticipate a future together, and in *Jazz* the same impulse provides accommodation between Violet and Joe Trace.

Morrison's strengthening of definitions and focusing of perception are reflected in the novels' narrative structures. In *Sula* and *The Bluest Eye* the movement is 'circular, although the circles are broken' (Tate, *Black Women Writers*, p. 124), and the circles echo the repetitious nature of despair, whilst a headlong flight into a vortex where the price of identity is death characterises *Song of Solomon*. In *Tar Baby* the structure echoes the frustration embodied in the interlocking but eccentric circles of Jadine and Son, who cannot find a common centre, and in *Beloved* the circularity of the structure reinforces the completed concentric circles of Sethe and Paul D. In *Jazz* the structure is determined by Blues jazz music, in which various voices work together to produce a lament for a past. Structural shape is controlled in all of her novels by skilful manipulation of narrative time in which she replaces linear progression with a series of moments in which past, present and future exist together. The structure of *The*

Bluest Eye cleverly juxtaposes two worlds, two cultures in tension within a double framework; one frame is the cyclical, seasonal one, the other the idealised world in a child's reading primer. The first frame, in which the narrative moves from Autumn, Winter, Spring to Summer, echoes the spiralling movement of Pecola's tragedy, and underlines the inevitability of natural processes which in Pecola's case become perverted and stunted. For such as Pecola, the world could never be a place of self-fulfilment. The larger society into which she is born, and by whose standards she will be judged, is, like the earth receiving the narrator's seeds, unyielding. The seasonal rhythm of planting and harvest is a cruel parody of Pecola's experience, as Summer brings both the death of the baby she bears to her father, and her retreat into madness. The novel questions not how this happened, but why: the answer suggested is found in the second frame, which contrasts white expectations with the reality of a black childhood.

In *The Bluest Eye* Morrison depicts the insidious inculcation of white societal 'norms' which begins in school. Any child, black or white, is confronted with a reading primer depicting an idealised version of a perfect, white, nuclear family. This model family is 'happy', lives in a 'pretty house' where sister and brother have a 'nice' mother who 'laughs' and a 'big', 'strong' father who 'plays'. The unfolding of Pecola's story parallels and directly refutes these concepts. Her home is not red, green and white, but a grey, dilapidated store-front. Her mother is not 'nice' to her, and her father's love-play destroys her. Dick and Jane's dog is replaced by Soaphead Church's landlady's dog, whose death Pecola believes signals her acquisition of blue eyes. As each concept is relentlessly belied by Pecola's experience, her dislocation is emphasised. In the figure of Pecola, Morrison illustrates how an unloved member of an underclass can be tragically destroyed and, in Claudia, the healthy survival of one cocooned by familial love. Nurtured in a home echoing with her mother's singing, assured of her father's protection and the loving friendship of a sister, Claudia's values are emotional, not materialistic. All she desires at Christmas is 'to sit on the low stool in Big Mama's kitchen with my lap full of lilacs, and listen to Big Pappa play his violin for me alone' (p. 24). Claudia's safety was indoors, with a family whose love gave reassurance of her value. Pecola lived 'outdoors' with a family who had surrendered totally to the negative socialisation upon which black inferiority is maintained in a white society: 'they lived there because they were poor and black and they stayed there because they were ugly' (p. 38). Pecola Breedlove imagined she was unloved because she was unlovely, in contrast to Claudia, whose home life provided an assured basis for growth towards fulfilment in self-love.

Claudia and her sister Frieda were not reared in the self-hatred which destroyed poor blacks like the Breedloves. Claudia methodically destroys the gift of a white doll symbolic of a value system which excludes black girls. Morrison describes the idea of physical beauty as 'the most destructive idea in the history of human thought' (p. 133). This idea is disturbing to all girls, but when the ideal of beauty is also white, black girls face a daily challenge to their personhood. The white world has assumed that every girl treasures this ideal embodied in the doll, but Claudia's one desire is 'to dismember it. To see of what it was made, to discover the dearness, to find the beauty, the desirability that had escaped me' (p. 23). She had not succumbed to the chillingly logical equation made by Pecola between blue eyes and love, between pale skin and happiness.

Like Hurston in *Their Eyes Were Watching God*, Morrison exposes colorism as a self-destructive and corrosive force, and economically delineates the resultant clash in cultural attitudes, embodied in the 'high-yellow dream child', Maureen Peal. Dressed as a Shirley Temple doll, in her velvet coat, muff, patent-leather and buckled shoes, Maureen Peal is a parody of the real thing, made manifest in the child of Pauline Breedlove's white employers who 'wore a pink sunback dress and pink fluffy bedroom slippers with two bunny ears pointed up from the tips. Her hair was corn yellow and bound in thick ribbon' (p. 100).

The emulation of the white film-star child, for which Maureen Peal's parents were responsible, exemplifies not only a fruitless striving for white values, but an acceptance of an equation between whiteness and desirability, between golden-haired beauty and normality. An adult version of Maureen is Geraldine whose mixed blood means she could pass for white, and whose self-hatred produces in her a blindness to any beauty in herself that didn't approach that of whites. She is seen as typical of a class of black girls who 'straighten their hair with Dixie Peach, and part it on the side. At night they curl it in papers from brown bags, tie a print scarf around their heads, and sleep with hands folded across their stomachs' (p. 77). Hair-straightening, as it was seen by Malcolm X in his autobiography, is a denial of black self, and a sign of a black subordination only made possible by an acceptance of inferiority. Tight, neat, loveless and 'colored', Geraldine imitates white living. Geraldine's failure to live naturally is governed by her perception of blackness as ugly, culminating in her reviling of Pecola as a 'nasty little black bitch'. Geraldine's creativity, channelled into the pursuit of a vicarious white life-style, has become perverted. Her denial of her blackness impairs the development of her son, who becomes sadistically vicious because of his alienation from other black children with whom he is forbidden to play. Although materially comfortable, Geraldine has suppressed all spontaneity in herself, and has never experienced the sexual joy once felt by the despised 'nigger' Pauline Breedlove. Yet Pecola, who gasps in wonder at Geraldine's potted plant and doilied home, can only see her as 'the pretty milk-brown lady in the pretty green and gold house' (p. 81). Utterly convinced of the intrinsic virtue of anything 'white', Pecola drinks milk avidly because it is served in a Shirley Temple mug, and buys Mary Jane sweets from a racist Mr Yacobowski (probably less of a 'native son' in America than was Pecola). His revulsion to her black skin, which he avoids touching when giving her change, affirms Pecola's conviction of her own ugliness. Her innate capacity for appreciating the natural beauty of dandelions is destroyed when she views them, as she herself is constantly defined, through white eyes: 'They *are* ugly. They *are* weeds' (p. 9).

The white values offered in the reading-book, reinforced by a Hollywood definition of female beauty which denies any to black girls, is unquestioned by Pecola or Maureen Peal. So brainwashed into an acceptance of black undesirability is Maureen Peal that she retails a screen story about a mulatta girl's hatred for her mother 'cause she's black and ugly' as a justifiable one. The impossible role model of Shirley Temple will be replaced in adulthood by the equally impossible Betty Grable and Jean Harlow. Even Frieda and Claudia are supposed to be complimented by the lodger's teasing reference to them as Greta Garbo and Ginger Rogers. There is a gradual intensification of evil associated with the desire to embrace white values seen in Maureen Peal, Geraldine and particularly in Soaphead Church who – disappointed, frustrated and half-white, from a family intent upon marrying 'whiter' – perverts Afro-American belief in magic. Bred into snobbery and madness by a mother who had learned 'to separate herself in body, mind and spirit from all that suggested

Africa' (p. 154), he decides to play God and convinces Pecola her eyes are blue.

Pecola's self-hatred is explained by Morrison as a learned response to a white world that denies self-esteem to black children. Those who taunt Pecola, Morrison depicts as consumed with contempt for their own blackness, so that when Pecola sees their 'exquisitely learned self-hatred', she covers her eyes. This defensive shielding of her eyes hides their offensive colour and blocks her self-reflection in those of her tormentors. Believing beauty to be a prerequisite for the deserving of love, Pecola longs for the blue eyes with which beauty began. Her self-loathing had been inherited from her mother Pauline, whose pathetic belief that 'somebody has to love you' was unfulfilled in a life of toil and spoiled dreams. Beginning life with a foot accidentally maimed, she falls in love with Cholly, and becomes emotionally crippled. Yet Pauline, resigned to a perceived sense of her own ugliness, was determined to love the unborn Pecola 'no matter what she looked like' – a determination irretrievably destroyed in the maternity hospital, where the doctor reduced Pauline's capacity for self-esteem when he spoke of her as an animal: 'They deliver right away and with no pain. Just like horses' (p. 115). Her new-born baby was, from then on, ugly. Pauline fills her need for a beauty she cannot find in her own life with her work for a white family. The kitchen she cleans she thinks of as 'my kitchen', the juice-spattered floor 'my floor'. Unable to create beauty in her store-front home, Pauline neglects it, as she does her children who are kept at bay in their address of her as 'Mrs. Breedlove'. Pauline Breedlove's creative urge, which Alice Walker's *In Search of Our Mothers' Gardens* argues is the unrecognised artistry of black foremothers, has been channelled into the creation of a pleasing harmony in a white woman's home. In her own life, artistry had been denied, although 'she missed – without knowing what she missed – paints and crayons' (p. 103). Divorced from her community when she and Cholly move North, she is out of tune with the harshness and squalor of her life far removed from the countryside. Sadly, but understandably, she expends her need for beauty and pleasing order in a white woman's kitchen, where she finds 'beauty, orderly cleanliness and praise'.

Social deprivation made of Pauline a living anachronism. Like the stereotypical plantation Mammy, she dares not love her children. In discussing motherhood in bondage, E. Franklin Frazier says:

> Where such limitations were placed upon the mother's spontaneous emotional responses to the needs of her children and where even her suckling and fondling of them were restricted, it was not unnatural that she often showed little attachment to the offspring – one would require a knowledge of the mother's experiences during pregnancy and childbirth and her subsequent relations with her infant in order to decide whether her behaviour was unnatural or extraordinary'.[12]

Irrevocably damaged by the cruelty of racism, Pauline's maternal love and creativity are focused on the child and home of her white employer. In her internalisation of black inferiority Pauline has allowed her emotional and physical self to become absolutely absorbed in service to whites. She is Morrison's illustration of the reductiveness of such absorption and is in contrast with Walker's depiction of Sofia in *The Color Purple*. Pauline's own home lacks the warmth of familial and communal love, in contrast to that of Claudia's mother, whose kitchen hosts a community of women exchanging gossip 'like a gently wicked dance'. Pauline does not have a supportive network of female friends and lives an emotionally isolated life.

Racist reductionism of blacks is graphically documented in the history of Cholly Breedlove, who was humiliated and reduced to impotence in adolescence when white hunters stumbled across him making love to a girl in the woods. His enforced 'performance' by these men who regard him as an animal, as the doctors had Pauline, results in a transference of hatred onto his partner rather than his tormentors. He is motivated into violence as Walker's Copeland men are in *The Third Life of Grange Copeland*. Unable to protect his girl, his hatred turns inwards: 'Never did he once consider his hatred toward the hunters' (p. 139). From that moment Cholly has a 'freedom' that is dangerous. His incestuous, drunken coupling with Pecola is not born out of intemperate lust, but an emotional complexity dominated by a need to love and protect. The Breedloves are driven by the needs to love, to be loved, and to find self-love, and the perversions of those needs are the mainspring of the story's tragic events.

Pecola's grasp on sanity, gradually loosened and finally destroyed, is enacted in the narrative structure, where Pecola's disintegrating sanity is reflected in the dislocation between the norms of the reading primer and the child's perception of the real world. The opening extract from the primer, clearly punctuated, makes sense, but as the story progresses, the punctuation disappears and sounds like a child who reads words without understanding, until finally there is a chaos of individual letters making no sense at all. Reading is a sophisticated use of the eyes. It is the end result of an intellectual translation of physical reality into a system of signs. The 'naming' process involved in this exercise helps children to make sense of the external world. This process assumes, however, that the writer and the reader share the same sense of 'reality'. What Pecola 'sees' in her life bears no relation to what white society and the educational process teaches her as being normal. What Pecola 'reads' does not equate with her 'reality' – what she 'sees' is at variance with what she reads. But instead of questioning what is seen, she questions her means of seeing. Eyes and ways of seeing dominate the novel. With blue eyes, Pecola thinks, she would see – and be seen – differently. What she sees when she visits Pauline's place of work, is the reality of the ideal home depicted in the reading-book, like a picture painted in primary colours on grassy green slopes against the blue of Lake Erie, where the sky was always blue. Pecola is unable to see with her inward eye that this is artificial – the windows are like shiny eyeglasses, there is no sign of life, and the lawn sports a painted wheelbarrow planted with seasonal flowers. Unlike Frieda and Claudia, who enthusiastically grub in the earth to plant seeds, to grow their own beauty in the world, Pecola's idea of beauty is glimpsed in the misuse of a wheelbarrow. She never learns self-love, so can never reach Claudia's health-giving realisation about Maureen Peal that 'The Thing to fear was the *Thing* that made her beautiful, and not us' (p. 49).

The exploration of values, community and love found in *The Bluest Eye* are more sharply focused in *Sula* and enlarged by a lengthening of narrative time spanning fifty years and three generations. Whereas the action in *The Bluest Eye* is compressed into the cycle of the seasons, *Sula*'s narrative is divided into two parts: the first, punctuated by named years from 1919 to 1927, depicts the childhoods and background of Sula and Nel; the second, from 1937 to 1965, their adulthood, the death of Sula, and the lonely ageing of Nel. Morrison describes the movement of *Sula* as more spiral than circular, and indeed the elongated narrative time-scale moves through named years like a coiled spring as past events reverberate in the narrative present. The story begins with a retrospective account of the black quarter, the 'Bottoms' now appropriated by the whites as a golf course. In a nostalgic lament for the lost community, Morrison mourns the clearing of beech trees, and 'the pear trees where children sat and yelled down through the blossoms to the passers-by'. The history of the Bottoms illustrates the abuse of white power, for the land had been given initially to a freed slave tricked into believing that the top land was superior because nearer the 'bottom' of heaven. This story had become part of the community mythology, a 'nigger joke' of the sort the 'coloured folks tell on themselves'. Like Hurston and Angelou, Morrison comments on the undertones of her people's laughter at their own gulling, saying, 'It would be easy for the valley man to hear the laughter and not notice the adult pain that rested somewhere under the eyelids' (p. 12).

Our perception of the Bottoms, disposed of and reappropriated by whites, begins and significantly ends with the National Suicide Day ordained by the shell-shocked war veteran, Shadrack. The significant entitlement of '1919' emphasises that Shadrack, like Sula's uncle Plum Peace, was destroyed by his involvement in a European war which he did not understand, and from which he would reap no benefit. The hospitalised Shadrack, unable to exorcise the horrors of war, looked at food and only saw 'the lumpy whiteness of rice, the quivering blood tomatoes, the greyish brown meat' (p. 15) that remind him of human carnage. Shell-shocked and unbalanced, his strategy to control the horrors of witnessed slaughter is to decree a National Suicide Day, as an invitation to all who so desire to commit suicide or murder. Bizarre as was this attempt to contain all slaughter in one ritualised day, the black community were able to absorb Shadrack, so that this proclaimed festival became an accepted feature in the community calendar. Tragedy strikes the community in 1941 when America entered another European war, and the townsfolk who previously had accepted but ignored Shadrack's summoning by bell to death had laughingly followed him to be accidentally drowned in the ice-bound river.

Mass death by water, a boy's accidental drowning, and two horrific deaths by burning, punctuate the novel with a violence that is never gratuitous. Each death, be it deliberate, accidental or natural, has a relevance to our understanding of the community and its place in the larger context of America, and illuminates the central relationship between Nel and Sula. In the chapters '1920' and '1921', Morrison places both girls in their familial setting, revealing that the attraction between Nel and Sula is founded on a shared experience of black femaleness, rather than a similar nurturing. Their backgrounds represent completely differing black aspirations. Nel's mother

Helene Sabat, the daughter of a beautiful Creole prostitute, has an inflated opinion of her superiority because of her inherited beauty and light colour. Like Geraldine in *The Bluest Eye* she presides over a neat, well-ordered, but unloving home. In the delineation of Nel's mother, Morrison addresses the historical fact of Creole women bred for sex, and also takes the opportunity to portray the hollowness of military victory for a nation that had Jim Crow laws. The shaping incident in Nel's childhood occurs during a journey to New Orleans on a segregated train, where she witnesses her mother's humiliating treatment by a white conductor and cringes at the manner of her mother's reply. The servile acceptance of humiliation in an apology, accompanied by a 'sir' and a placatory smile, is reflected in the watching eyes of returning black soldiers who hate this reminder of their own impotence. For the first time in her life outside the small community of Medallion City, Nel faces the reality of segregation. The insignificance of the blacks in the eyes of whites leaves her feeling dispossessed. She can receive no succour from her Creole grand-mother as contact with her is limited and deliberately curtailed by her aspiring mother. Made aware of her inferior social placing by colour, Nel emotionally rebels and determines on a search for self-hood: 'I'm me. I'm not their daughter, I'm not Nel, I'm me. Me' (p. 32).

Sula's experience of home as an untidy, busy household, overflowing with lodgers, is very different. Hers is dominated by a grandmother who is capable of a love of frightening ferocity. In the creation of Eva Peace Morrison conveys a mother love as intense as Sethe's in *Beloved*. Deserted in young motherhood by her husband, Eva Peace had thrown herself in the path of a train, not to kill herself, but to claim compensation for the leg she loses. She is determined to raise and protect the children she has borne, even if this involves sacrifice. Equally she will exercise the right to end the life she has fought to preserve if she sees it being slowly destroyed. In *Beloved* the choice of the mother to kill a child rather than let her live as a slave, is the end-product of the system of slavery. In the same way Eva Peace chooses to burn her beloved son to death rather than witness his enslavement to a drug addiction which is the legacy of his war service. Shocking as this episode is, it does not make a monster of Eva in the reader's eye for, like Cholly Breedlove and Sethe, she demonstrates a parental love that is curiously protective. In this environment, Sula is conditioned to regard death with a fascinated rather than a fearful interest, as she does when her mother perishes in a fire. Immured from shock at death, and having overheard Hannah once say she loved – but didn't like – her, Sula watches her dying mother – 'a flaming, dancing figure' – not in paralysed horror, but interest. The only abiding relationship for Sula is her love for Nel, which in girlhood was uncomplicated by jealous competition between them for boyfriends. So when in 1927 Nel marries Jude, Sula is unimpressed, as she could envisage no disruption of their friendship. Marriage for Nel is an escape from an undemonstrative family, but it holds no attraction for Sula, who leaves the Bottoms to live life on her own terms. Sula's upbringing is unimpeded by the stultifying restrictions of bourgeois white values, thus allowing her a freedom denied to Nel, to 'make' herself.

Sula and Nel develop an intimacy which some feminist critics interpret as subconsciously lesbian. This is a relevant reading of their attachment in that they are truly loving of each other. In adulthood both girls find sexual fulfilment in heterosexual relationships, and even allow these to subjugate an emotional bond founded in the lonely interdependence and the shared dreams of girlhood. Together they discover sexuality in the tentative sexual invitations thrown out by boys. They also learn that as females they are destined to become sex objects in an hierarchical society which assigns them the least important role. They grow into a world fashioned first for whites, then for males and lastly for black women. In a society constructed on racial and gender differentiation they discover that 'all freedom and triumph was forbidden to them'. Their answer to these social realities is to establish a 'something else' in a friendship so intense that, when Nel is threatened by young white boys, Sula, like Eva, is prepared to mutilate herself, cutting her own finger with her knife, with the warning, 'If I can do that to myself, what you suppose I'll do to you?' (p. 55). This initiation into blood intimacy, which is traditionally associated with the initiation of men into brotherhood, is emphasised in a strangely sexual and ritualistic digging and filling of a hole, as if the girls are subconsciously anticipating an adult sexuality that they know will signal the end of girlhood. This communion of shared but unspoken knowledge is consummated in their joint complicity in the accidental drowning of a small black boy.

Part two of *Sula* takes up the narrative after a ten-year break, in which Sula's return to Medallion City is accompanied by an ominous plague of robins that alarms the townspeople. In her ten years of absence, Sula had lived an 'experimental' life in which she had free-wheeled amongst lovers for whom she never felt possessiveness. Singularly free of personal vanity, competitiveness or ambition, she had lived by no rules of conduct but her own, governed neither by acquisitiveness nor by conscious malice towards others. She returns wearing the finery associated with 'fast' white women, and her strange rose-shaped birthmark seems more prominent to a community who regard her with suspicion. Only Nel recognises that Sula has come 'home' and welcomes her. Wearing a yellow dress like the ancestor in *Tar Baby*, Sula brings forgotten sunshine and laughter into Nel's life. She spends 'easy sun-washed days' with 'lemon yellow afternoons bright with iced drinks and splashes of daffodils' (p. 87). As in *The Bluest Eye* where Claudia's green, 'living' house is contrasted with Pecola's 'sterile', grey one, colour imagery is used to depict emotional as well as physical realities. The friends' reunion is refreshing, regenerating and mutually beneficial. Nel becomes 'soft and new' again, and Sula is healed in the haven of friendship. The question raised, however, if Sula had lived as she had pleased, is why she needed to return. I think that Morrison's answer is that, completely divorced from the community which had supported and succoured Eva Peace, Sula could not flourish. She needed the community whose history was one of survival, and who perceived evil as something to survive rather than defeat, along with 'floods, white people and tuberculosis'.

Nel and Sula are mutually nourished by their friendship which eventually founders on the rocks of sexual politics. Sula entertains Nel and her husband with a witty tirade about the dynamics of the sexual politics governing the relationship between black men and whites, and between black men and black women. Laughingly Sula sketches in the function of the black male in white society as sexual scapegoat:

> White men love you. They spend so much time worrying about your penis they forget their own. The only thing they want to do is to cut off a nigger's privates. . . . And white women? . . . They think rape soon's they see you. . . . Coloured women worry themselves into bad health just trying to hang on to your cuffs. (p. 95)

Sadly, Nel and Jude miss the seriousness of Sula's comments. Incapable of feeling possessive herself, Sula does not regard Jude as Nel's possession, and views her own ensuing affair with him as a sharing rather than a dispossession. Nel, however, sees it as betrayal, and both marriage and friendship are destroyed.

The chapter '1919', delineating the disillusioned aftermath of the First World War, is echoed in '1939', the year heralding the Second World War, when Sula begins a love affair with the golden-eyed Ajax, and she loses her previous disdain for possessive love. Ajax loves Sula because of her seeming difference to other women, in her willingness to luxuriate in a sexual relationship based upon free will rather than marital obligation. He backs away when Sula develops a dependence on him, and a desire to domesticate him from which he flees as the 'scent of the nest'. With his defection, Sula's thoughts turn to Nel, as the one permanent relationship in a community from which she has become isolated. The townspeople regard Sula as a deviant who had disregarded communal commitments. She had broken Nel's marriage and rejected family when she forcibly institutionalised her grandmother. The women see her as a sexual threat, the men hint that she sleeps with white men. In all, unable to understand her, they simply think of her as bad medicine. Her isolation is complete. The blemish on her forehead is no longer seen as a rose, a symbol of passion, but a snake, symbol of evil betrayal. Paradoxically, although the community keeps its distance, it does not try to eject her. The townsfolk work round her, seeing her as a natural aberration and 'it was not for them to expel or annihilate it' (p. 107). If she was a source of evil, she was, as experience had taught them, to be accepted and survived. Indeed, her presence has a beneficial effect on the community who, in their fear of her supposed power, nurture children and husbands with greater attention.

When in 1940 Sula is terminally ill and alone, only Nel visits her, with the simple statement, 'But you a woman and you alone'. What follows is a brilliant demonstration of how effective novelistic dialogue can be. As the friends talk, the directness and energy of their exchange is not disturbed by the introduction of any but the barest minimum of authorial description. No extraneous adverbial phrases detract from the reader's involvement in what, for me, is the most moving exchange in the novel. Greeting Nel as if there had been no disruption in their friendship, Sula both answers Nel's accusation of betrayal and questions the values responsible for Nel's interpretation of that episode. Their differing attitudes leave the reader, like Sula, asking Nel if she is so sure she was right. At least, Sula claims, if lonely, her loneliness was of her own making, whilst Nel's loneliness had been created externally by loss of husband and natural defection of children. At the moment of death, Sula's abiding thought is of Nel, to whom she'd like to say how easy it is to die. The community are relieved when Sula's death removes a source of unease, yet they are not content but become strangely irritable despite the improvement in economic conditions which 1941 brings. It is at this point in the narrative that Morrison completes the narrative link with 1919, and the events of a National Suicide Day for which Shadrack had lost his enthusiasm. The containment of violence and death which had been Shadrack's initial purpose is no longer possible for a nation at war, and Sula's death finally persuades him that he had failed in his desire to convince her as a child that some things are for 'always'. The townspeople, like lemmings, follow Shadrack to a death which is a metaphor for the ensuing holocaust of war: 'A lot of them died there' (p. 144). As the Bottoms 'collapse' and America enters the war, the community is dispersed. That which survives is recognised by Nel, as love. Reassessing in 1965 what she had enjoyed and valued in life, she realises that her love for her children was like 'a pan of syrup too long on the stove', making a sweetness as eventually non-nutritious as Valerian's sweets in *Tar Baby*. The real loss was not of husband or children, but of friendship, as she discovers:

> 'All that time, all that time. I thought I was missing Jude' And the loss pressed down on her chest and came up into her throat. 'We was girls together', she said, as though explaining something. 'O Lord Sula', she cried, 'girl, girl, girl girl girl' (p. 154).

Sula's death coincides with the destruction of the Bottoms, as those who had made money during the war moved into the valley – whilst the whites built homes in the hills. A complete reversal had taken place, and Morrison laments the fragmentation of a community into 'separate houses with separate televisions and separate telephones'.

In *Sula*, Morrison points to what can be lost when community disappears. Technological progress had brought isolation; a distancing of individuals from the emotional nutrition which had characterised the Bottoms, where once the air had 'got heavy with peeled fruit and boiling vegetables. Fresh corn, tomatoes, string beans, melon rinds'. Morrison suggests that in striving to acquire the artefacts of twentieth-century America, black Americans will only survive 'whole' if they nourish, and are in turn nourished by, their own community. With this they can preserve the sense of identity which Nel and Sula, in their own ways, had set about finding. One of the features of that community had been its acceptance of the grotesque,

in the one-legged Eva Peace and the incredible Deweys. Another was
the awareness that reality is more than physical. Hannah's death is
presaged by dreams of being married in red and premonitions of
disaster. In this, Morrison begins to introduce into her writing a sense
of magic, a juxtaposition of the credible and the seemingly incredible
which throws her preoccupations into startling relief. Other concerns
with community, friendship, and an insistence that black identity can
only be found and retained by a cleaving to ancestry, are developed
in *Song of Solomon* and *Tar Baby*. Her more conscious focusing on
African cultural roots is signalled by the titles, both derived from
Afro-American folk-history. *Song of Solomon*, a compelling and
complex story, draws upon the Afro-American myth that Africans,
like their ancestor Solomon, could fly from enslavement back to
Africa, whilst *Tar Baby* echoes the folk-tale of the rabbit who has to
be thrown into a briar patch in order to free himself from the tar-baby
trap laid by the (white man) fox.

Song of Solomon is a fable underlining how separation, both
physical and spiritual, hinders growth. To emphasise the dangers of
a further diaspora as Southern black communities disintegrate in
Northern migrations, Morrison uproots her fictional characters from
the rural South and locates them in the urban, industrialised North.
Even there, they cannot escape the violence of racism which invades
them in the account of the boy murdered in Mississippi, where he
'had whistled at some white woman, refused to deny he had slept with
others, and was a Northerner visiting the South' (p. 83). Paradoxically,
despite the viciousness of endemic Southern racism, the uprooted
blacks, like those in Alice Walker's fiction, love their Southern
homeland. Being cut off from the vitality and regenerative properties
of Nature, leaves even the white-hating Guitar with a deep loneliness
and longing, and is the source of tragedy in *Jazz*. In migrating, blacks
suffered a double dispossession, for in leaving the Southern homeland
they left their living contact with African ancestors. Morrison's
professed purpose in *Song of Solomon* is to keep that contact alive:

> When you kill the ancestor you kill yourself. I want to point out the
> dangers, to show that nice things don't always happen to the totally
> self-reliant if there is no conscious historical connection, to say 'see –
> this is what will happen'.[13]

To explore the possible consequences of a denial of roots, *Song of
Solomon* is structured in two parts, the first depicting the black

sterility of dispossession, the second the joyous triumph of rediscovery as Milkman finds his ancestry in Shalimar.

The inhospitality of the setting into which Milkman is born echoes that of Pecola Breedlove. It is a cold world, whipped by a gusting wind and white snow against which the black people, whose ancestors had been forcibly removed from the African and then the Southern American sunshine, stand in stark relief. They have gathered to witness an announced 'flying' by an insurance salesman. This seemingly insane act is transformed at the end of the novel when Milkman believes that he also possesses the power of flight inherited from his fabled ancestor, Solomon. The flight is a sustaining motif symbolic of the physical flight of Milkman from Hagar and the spiritual freedom gained from a discarding of materialism. The need to be stripped of the accrued luggage of possessions is epitomised in Guitar's observation that the flightless peacock has 'Too much tail. All that jewelry weighs it down. Like vanity. Can't nobody fly with all that shit. Wanna fly, you got to give up the shit that weighs you down' (p. 180). Unlike Jadine in *Tar Baby*, whose accumulated jewels entrap her into a false value system from which she cannot fly, Milkman Dead is guided to the freedom to be found only in true identity.

The intention of Northern white society to suppress black people's identity and consign them to invisibility is palpable in the white, bureaucratic insistence that Mains Avenue was not 'Doctor St'. The resilient determination of the dispossessed who had named it because a black doctor had lived there, triumphs in their persistent reference to it thereafter as 'Not Doctor St'. Humorous as this is, the underlying indignity offered to the black townspeople is not missed. As seen in Angelou's works, the power of naming is white, and the struggle for black identity begins with an insistence upon being named correctly. The reductiveness of 'gal' as an address to Nel's mother in *Sula*, and the inability of Jadine to remember that the servant 'Mary's' name was actually Alma Ester, are pertinent reminders of white oppression. Even in freedom slaves could be misnamed, as occurred when Macon Dead was given his bizarre name 'in perfect thoughtlessness by a drunken Yankee'. From this follows Macon's determination to preserve and establish a tradition in which the male offspring were called Macon and the girls named by random opening of the Bible. Hence his daughter was named Pilate and his granddaughters First Corinthians and Magdalene.

Orphaned when their father dies defending his land against white appropriation, the second-generation Macon and his sister Pilate drift separately northwards to settle in the same town. It is in this transposition that the brother and sister embrace values which are diametrically opposed. Macon marries Ruth Foster, daughter of a colorist doctor, whose aspirations lead him to refer to his black patients as cannibals, and whose only concern for his grandchildren is the lightness of their skin. Infected by her father's false ideas, Ruth Foster, like Mrs Wright in *Sula* and Geraldine in *The Bluest Eye*, is detached from a community and husband she regards as inferior. Repelled by Ruth's inordinate adoration of her dead father, on whose reputation she had sucked as she had his dead fingers, Macon is impelled to achieve the trappings of white capitalist success. He pours his energy into a material acquisitiveness which leaves him spiritually bankrupt. As a landlord he is unrelenting to his black tenants and, unlike his father who had died for the love of his land, Macon lives only for the love of his houses. This difference in attitude towards the land as opposed to buildings is the same as had driven the Boyces apart in Marshall's *Browngirl, Brownstones*, and springs from the same difference in values. Macon Dead becomes earth-bound, and like Marley's ghost is weighed down with rental accounts, ledgers and keys that closed and imprisoned, rather than opened, possibilities. Guitar's mother, who falls economic victim to Macon Dead, observes: 'a nigger in business is a terrible thing to see' (p. 27). His steady accumulation of wealth had completely ruptured any wholesome communion with his people, creating in him an isolation he passes on to his son, Milkman.

Saddled with a mischievous nickname because in her need for emotional comfort his mother had continued to suckle him into boyhood, Milkman is dispossessed more surely than his friend Guitar. The economic deprivation of urban blacks had fostered in Guitar the intensity of hatred for whites encountered in the earlier part of Malcolm X's autobiography, but also a sense of fraternal kinship with his own people. As a member of the secret association, the 'Seven Days', Guitar is committed to the indiscriminate and retaliatory murder of whites, believing 'there are no innocent white people, because every one of them is a potential nigger-killer, if not an actual one' (p. 157). Politicised, angry, and actively engaged, Guitar has an identity denied to Milkman whose mirrored reflection 'lacked coherence', failing to present a 'total self'. Born to parents whose lives denied the values associated with their ancestral heritage, Milkman is rootless, his life and relationship futile. When Guitar says to him, 'You don't live nowhere, NOT Not Doctor St *or* Southside', he refers to something more than a geographical location. Milkman doesn't belong. The dead hand of materialism is stifling Milkman as it had his father, whose lack of spiritual soaring and direction is epitomised by the status-conscious driving in his Packard. Although as yet unawakened to the cancer eating away his spiritual life, Milkman, who often dreamed of flying as a child, felt uncomfortable riding backward in that car: 'It was like flying blind, and not knowing where he was going – just where he had been, – troubled him' (p. 36). Unconsciously Milkman was missing a past which had been denied him by 'upwardly mobile' parents.

Morrison demonstrates that Macon Dead's life of business success had only fattened his bank balance at the expense of his spirituality. His loveless domestic life is characterised by tasteless, hastily prepared meals, in contrast to those of his miraculous sister, Pilate, who lives spontaneously with her daughter and granddaughter eating 'like children' whatever was naturally abundant:

> or there might be grapes, left from the winemaking, or peaches for days on end. If one of them bought a gallon of milk they drunk it until it was gone. If another got a half bushel of tomatoes or a dozen ears of corn, they ate them until they were gone too. (p. 36)

Born without a navel, Pilate is the ancestor, an 'original' first mother who, like the African woman in *Tar Baby* who holds eggs aloft in a Parisian market, offers eggs to Milkman and Guitar. She is the ancestral mother whose contact with the natural world has remained unbroken and whom her offspring deny at their peril. With blueberry lips constantly chewing seeds and pine kernels, Pilate is succoured both by natural food, and by the relics of her past carried in the green sack of bones and the ear-ring containing the paper on which her father had written her name. Both are relics which affirm her identity and connectedness with the ancestral dead. Unmindful of possessions, her spirituality gives her unquestioning acceptance of an other-world reality. Whereas Ruth Foster's only contact with her father is in midnight visits to the graveyard, Pilate remembers how she and Macon had been visited by their Papa's ghost. Pilate's retention of history is strengthened by this ghost who leans in at the window and urges her to 'Sing, Sing'. She moves through the novel as a miraculous presence, associated with round and juicy words, 'berries', 'cherries', 'eggs', 'oranges'and 'tomatoes'. In contrast, the language Morrison uses to describe her brother Macon is precise, sharp and evocative of an atrophied vitality:

> His hatred of his wife glittered and sparkled in every word he spoke to her. The disappointment he felt in his daughters sifted down on them like ash, dulling their buttery complexions and choking the lilt out of what should have been girlish voices. (p. 16)

Pilate enjoys a relationship with her womenfolk envied by Macon as he watches them through a window. The generational matriarchy of Pilate's household reflects that of Eva Peace's, and interestingly Morrison does not suggest that either will ultimately flourish. Death results for Sula and Hannah, as it does for Hagar, demonstrating Morrison's holistic approach to gender interdependence. As Sula's and Hagar's contact with ancestors is diluted and as they are separated from their men, so they find it harder to survive; when the men are driven out of 124 Bluestone Road in *Beloved* the three-generational matriarchy left does not thrive, but is torn by unresolved tensions. In *Song* it is Milkman, not Hagar, who is guided to Shalimar; his soul at stake in the clash between the materialism of the new middle-class negro, and the spirituality of the Ancestor. Milkman's quest ultimately tests his father's assertion that 'Pilate can't teach you a thing you can use in this world. Maybe the next, but not this one' (p. 59). Eventually Milkman learns that his father and aunt represent two cultures as different in kind as the two medicines on offer: the cold, unloving white medicine grudgingly administered by his grandfather, and Pilate's naturally curative powerful root medicine.

In a tautly interrelated narrative network, structured to enable each participant to furnish the present with a past, Part 1 establishes the parameters of conflict. Suspense is created and maintained through Morrison's controlled unfolding of narrative fact. Simultaneously with Milkman, the reader is made aware of the remembered history of Macon Dead, and has to reconstruct events from proferred versions of that history. This involves no narrative sleight of hand or assumed pre-knowledge on the part of the characters, in whose episodic recounting and recalling the reader and Milkman are simultaneously prepared for the gathering pace of narrative events in Part 2. When Milkman retraces his forebear's journey from Shalimar, there is a noticeable quickening in narrative pace likened by Morrison to a 'locomotive'. The further he is removed from Northern influence, the deeper Milkman penetrates the Southern homeland of his ancestors, the stronger is the sense of magic. Hoping to discover hidden treasure, he encounters the impossibly old Circe – 'But Circe is dead. This woman is alive' (p. 241) – who had sheltered Pilate and Macon from their father's murderers. Sorceress, root-doctor, with the voice of a young girl, Circe points him towards the truth of his ancestry. The exciting prospect of imagined treasure pales before the thrill of discovery that his ancestor's past is part of Shalimar folklore, kept alive in children's song. The stripping of the 'shit' which had hindered the peacock's flight is echoed in Milkman's discarding of materialistic bonds. He arrives in the South with all the appurtenances of a slick, visiting Northern cousin to live with Backwoods people who carried nothing: 'The women's hands were empty. No pocketbook, no change purse, no wallet, no keys.' The trappings of property and capitalism were not needed where man and nature live in harmonious relation. In Shalimar his initiation into self-awareness is completed in the hunting trip, when survival rests upon his own physicality – 'eyes, ears, nose, taste, touch – '. He learns to listen to his own body and the sounds of the natural world, so experiencing a spiritual communion with forces he had never known existed. The animism of his African ancestors survives in the life of the Shalimar hunters in a communication pre-dating language: 'Language in the time when men and animals did talk to one another' (p. 279).

Milkman's treasure turns out not to be the lusted-after gold, but something more glorious: the wholeness of finding a real identity with his discovery of his ancestry. His spiritual health is matched by a physical one, as the limp he had been born with disappears during the hunt. The process of birth and death with which the novel opens is repeated in the final chapters. As he plunges naked into the water beneath Solomon's Leap, he is born and baptised anew. His physical birth (in the North) coincides with a spiritual death; his physical death (in the South), with a spiritual birth. Magic had supposedly aided his conception, as Ruth Foster had sought Pilate's root medicine to persuade Macon to impregnate her, and his belief in the magic of his flying ancestor willingly makes him leap into the air to meet possible death. He had learned that 'If you surrender to the air, you could *ride* it' (p. 336). Milkman lives most intensely in the moment he is willing to surrender his life to Guitar. He is prepared to be wildly lavish of self, when formerly he had vacillated between careless dissipation of his capacity for life and a selfish taking from others. His sister Lena complains of her girlhood spent in satisfying his needs, and remembers his 'peeing' on her maple tree. Lena feels Milkman had spent his life repeating this action, and that those he touched, like the maple tree, had shrivelled and died. Milkman's soul is the trophy for which Macon and Pilate compete, but the victory which left Pilate dead and Macon dispossessed of a male heir, is Milkman's alone.

The scenario of struggle is rehearsed again in *Tar Baby*, but here it is situated not in the past, but the present generation in the figures of Jadine and Son, who engage in a deadly combat for the supremacy of the different values they have embraced. As in *Song of Solomon*, the narrative impulse sets in motion and traces the outcome of this conflict, embodied in the black woman who eventually opts for white European materialism, and her black lover whose destiny will be decided on the island where African slaves had made landfall and had been mysteriously struck blind. Morrison's skill as a storyteller is apparent in the arresting openings of her novels. The reader is immediately intrigued by the reading-primer context of *The Bluest Eye*; the provocative announcement of unassisted flight in *Song*; the disappearing community in *Sula*; the sense of danger and reprieve at the beginning of *Tar Baby*; the attempted mutilation of a corpse in *Jazz*; the haunting of a house in *Beloved*. These openings are not cosy preambles allowing slow access to the narratives, but thrust the reader immediately into a provocative fictive world. *Tar Baby* begins with an expulsion of held breath – 'He believed he was safe' – but 'his', and the reader's, pounding heart is only temporarily quieted. Physical danger might be averted, but Morrison's language alerts the reader to the more dangerously seductive danger of sexual attraction: 'Queen of France blushed a little in the lessening light and lowered her lashes before his gaze. Seven girlish cruisers bobbed in the harbour' (p. 1). The liner holds the beautiful Jade, who is to ensnare Son as surely as the tar baby did the rabbit.

In contrast to the Northern worlds created in *The Bluest Eye*, and *Song of Solomon*, *Tar Baby*'s setting is exotic, lush and captivatingly sensual. The Caribbean island is riotously fecund, with abundant fruit and flowers, ants that march inexorably to retrieve chocolate flakes, and honeyless bees that do not sting. As magical as Prospero's island, Ile de Chevaliers has an untameable, dark and exotic life, clamorously striving to be seen and heard. It also houses the lurking danger in the tarry bog of Sein de Vielles (witches' tit). The metaphorical framework of *Tar Baby*, rests on increasingly dominant and divergent images of tar. The bog is 'seeping' with a thick, black, cloying and dangerous 'substance', with a consistency variously described as like treacle, or oily molasses, or jelly-like. Such descriptions connect the bog to the boiled-sugar confectionery on which the white man Valerian's wealth was built. The connection between Valerian's inherited wealth and the exploitation of island blacks is not an arbitrary one, as Morrison makes explicit the link between the oppression of African slaves who had worked the sugar plantations and Valerian's continuation of that exploitation into the twentieth century. Valerian, whose name resonates with imperial associations and reflects his attitude towards his island 'empire', epitomises the destructiveness of colonisation. With no contact with the natural world except a desire to subdue it, he represents artificial, life-suppressing forces: 'Anybody builds a greenhouse on the equator ought to be shame' (p. 11). He is deaf to the island's natural rhythm and music, which are overlaid by his recordings of classical music. Valerian is both agent and victim of white rapaciousness. Born into a rich family, like Milkman Dead he had reaped the unhealthy harvest of capitalist exploitation. Neither relationships nor greenhouse plants flourish for Valerian, as both harbour a canker which destroys as insidiously as candies rot teeth. Valerian had been conditioned to desire and to consume the artificial. His love for Margaret was triggered by her red-and-white appearance as the 'Principal Beauty' on a float, where she appeared to him like the incarnation of a 'Valerian' candy. The intruder, Son, whose arrival disturbs the well-ordered artificiality of Valerian's retreat from life, recognises in Margaret 'that inside that white, smooth skin was liquid sugar, no bones – no cartilage – just liquid sugar' (p. 197). Even Valerian's one friendly neighbour, Mr Michelin, is associated with the corruptive disease resulting from over-sticky foods. As a dentist Michelin's livelihood depends on treating decay caused by over-indulgence in an unnecessary product, but like the dentist remembered by Maya Angelou, he refuses to tend black patients. Neither Michelin nor Valerian can recognise the humanity of the island blacks, or see their own part in an exploitative process which was set in place with colonisation and enslavement. The cheap, decay-producing sweets named in honour of Valerian's birth sold well only to poor Southern blacks: 'Jigs buy 'em'. The candies are emblematic of a continued exploitation which Northward-migrating blacks, who stop buying these confections, are hoping to escape: 'They're *leaving* the South, when they move out they want to leave that stuff behind' (p. 48). What they look for in the North is something with 'nuts' in them, perhaps symbolic of a belief that in an imagined freer environment their manhood would reach full potential.

Valerian's status and authority as a wealthy white are underlined by the likening of his face to one stamped on a coin. He is associated with currency and the white power it represents. His eyes, accustomed to survey a world his wealth has bought, are as blind as those on a coin. He fails to see that his attempted moulding of his young wife, and the defection of his son, are connected, or that his power base is economic rather than personal. His black servants, like Walker's Sofia in *The Color Purple*, subtly overturn the power relationship between themselves and their employer whose folly fills them with contempt. Sydney tells the tetchy Valerian, 'I can't stand here all morning. You got corns, I got bunions' (p. 17). Real life is not found 'upstairs' where the Streets live in separate cocoons, but 'below stairs' in Ondine's kitchen. Clearly the island is full of surprises. Sydney is more dominant than his master, the childless Ondine more maternal than her mistress, and the white son born to wealth rejects it whilst the black girl Jadine rushes to embrace it. Jadine is a black girl whose photographed natural beauty – which had 'Made those white girls disappear. Just disappear right off the page' (p. 37) – is in contrast with Margaret's fading, bleached and cosmetic beauty.

In Jadine it would seem that Morrison gives us a black female protagonist whose potential for tragedy lies not, as did Pecola's, in self-doubt regarding her attractiveness, but in her corruption by acceptance of white manipulation. Educated at Valerian's expense and finding acclaim from a European world who saw her beauty as 'exotic', Jadine resembles the peacock in *Song*. Weighed down with materialistic concepts, her idea of beauty is as artificial and dead as the dearly bought pelts of baby seals in which she wraps herself. When Son encounters her, she is already tainted by the mores and values of white society in which are inscribed notions of black inferiority. Implicit in her ministrations to Valerian is her continuation of the social hierarchy of the Southern plantations from which Son recoils in horror as the embodiment of black female exploitation, seeing her as 'Gatekeeper, advance bitch, house-bitch, welfare-office torpedo, corporate cunt, tar baby side-of-the-road whore trap' (p. 221). It is to save her from falling irrevocably into the stereotypical role of tragic mulatta that Son tries to pull her away from the Streets and their sphere of influence.

The Streets' perception of the non-importance of blacks in any capacity except service had so infected Jadine that she addresses the gardener as 'Yardman', and the laundrymaid as 'Mary' until Son reminds her of their actual names. Son's disrespect for the Streets' assumed superiority and the real nature of Valerian's role is shown in the name he gives him – Mr Sheek. Son's confidence comes from a self-esteem which is as natural as his knowledge of how to make cyclamens open their blossoms: 'Shake it' – 'They just need jacking up'. His shaking into awareness of the plant metaphorically echoes his deliberate shaking of Jadine into self-awareness as a black woman. When the deodorised Jadine falls into the swamp she feels defiled; but the blackness of tar, smelt by Son on Jade's sleeping breath, is a visible sign of blackness equated with Son's exciting, un-deodorised animal smell. Like the African woman with skin 'like tar against the canary-yellow dress' who haunts Jadine's dreams, Son disturbs Jadine's complacent acceptance of white values. His warning of her loss of black identity is underlined when he mocks her with: 'Rape? Why you little white girls always think somebody's trying to rape you?' (p. 121)

Attracted by Son's animal beauty and magnetism, Jadine begins to see through his eyes. She had initially called him an 'ape', but later bristles when Margaret refers to Son as a 'gorilla'. The sexual magnetism between Son and Jadine is capable of pulling Jadine out of white orbit and silencing her disquieting dreams, one of which features women wearing the large hats symbolic of conspicuous and artificial consumption. Sula had returned to Medallion wearing such a hat, as had Milkman when he first went to Shalimar, and Pauline Breedlove had longed to wear one. This subconscious reminder of materialistic values is given definite shape in Jadine's memory of a disturbing encounter when she is shopping in Paris for ingredients needed for an exotic but false meal, 'a rich and tacky menu of dishes Easterners thought up for Westerners in order to indispose them' (p. 42). As in her depiction of Pilate, Morrison uses food imagery to emphasise the link between spiritual and physical succour afforded by community. Even Valerian's wife's desire to make olliebalan, a dish she remembers from childhood Christmases, represents a desire to return to a meaningful life. Jadine's heritage is represented by the

majestically beautiful and haughty African woman whose shopping
consists of simple eggs held aloft in her 'tar-black fingers'. Like Pilate,
the African woman is the ancestor denied by Jadine. Gasping at the
beauty of 'that woman's woman – that mother/sister/she', Jadine is
transfixed by a beauty that is not 'white'. This woman and Pilate are
too tall to be 'fashionable' and beneath the African's ethnic dress there
is too much bust and hips for the cover of *Elle* magazine. The woman
spits contemptuously at Jadine, who is left feeling 'lonely and
unauthentic'. Morrison's point is that just as Valerian's wife's
chocolate-box beauty had been manufactured to please a man's palate,
so Jadine's beauty is packaged to suit the taste of white men, for whom
she is the 'Black Beauty', the sexual fantasy of white men who long
for the exotic. Her success as a model in Paris is merely a form of
prostitution; the devouring of her magazine-cover picture by white
males, a form of rape.

Son's perception of Jadine's spiritual danger is matched by his
unblinkered view of Valerian's unconscious, but autocratic and
careless, cruelty towards the blacks. When Valerian fires Gideon for
stealing apples, Milkman's careless 'peeing' which had killed his
sister's bush is echoed in what Morrison describes as Valerian's
relentless moral defecation. Son sees whites who 'could defecate over
a whole people and come and live there to live and defecate more'
(p. 204) as inferior to animals: a neat turning of the white opinion that
blacks deserved inferior status because they were no better than
animals. Son's perceptions, sharpened by his return to the site of his
ancestors' slavery, are realised through his 'savanna' eyes which smack
of the golden life of Africa. Like Sula's Ajax and Milkman's friend
Guitar, Son's golden-flecked eyes are the sign of his embracing an
ancestral past. The ensuing struggle between the demands of ancestry
and those imposed by white exploitation reaches a climactic emotional
blood-letting on Christmas Eve. The anticipated traditional feast
turns into a dramatic bean-spilling, when black and white sit down
to eat for once together and slumbering racial resentment is released.
In swift, economic dialogue, Morrison shows how quickly the tinder
of resentment can flare into uncontrollable conflagration when, social
niceties abandoned, Ondine calls Margaret a 'white freak', and
Margaret screams 'nigger bitch' at Ondine. As the reality of prejudice
is faced, Valerian surrenders in his battle against the ants and admits
the impossibility of his jungle greenhouse, whilst Margaret, freed
from the need to be beautiful, allows her hair to grow out, and is 'even

lovelier now that her hair had no spray on it, that it was not tortured into Art Deco' (p. 239). The barriers created by the social constructions of race, once admitted, come down and allow for a real connection between the older generation of characters as the regenerative powers of the island work on those who remain there.

Son and Jadine flee from the island to New York, the city which is the summation of white capitalist society, where the clash between their values is exacerbated and crystallises in the question each asks of the other: 'Mama-spoiled black man will you mature with me? Culture-bearing black woman whose culture are you bearing?' (p. 272). The geographical locations of their desired life-styles are polarised between the North and the South, and neither feels comfortable in the other place. The hectic urban bustle which excites and stimulates Jadine – 'This is home' – chokes and confines Son, who sees New Yorkers as 'ridiculous, maimed and unhappy' and in need of 'the blood-clot heads of the bougainvillea, the simple green rage of the avocado'. What to Jadine is sophistication, to Son is suffocation and he persuades Jadine to visit the small Southern rural community of Eloe where he was born. In Son's eyes the Eloe community is one built on friendship, where doors are open to neighbours and the companionable porch and a kitchen with an ever-simmering pot invite intimacy. Here, where Jadine feels as entrapped as Son had in the city, her dreams become more clamorous as her sleep is filled with the nakedness of black women revealing their breasts. Jadine recognises these 'night women', dominated by the African woman holding three eggs, as her female ancestors offering a succouring she has rejected. The lovers' mutual inability to accept the other's values suggests that harmony will only result from compromise. Neither one has it completely right. Jadine can only see the Eloe community as art to be frozen in photographs, but Son too recognises that his memories of Eloe are idealised. Some new, common ground needs to be found.

The lovers are finally pushed apart by their conflicting aspirations, and as Jadine flies to Paris and her white lover, Son returns to the Caribbean island in search of her. The half-blind ancestor-figure, Therese, believes that Son is returning to join his mythicised forebears who, blinded, ride the island naked on horseback. Her belief in African voodoo is intact and in Son's sight she burns his hair clippings to show she means him no harm. Her disbelief in white technology is expressed in her bewilderment at blood banks and sex-change operations and the cultivation of avocados as decorative plants. In her deliberate ferrying of Son to the wild side of the island, she tells him that only there can he make a choice to free himself of the tar baby Jadine, who 'has forgotten her ancient properties'. As, rabbit-like, Son runs 'lickety spit' on to the island, the reader is left suspended in uncertainty. The fog that had descended during their river crossing might herald the physical blindness with which Son's slave ancestors had been struck, but which had not hindered their development into sure, free horsemen. As Son runs up the shore he begins to see clearly, but whether he is to join his fabled ancestors or discover Jadine's whereabouts is not resolved. The individual quests of Jadine and Son represent two circles which cannot find a common centre, and their orbital paths return them to their separate starting-points in the novel, Jadine to Paris and Son to the Ile de Chevaliers. The separate magnetic forces to which they are attracted eventually repel rather than attract, but Morrison leaves the reader in no doubt that Son's return to his past will be more fulfilling than Jadine's defection.

Morrison continues to explore the significance of past events in *Beloved*, which has a determined historical setting covering two generations and three decades in the nineteenth century. Focusing on events arising from the Fugitive Slave Act, enacted in 1856, Morrison describes the horrendous consequences of a flight from slavery for Sethe and her children. Significantly, narrative time begins eighteen years after Sethe's break for freedom in the historical period of Reconstruction, which Morrison interprets as the time when her people, deprived of their past, had to face their own painful process of self-reconstruction. She alerts the reader to a reappraisal of a time which is often recorded in white history in terms of economic reconstruction alone. The fixed location in which past and present events are revealed is No. 124 Bluestone Road, where Sethe had sought sanctuary with her already freed mother-in-law, Baby Suggs. Sethe's murder of one child, and attempted murder of her others when tracked down by slave-holders bent on retrieving their property, is historically authentic. Events are based upon the trial in Cincinnati of Margaret Garner, who with her husband and seventeen other Kentuckian slaves had crossed the Ohio and been lodged in a supposedly safe house. Finding themselves surrounded by pursuers, with her husband overpowered, Margaret Garner acted:

At this moment, Margaret Garner, seeing that their hopes of freedom were vain, seized a butcher's knife that lay on a table and with one stroke cut the throat of her little daughter . . . she then attempted to take the life of the other children and to kill herself, but she was overpowered and hampered before she could complete her desperate work.[14]

Garner was tried for theft, on the grounds that the child she had killed was the legal property of her owner. Newspaper reports claimed that Garner would have killed her 4- and 6-year-old boys and other baby girl rather than see them taken back into slavery. With daring skill Morrison locates these verifiable happenings within a ghost story, skilfully interweaving the extraordinary with the commonplace of slave experience. The strategy, Morrison admits, is deliberate: 'I could have an incredible thing – ghosts, help the reader deal with a factually incredible thing which was slavery' (BBC Interview). The novel opens with an acceptance of a haunting: 124 Bluestone Road is disturbed by the uneasy spirit of the 2-year-old child killed by the fictional Sethe. When Beloved's ghost later materialises physically as an 18-year-old girl, she is more than the shade of a child. Beloved has to be understood as the visible manifestation of slavery which haunts her people, who had tried to repress the pain of its memory, but which has to be faced and exorcised.

The three-part structure of the novel emphatically underlines the interrelation between the specificity of location and the demands of the ghost for audience and attention. Part I opens with '124 was spiteful', Part II with '124 was loud', and Part III with '124 was quiet'. These simple statements chart the progress of the haunting, from the fretful mischief of a poltergeist, through the clamorous demands of a materialised spirit, to the final freeing of the haunter and the haunted. At the same time, they reflect the gradual pacification of an aggrieved child, whose demand for attention, when fulfilled, allows a final slipping into easy sleep. Greedy for the mother-love of which she was deprived by violent death, Beloved's ghost returns to demand attention from a mother overcome with grief and guilt, yet overflowing with maternal love. Beloved's materialisation occurs when Sethe's plantation past re-emerges with a visit from a fellow ex-slave, Paul D. This encounter with her own history, when Sethe is offered the possibility of new life and love by Paul D, triggers the materialisation of Beloved who is clamorously jealous for recognition as the living proof of her mother's deed. Sethe's guilt and the manifestation are mutually sustaining, one feeding on the other. For eighteen years, the memory of her child-murder had disturbed and prevented peaceful co-existence for those living at No. 124. The initial shock horror of the event had destroyed Sethe's mother-in-law's will to live and the continuing disquiet had driven Sethe's two sons to steal away from home as soon as they reached adolescence.

What follows takes the reader into an ever-deepening, spiralling mystery. The clues necessary to unlock the events of eighteen years past are slowly revealed and pieced together during the painful re-awakening of memory. The narrator does not stand in a position of obvious omniscience, but encouragingly supports the reader's entry into a re-creation of events which are unbearably shocking. To do this Morrison moves around and amongst the participants, allowing each one in turn – Baby Suggs, Paul D, Stamp Paid, Denver, Sethe and Beloved – to share with the reader their perception of events. This multiple narrative viewpoint enables her to give substance to a fictive past arrived at from many angles. The accumulated voices of various agents act together as chorus and witness to Sethe's experiences. Baby Sugg's horror at her grandchild's murder, Paul D's memories of Sweet Home and chain gangs, are given as much narrative weight as Sethe's account of events, or even Beloved's impressions from the grave. Each account of personal suffering has the haunting of 124 as its geographical epicentre, whilst the causative events scribe an ever-widening circumference embracing the composite experience of slavery. The enormity of the central experience focuses on the triple burden carried by black women, who had no control over their husbands, children or their own bodies. Sethe's life at Sweet Home, where she was expected to breed, offered a limited choice: she could marry any one of the Sweet Home slaves. The powerlessness of black women as illustrated in *Beloved* is yet another challenge to the conclusions of the 1965 Moynihan Report about the power of black matriarchy. In my discussion of Maya Angelou I have already drawn attention to the angered response of black women to this report and Michelle Wallace's refutation of the myth of black matriarchal power: 'The American black woman is haunted by the mythology that surrounds the American black woman. It is based upon the real persecution of black men, castrated black men'.[15] Gerda Lerner in her documentary history of *Black Women in White America* also dismisses Moynihan's thesis: 'The question of black "matriarchy" is commonly misunderstood. The very term is deceptive, for "matriarchy" implies the exercise of power by women, and black women have been the most powerless group in our entire society' (Lerner, *Black Women*, p. xxiii). Sethe was powerless to keep her children from enslavement except by killing them. Morrison engages in the debate aroused by the Moynihan Report in *Beloved*, where she emphasises both the enormity of slavery and the powerlessness of the black slave woman.

Sethe could not even keep the milk from her breasts to give to her baby, and is violated by her white masters who hold her down while her milk is taken from her. The sexual violation to which black women were subjected is abundantly documented in the collected memories of enslaved women, who record constant sexual ambush: 'My mamma said that a nigger 'oman couldn't help herself, fo' she had to do what de master say'.[16] Morrison builds *Beloved* upon the actuality of the slave narratives, and imaginatively re-creates this in the information given to Sethe about her mother by Nan, who supervised the children in the nurse-house while their mothers worked in the fields. The despoliation of African women began at the moment of capture: 'She told Sethe that her mother and Nan were together from the sea. Both were taken up many times by the crew'. Rape and impregnation took place on the journey. Sethe's mother threw away the children of white fathers, exercising the choice to kill, only keeping Sethe because her father was a fellow slave. This willingness to kill the rapists' offspring was born out of an intensity of hatred for the oppressors, matched by the love Sethe felt for her own children. For both mother and daughter the choice to kill was the ultimate act of resistance. Later Sethe's rebellious mother was hanged and mutilated, but not before she had tried to impress her identity upon her child. Like countless slave mothers whose contact with separated offspring was hurried and furtive, Sethe's mother felt impelled to preserve a matrilineal link, however tenuous. In Sethe's case her mother's identity was impressed upon her by her mother's pointing to the scar of a brand which had been burned on her body as if she were a farm animal. The treatment of black women as productive livestock, whose children were regarded as valuable economic units, was a fact of slave life. Morrison forces recognition of this in her account of Baby Suggs' life:

> Men and women were moved around like checkers. Anybody Baby Suggs know, let alone loved, who hadn't run off or been hanged, got rented out, loaned out, bought up, brought back, stored up, mortgaged, won, stolen or seized. So Baby's eight children had six fathers. What she called the nastiness of life was the shock she received

upon learning that nobody stopped playing checkers just because the pieces included her children. (p. 23)

The terminology used here is drawn deliberately from capitalism, denoting a world of commerce and traffic in goods. The horror comes from the knowledge that in slavery the merchandise was human. Having had to endure the enforced tearing asunder of maternal bonds, Baby Suggs is incapable of understanding Sethe's murder of Beloved. Sethe's actions are incomprehensible to a woman who never had been in a position to challenge the proprietorial 'rights' of a slave-owner. Only one child, Sethe's husband, had been spared to Baby Suggs, and he had worked to buy his mother out of bondage. The difference in attitudes between Sethe and Baby Suggs springs from the opportunity choice afforded. As a chattel valued only as a breeding machine, Baby Suggs had adopted a strategy for survival by which she had not allowed herself to become attached to babies who could be, and were, sold from her. Sethe's life at Sweet Home under her original owner had been less harsh than Baby Suggs', deceiving her into believing that she and her husband could work to buy freedom for themselves and their children. A change in Sweet Home ownership denies this possibility, but by then Sethe's bonding to her children is complete. In her escape from slavery this bond is intensified. For the first time in her life, Sethe feels able to love her children unreservedly: 'Look like I loved em more after I got here. Or maybe I couldn't love 'em proper in Kentucky because they wasn't mine to love' (p. 162). This experience of unrestrained mothering had never been afforded to Baby Suggs, whose emotional survival had been possible because, as Paul D says, she had 'loved small'. Sethe's vision of real freedom was of 'a place where you could love anything you choose – not to need permission for desire – well now, that was freedom' (p. 162).

Sethe's instinctive reaction to kill her children rather than have them returned to slavery is only incredible if viewed from the outside, where other characters and white readers are positioned. From where Sethe stood, it seemed the only thing to do. The intensity of her grief is matched by her love, which is the source of Beloved's power:

'For a baby she throws a powerful spell' said Denver.
'No more powerful than the way I loved her' Sethe answered and there it was again, the welcoming cool of unchiselled headstones, the one she selected to lean against on tip toe, her knees wide open as any grave. (p. 4)

Sethe's present is shaped by the inescapable memory of Beloved's death. The tombstone erected over her grave is paid for by Sethe with sex, the stonemason offering to carve it 'for free' with the implicit assumption that the giving of herself costs the black woman nothing. The abomination of this transaction, witnessed by the engraver's son who watches with an anger 'in his face so old, the appetite in it quite new', explicitly demonstrates the sexual politics of slavery. Sethe, like Pauline Breedlove, is both seen and treated as an animal. The reality of Sethe's suffering is in her consciousness of her dead baby, in whose tombstone she sees the delicate pearly pinkness of a child's fingernails. The ten minutes allotted to the coupling seem to her like an endless dying, and the womb which had sheltered Beloved a place of death. On Beloved's unexplained arrival outside 124, the connection between womb, birth and death is made. Like a new-born baby, Beloved appears wet and bedraggled, and her sighting is accompanied by a sudden, uncontrollable venting of Sethe's bladder like the water rush signalling the rupture of the birth sac. Beloved's neck, slashed by a frenzied mother, droops at a peculiar angle and her forehead bears scratches like baby hair. Her hands, like a baby's, are fresh and new. She drinks greedily and craves the sweetness of a baby's soothing sugar-tit. With mounting amazement, the reader learns to accept the reality of the ghost as do Sethe and Denver.

Faced with this other-world reality, a white reader's initial response of incredulity can only be dispelled by an acceptance of Afro-American spirituality. What has become for the urban, industrialised, Western white a world in which the material and the spiritual are kept in separate compartments, is a view not shared by the African. It is interesting to see in the Africa of today the incorporation of African animism into the Christian faith, in the many independent Christian communities who choose to worship out of doors in palpable contact with the natural world. Such a spirituality informs the activities of Baby Suggs who preaches the gospel of love in the clearing, 'a wide open place cut deep in the woods nobody knew for what'. Her message to the congregation is that individual happiness is commensurate with a recognition of each and every one as manifestations of their Creator. She urges them to love themselves as proof of their love of God:

> 'Here,' she said 'in this here place, we flesh; flesh that weeps, laughs, flesh that dances in bare feet in grass. Love it. Love it hard. Yonder they do not love your flesh. They despise it. They don't love your eyes;

they'd just as soon pick em out. No more do they love the skin on your back. Yonder they flay it. And O my people they do not love your hands. Those they only use, tie, bind, chop off and leave empty. Love your hands! Love them. Raise them up and kiss them. Touch others with them, pat them together, stroke them on your face 'cause they don't love that either. *You* got to love it, *you*! And no, they ain't in love with your mouth . . . *You* got to love it. This is flesh I'm talking about here. Flesh that needs to be loved.' (p. 88)

Baby Suggs' sermon retains the traditional rolling cadences designed to exhort and inspire the listeners, which Hurston recorded and analysed in her work on black language. The beauty is no less than, but different from, that of traditional sermons, although the language is free of biblical allusions and vivid imagery. Using very simple language Morrison rewrites the sermon with a challenging redefinition of the way to worship the Creator. Those black sermons collected by Hurston had stressed the might, power and beauty of God; Baby Suggs' questions the inscription of racial inferiority in slavery which denies the benevolence of that Creator. Her sermon does not advocate a heaven delayed until death, but the promise of amelioration in life which will not come from an outside but an inside agency. The African animism of pre-Christian worship in her congregation's barefoot contact with the earth, emphasises Baby Suggs' message that the material and the spiritual cannot be separated, and only flourish when together. This sermon effectively interrogates an interpretation of the Christian message which had been perverted by some to accommodate the systematic degradation of blacks. It is also a summation of the urgings of other black women writers whose works preach a re-evaluation of the physical black self.

For a people whose negative socialisation has associated blackness with every connotation of evil and ugliness, self-love is difficult to foster. Reconstruction can only be achieved with a complete rejection of all that had fractured black identity in slavery. Morrison joins other black women writers in an attempt to show the historical roots of this negativity which, when understood, can be overcome. Her novels all stress that love of self comes from a discarding of labels imposed by whites and begins with a self-definition previously denied by their 'naming' or 'non-naming' by whites. This negation of individual humanity is epitomised in the naming of the Sweet Home men as Pauls A, D and F Garner, and of Sixo, who at the moment of death announces his impending fatherhood by shouting 'Seven O'. In the knowledge that his child will be born in freedom, Sixo triumphantly names his own child. The ex-slave Joshua asserts his free identity in the name 'Stamp Paid', reflecting the price paid for freedom, which was the enforced concubinage of his wife to their white owner. When he encounters Sethe, newly delivered of the baby she chose to name Denver, he is appalled at Sethe's lacerated back: even in advanced pregnancy she had not been spared a lashing by 'Schoolmaster'. Sethe remembers how a hole was dug to contain her pregnant belly, to prevent any harm to the unborn 'property'. Documentary evidence of such practices exists. An ex-slave remembers: 'When women was with child they'd dig a hole in the ground and put their stomach in the hole and beat 'em'.[17]

The decision of the Sweet Home slaves to flee is made when under Schoolmaster's regime the reality of the enslaved condition is brought home to them. The vulnerability of slaves under any change of ownership is dramatised in the inheriting of Sweet Home by Schoolmaster on Mr Garner's death. Sweet Home had been comparatively 'sweet' under the Garners, but Morrison does not allow a confusion to arise between paternalism and freedom. Mr Garner's pride in his slaves did not diminish his wielding of absolute power over them. The difference between him and Schoolmaster was not in the scope of that power, but the way in which it was exercised. The power base was still the same: an assumption that the black body did not house a soul commensurate with that of whites, thus justifying their treatment as non-sentient human beings. Schoolmaster is no less bestial than Stowe's infamous creation Simon Legree in *Uncle Tom's Cabin*. A proponent of the doctrine of black racial inferiority, Schoolmaster embodies the desire of some whites to provide scientific evidence as justification for their treatment of slaves. He obsessively records physical measurements of his human property and encourages his nephew to compile a profile of Sethe's human and animal characteristics, noting her 'human characteristics on the left; her animal ones on the right' (p. 139). Overhearing this determines Sethe to escape. In a vividly economic passage Morrison sketches in the historical record of the corrosive racial prejudice on which slavery was perpetuated and which threatened to destroy the humanity of both the oppressors and the oppressed. Blacks always had to *prove* their humanity to whites, and those who achieved middle-class status became the over-burdened representatives of their whole race, under constant pressure to prove a humanity they never felt they lacked.

The frustration and bitterness induced could only nurture a destructive racial hatred she sees as a cancer:

> And it grew. It spread. In, through and after life, it spread, until it invaded the whites who had made it. Touched them every one. Changed and altered them. Made them bloody, silly, worse than even they wanted to be, so scared they were of the jungle they had made. The screaming baboon lived under their own white skin; the red gums were their own. (p. 199)

Sethe's horrified realisation that Schoolmaster believes her to be sub-human is the same as was Pauline Breedlove's when she was being delivered of Pecola. Schoolmaster's inability to recognise black humanity, still represented as intact 100 years later in *The Bluest Eye*, is reinforced when he witnesses Sethe's murderous attack on her children. Unable to recognise Sethe's anguish as a natural human response to her situation, he interprets her rage as a petulant reaction to a beating, and the killing as the consequence of 'a little so-called freedom' for a woman who needed guidance to be kept from the 'cannibal life' her people 'preferred'. Morrison graphically delineates how a lack of black self-esteem is the inevitable consequence of such systematic brutalisation, which can only be expunged by the constant reiteration of the beauty of self, and a self-construction as preached by Baby Suggs.

In the following years of freedom, in which Sethe has to reconstruct a self previously defined by white slavery, she is drawn into memories of an African past. She recalls a language now lost which was spoken by Nan and her mother, and remembers slaves who sang and 'danced the antelope'. The ancestral link sustained in black culture is an agent in her recuperation and growth into self-identity. The vitality of a black culture expressing a close spiritual as well as physical communion with nature – a major theme in Hurston's, Walker's, and Marshall's work – is spelled out in *Beloved*. Passing on to Denver her animistic conviction that memory has the power to keep things alive, Sethe describes the palpable spirit of place which transcends physical materialism:

> 'Some things just stay. I used to think it was my rememory. You know. Some things you forget. Other things you never do. But it's not. Places, places, are still there. If a house burns down it's gone, but the place – the picture of it – stays, and not just in rememory, but out there, in the world.' Denver picked at her fingernails. 'If it's still there, waiting,

that must mean that nothing ever dies.' Sethe looked right in Denver's face, 'Nothing ever dies', she said. (p. 36)

This spirituality is crucial to an understanding of the incredible in *Beloved* where nothing ever dies, and time is not depicted as a linear progression but as an ever-lengthening, ravelling thread, like the ball of wool in *Sula* which Nel imagines is hovering near her shoulder. Nel's grey ball of emotions is a compelling image for the complexities of her interior life, and its air of persistent malevolence springs from her refusal to examine it. The concept of experiential complexity has deeper and wider resonances in *Beloved* where time is presented as an interweaving of past and present events in an ever-widening circle. This circularity of experience necessitates a confrontation by Sethe and Paul D with their past. In Paul D's gradual quilting of the facts of Beloved's death, Morrison succinctly images her own narrative technique: 'It made him dizzy. At first he thought it was her spinning, circling him the way she was circling the subject. Round and round, never changing direction, which might have helped his head' (p. 161).

Morrison admits that the translation into fiction of the facts of slavery which are almost too abominable to countenance, but which *must* be faced, involved the careful use of narrative strategies which would not alienate the reader: 'You have to permit the reader to go through the horror as an outsider before allowing him in or encouraging him to go through it as an insider' (BBC Interview). So the facts surrounding Beloved's death are slowly revealed in a roundabout way, as the reader's knowledge of the events is pieced together. Morrison's awareness of the inadequacy of language to convey the experience is admitted by Sethe who, when explaining the circumstances surrounding her killing of Beloved to Paul D, 'knew that the circle she was making around the room, him, the subject, would remain one. That she could never close in, pin it down for anybody who had to ask. If they couldn't get it right off – she could never explain' (p. 161).

Sethe's difficulty in articulation reflects the experience of women writers, both black and white, who struggle with the inadequacy of phallocentric language to convey female experience. When taxed by Paul D with the old newspaper account of her trial, the barely literate Sethe instinctively knows 'that the words she did not understand, hadn't any more power than she had to explain' (p. 161).

The need for a sufficient language is something Morrison grapples with in Part II, where she uses language experimentally to portray both the overtly impossible materialisation in flesh and blood of a child long dead, and the enormity of the diaspora which it represents. In three consecutive passages she conveys simultaneously the impressions of the short life experience carried by the baby ghost, and the bewildered horror of a captive people. In an unpunctuated series of impressions, she suggests the brevity of a life violently cut short and the agonies of the 'middle passage'. The child's unformed consciousness is dominated by the pre-oedipal need to cleave to the mother, echoing also the terror of the Africans torn from their homeland: 'how can I say things that arise in pictures – I am not separate from her – there is no place where I stop – her face is my own' (p. 211). The baby's awareness is dominated by the smiling, ear-ringed Sethe, who offers safety, and the white men terrifyingly seen as 'men with no skins'. Struggling to materialise, Beloved's task is to arise from the dead and rejoin her severed head. In this she enacts the need of her people to reclaim an African heritage from which slavery had separated them. At the point of materialisation Morrison's prose becomes a controlled questioning of Beloved's struggle to reclaim connection with her mother: 'Three times I lost her: once under the bridge when I went in to join her . . .' (p. 214). Morrison then abandons prose entirely in her effort to re-create the willing communion of Sethe with her dead child, and with it the reclamation of a past:

> Tell me the truth. Didn't you come from the other side?
> Yes. I was on the other side.
> Ya came back because of me?
> Yes.
> You rememory me?
> Yes. I remember you.
> You never forgot me?
> Your face is mine.
> Do you forgive me? Will you stay? You safe here now.
> Where are the men without skin? (p. 215)

Morrison circles the subject of slavery and inexorably draws the reader into confrontation with the unspeakable; to the very heart of the slave experience of which Beloved's ghost is a manifestation. *Beloved* is Morrison's attempt to lay the ghost to rest by looking at and listening to it. She knows that her people never can, nor should they, forget their enslaved history, but she wants confrontation to effect a growth. For this, it seems she places dependence upon the humanity of her own people. The reality of racial prejudice does not disappear when one closes one's eyes. Part III of the novel emphasises this in her focus on the daughter who had escaped Sethe's murderous intentions. Never having left 124, Denver had never encountered white people until forced to seek help from her community when she recognises the danger Beloved poses to Sethe. Denver's personal growth begins when in the house of the paternalistic white man who had given 124 free of rent to Suggs, she sees the effigy of a black boy used as a money-box: 'Painted across the pedestal he knelt on were the words "At Yoh Service"'. She realises that help from the man who owns this statue is helping to perpetuate racism. Her eventual freedom to live results from an individual act of will only made possible with the support of the black community.

In *Beloved* Morrison demonstrates once again that community is necessary to growth. Significantly, Sethe's release from the past is through the intervention of the thirty-strong company of women who gather outside 124 in rescue. They overcome their old hostility to a woman whose violence had shocked them, because she is in need. Ella leads the women, believing that: 'The future was sunset; the past something to leave behind. And if it didn't stay behind, well, you might have to stomp it out' (p. 256). Armed with tokens to ward off evil they slowly gather at the same time as the white owner of 124 rides towards his property. Transfixed in a reliving of Schoolmaster's arrival eighteen years before, Sethe, ice-pick in hand, attacks. But this time, she strikes out at the white man instead of her own child. This is the act which frees her and causes Beloved to disappear, allowing a quietness to descend on 124. Whilst not an incitement to white murder, Morrison seems to be saying here that the hatred engendered by oppression had been wrongly internalised by blacks into a hatred of self. In killing her child Sethe had turned her rage into an attack upon the wrong object, and in her attack upon the representative of oppression she had destroyed the power of the past on which the blacks' feelings of guilt and inferiority had fed. Freed from her violent past Sethe is at last able to anticipate a future with Paul D, who points the message of the novel: '"Sethe", he says, "me and you, we got more yesterday than anybody. We need some kind of tomorrow"' (p. 273).

Beloved is an extended slave narrative whose meaning is only fully understood if it is read as a re-creation of the history of American ancestors. Morrison's focus in this novel is on race and the consequences of slavery, whereas that of her previous novels had been on differing constructions of gender and culture. Although centred on Sethe, *Beloved* is the encapsulation of a people, not simply a woman. The double agony of a slave mother, heard in original slave narratives, is depicted alongside that of Paul D Halle and Stamp Paid, whose agony was different but no less than Sethe's. The possible wholeness of Sethe and Paul D symbolises the joint potential of a people united, not held apart by white constructions of race or gender. In this novel there is a widening of Morrison's vision which embraces men and women. By concentrating on the oppression of the race she avoids the divisiveness of sexism, producing a completed narrative fabric no longer white, black and grey but 'patched in carnival colors'. In *Beloved* colour imagery is an effective commentary on spiritual health. When Baby Suggs had arrived in Cincinnati, her quilt, symbolic of the fabric of her life, had so few splashes of colour that she spent her dying days contemplating the colour she had missed in life. For eighteen years the last colour Sethe could remember was the pink of Beloved's dearly bought headstone. When Sethe's life is pieced together Baby Suggs' quilt is seen to blaze with colours and Paul D reflects that his need for Sethe is like Sixo's for his thirty-mile woman: '"She is a friend of my mind. She gathers me, man. The pieces I am, she gather them and give them back to me in all the right orders"' (p. 272). This quilt image both exemplifies the holistic quality of sexual interdependence, and aptly describes the narrative techniques Morrison uses to make a wholeness of disparate views of the same event. I think *Beloved* is a brilliantly crafted, challengingly structured novel. The lyrical beauty of language and imagery of her previous novels reaches new heights in its efforts to present the co-existence of spiritual and physical realities. The rooted magic of *Tar Baby* and *Song* becomes a palpable and unquestionable reality.

All of Morrison's novels are underpinned by her drawing upon Afro-American oral tradition in her incorporation of folkloric myth. In her *listening* to the language and stories of her people she also hears the music into which her enforcedly illiterate ancestors had poured their souls. This music, often used as indicative of emotional states, is woven into her fictions in both content and structure. In *The Bluest Eye* music is a sign of family happiness – Claudia's mother sings while working, and the family gather to make music; in *Song of Solomon* Pilate, daughter of the half-Indian woman Sing, is the ancestral singer of songs who croons the 'Sugarman' song of her ancestors. In *Beloved* the music is woven seamlessly into a narrative fabric which is a composite articulation of the infinite variety of oral tradition. Paul D's Sweet Home song is one of sweet yearning for love: 'Stone blind; stone blind/ Sweet Home gal make you lose your mind', and work songs evoking the physical hardships of enforced labour in reconstruction are described as 'flat headed nails for pounding and pounding and pounding'. The importance of music as an expression of emotions is summed up in Morrison's evocation of the chain gangs: 'They sang it out and beat it up'.

Music comes to the fore in her most recent novel *Jazz*, in which Morrison undertakes an imaginative interpretation of a specific and transitional period in the history of her people. The time is the 1920s, the place Harlem. Morrison's focus is not upon the 'niggerati' described by Hurston, but on the hopeful Southern blacks who were forced by Reconstruction from rural homelands into the 'City', in the belief that 'History is over, you all, and everything's ahead at last' (p. 7). The vehicle for her reconstruction of this second diaspora is the story of the middle-aged couple, Violet and Joe Trace, whose relation to this new environment is realised in Morrison's examination of Joe's affair with the 17-year-old Dorcas. Morrison's choice of title aptly embodies both the structure of the novel and the significance of jazz music as an expression of black experience. Blues and jazz music, now incorporated into the cultural heritage of all Americans, owes nothing at all to white cultural models. It is an artistic expression of a black experience untainted by white association or cultural models: 'She knew from sermons and editorials that it wasn't real – just colored folks' stuff; harmful, certainly, embarrassing, of course; but not real, not serious' (p. 59).

When at the turn of the century many blacks left the South for the North they took with them an African music from which jazz emerged. The resultant music differs from the distinctive Blues of Southern rural blacks, being a synthesis of the individualistic lament of Blues and the new consciousness of a dispossessed community. It is an urban music created by a new urban community, sharing with Blues a sense of extemporaneity yet with a more sophisticated structure, depending as it does upon the complex harmonising of a variety of single expressions.

Morrison questions the adequacy of language alone to conjure up the past of those long dead, and bows to the power of music as a metaphor for their lives. She imagines the new Harlemites living in an atmosphere full of the inescapable throb and pulse of music, coming across radio wires and into their homes on records. The spell of jazz lies in its promise of an engagement with life, and in Morrison's Harlem it was an accompaniment to all of life's activities. Violet's near-abduction of a baby had been facilitated by the sister who had rushed indoors to get a record of 'The Trombone Blues', and Dorcas's young friend Felice bought butcher's meat at the same time as she bought Okeh music on record. Dorcas's budding sexuality was excited by the open invitation of song lyrics where women told men: 'They had the right key baby but the wrong keyhole'. The seductive sounds emerging from the clarinet, saxophone, trumpet and trombone underlined such a pervasive sexuality that there was 'no place to be where someone was not licking his licorice stick, tickling the ivories, beating his skins, blowing off his horn' (p. 61). The highlights of Dorcas's affair with Joe are those times spent in darkened clubs listening to music, and the shooting which leads to her death happens when she is dancing to black music with a new young lover. The music speaks simultaneously of the passion, tragedy and hope in Harlem life, so that Joe and Violet's reconciliation is marked by a spontaneous dancing together to the Okeh record, and Violet's sick bird recovers outdoors to the sound of jazz. The therapeutic release for the blacks into a beauty which is their own, is realised when Morrison describes how the music enables the rural past to enter and become part of city experience:

> You would have thought everything had been forgiven the way they played. The clarinets had trouble because the brass was cut so fine, not lowdown the way they love to do it, but high and fine like a young girl singing by the side of a creek, passing the time, her ankles cold in the water. (p. 197)

Jazz was disturbing to the old in its newness, who saw it as symptomatic of changes in social organisation which shocked them: 'The dirty, get- on- down music the women sang and the men played and both danced to, close and shameless or apart and wild' (p. 58). They associated youthful misbehaviour with jazz, yet at the same time were not immune themselves to the chords deep within themselves which it struck. Even Alice Manfred, the conservative righteous guardian of Dorcas, was caught by the connectedness of African drums and jazz when she watched a Fifth Avenue parade of black war veterans protesting against race violence in St Louis East. The excitement of removal to New York, where in Harlem the blacks had felt 'safe from the fays', had persuaded the older generation that city life was a lot better than the one they had left, and in this transposition they had lost contact with the life-giving force only met in daily communion with nature. Joe Trace, whose young manhood had been spent in a South he had never dreamed of leaving, now made a living selling cheap cosmetics from his sample case, a far cry from a youth spent in the woods and the fields. He missed, without knowing it, the succour of his rural life and community, and dreamed that in Dorcas's young love he could recapture his own lost youth. His uncharacteristic infidelity in middle age is not to satisfy an old man's lust, but is a response to a past which is captured in the music of Harlem. He dreams of recapturing the idyll of an Edenic youth and the tasting of Adam's first bite of the apple.

The Harlem which Morrison re-creates is built upon the historical fact that 'The wave of black people running from want and violence crested in the 1870's, the 80's, the 90's' (p. 33), of which the Traces are an example. They were fleeing from dispossession and racism, in the belief that each mile nearer to New York was one nearer to a place free of the racism in the South. As Morrison shows, their dreams were without substance. Migration to the North merely gave oppression a wider geographical location and more concentrated outbreaks of race riots in Northern cities. The delight of Harlem blacks was in their being together, rather than in an increased share in America's good life. They thrilled to the city bustle in a black ghetto where there was a 'postbox (but no high schools)', where the streets boasted furniture stores, 'street vendors, the bootleg houses (but no banks)'. They were marginalised in New York, as they were in America as a whole, and realised that the racist violence from which they had fled was on their doorsteps still. Disillusioned, but with the caution of a people long used to oppression, the elders tried to teach the first-generation Harlemites the defensive strategies of self-effacement which had aided black survival in the past. Dorcas was trained to be 'deaf' and 'dumb', to 'crawl along the walls of buildings, disappear into doorways . . . how to do anything, move anywhere to avoid a whiteboy over the age of eleven' (p. 55). Such teaching might have proved effective but for the insistent call to life signalled by the emergence of jazz.

Jazz not only urged the young to live, it urged the old to remember, and it is in the act of remembering that the protagonists in *Jazz* find a self they had lost in the city. All had encountered violence, summed up in Joe's seven attempts at making himself over in seven new starts, in which he had moved North in progressive bids for a life free from white domination. His wife's childhood had been marked by the violent turning-out of her mother, Rose Dear, with her children, from their home. While nursing a baby, Rose Dear had been tipped from a chair as one would remove a cat, an event which so traumatised the young Violet that she decides never to have children of her own. Even the young were fleeing from white violence. Dorcas had been orphaned in the St Louis East race riots in which she had seen her mother burned to death, and Felice, like Sethe in *Beloved*, barely knew her parents who had to work away in another city. In each case violence done to mothers is a key factor in their experience, and all are depicted as trying to find a way to compensate for matrilineal dysfunction. Felice explains her mother's theft from Tiffany's as an act of revenge against racist shop assistants, Violet is haunted by her grandmother's stories of the mulatto boy Golden Gray, and Joe wants to know if the wild woman in the woods of home is in fact his mother. The characters described in *Jazz* each bring separate histories of emotional separation and racist violence which have not been resolved in their present. It is the music of Harlem which is their salvation; enabling a renewing of contact with ancestral vitality. The inter-relationships which develop allow for a sorting out and an identifying of discordant and disruptive memories. Each personal history is one in which life's harmony has been destroyed by the intrusion of something or somebody white. The source of their misery is left in no doubt: even the girl Dorcas is viewed by Violet as being more dangerous because she is half-white, with hair that didn't need straightening and a 'creamy loon' complexion. Violet's grandmother's devotion to the child of a white 'lady' and a black hunter takes her away from her own children in a time of their greatest need. Miscegenation and its consequences resonate in the strange tale of Joe's mother, and the interdependent network of mixed alliances is sewn together in the narrative revelation that the Golden Gray of Violet's childhood is the man who eventually cared for Joe's wild mother. The dominant 'whiteness' of society is a common burden.

As in *Beloved*, narrative time in *Jazz* is non-linear. The violence at Dorcas's funeral with which the novel opens is in a specific fictive present, 1926, but the events giving shape to this present occurred fifty years earlier, in the 1880s. The seeds of the tragic involvement of Joe, Violet and Dorcas were planted in the days of Reconstruction, and Morrison's concern is to emphasise the inescapability of the past. She achieves this by allowing different voices to react to, or try to explain, the death of Dorcas. As the tale unfolds Morrison impresses upon the reader that actions are subconsciously motivated by past events beyond individual control. The past is a particular stream of events upon which each human participant puts her/his own gloss, just as jazz musicians will take up and reinterpret a melodic strain. In *Jazz* the structuring narrative voice which gives initial shape to events is that of the thoughtful narrator who is, as Morrison was, trying to impose meaning on to the flux of experience. The voice is interior as the reader is drawn into the narrator's reminiscences and an uncertain, yet honest, groping towards the truth. Authorial unwillingness to be dogmatic in interpretation comes in such admissions as, 'I've often wondered about that' and 'I can't say'. What begins as an omniscient authorial stance dissolves as other voices take up the story, fade in turn, and give way again to the 'I' of the narrator. The danger of accepting any one version of history is emphasised in the narrator's admitted manipulation of her imagined characters, upon whose fictive lives she had tried to impose order: 'I thought I knew them and wasn't worried that they didn't really know about me. . . . They knew how little I could be counted on; how poorly, how shabbily my know-it-all self covered helplessness' (p. 221).

Jazz is Morrison's attempt to understand a time in black American history which had seemed to promise so much that remained unrealised. It also reiterates her constant concern that black Americans should reclaim, reinterpret and rewrite their own history, and not allow it to be 'whitewashed' by white historians. The informing impulse in Morrison's writing is the same as that of feminists who demand a rewriting of history from which they had been written out, knowing that to demand is not enough. They have to set about the task themselves, which is what Morrison does in her novels. *Jazz* works because, like a quilt, it is an harmonising of apparently different materials. The quilt is controlled by tradition and design, but the texture and colour is left to the imagination of the makers; Morrison's *Jazz* is given coherence by her use of a recognised and specifically black musical form. The materials Morrison uses are taken from her consciousness of herself as a black woman, as part of an historical process which must be understood. Her novels to date are a consummate gathering of the 'pieces' of the experience and preoccupations of the black woman in America, and are an integral part of the literary 'quilt' which black women writers are still making.

— 7 —

Alice Walker (b. 1944)
The spiritual inheritance

The personal and literary career of Alice Walker, born in Georgia in 1944, exemplifies the hopes and dreams which characterised the 1960s. The distinguishing voice of that decade, whether it emanated from emergent African nation states, the Civil Rights Movement in America, or the Women's Movement internationally, had called for liberation. Aspiring young writers like Walker set about reclaiming their cultural heritage and identifying the literary tradition to which they belonged. Courses on black American writing tentatively appeared, and women teachers rediscovered the neglected works of their female antecedents. In an article for *American Scholar* in 1967, Walker summed up the identifiable gains made by her people as a result of the Civil Rights Movement as 'knowledge and pride', providing a 'purpose for living' in a future built upon a breaking of 'the pattern of black servitude'.[1] Her optimism about black advancement had survived the painful confrontation with the violence of white racism, but was mitigated by her fear of black sexism, causing her to question whether the pattern of black servitude had been broken in equal measure for men and women. Walker's published writing now spans a quarter of a century, and is an ongoing record of a highly personalised self-examination as a woman and artist who is also black. It began with some suicidal despair in *Once*,[2] her first published volume of poetry, and has culminated in a visionary hope for a New World in *The Temple of my Familiar*.[3] With the confidence arising from published success, Walker has spoken with increasing clarity on the issues of race and gender which preoccupied her own generation of black women writers just as intensely as they had earlier ones.

Walker's writing springs from her introduction to the realities of racial and sexual politics with which she engaged as a young student, and is a measure of readjustments she made in answer to the increasing complexities of political debate. Her early concern to challenge the racist stereotyping of blacks in literature was enlarged to include the relevance of a feminist movement to black women; sexism, which she sees as corrosively damaging to relationships as racism; and an embracing of a problematic spirituality. I say 'problematic', because although her early work reveals an affinity with African animism, her later work has enlarged this into a visionary and speculative world, much less obviously rooted in the black experience. Yet Walker warns white readers and critics to beware of passing judgement on the work of a black writer who will introduce them to a spiritual awareness, as expressed in Marshall's writing, of which the white Western world has long lost sight. The inadequacy of white response to black writing is perhaps summed up in the words of the writer in 'Fame' in *You Can't Keep a Good Woman Down* (1981),[4] who, weary of probing white interviewers, says, 'one never expected them to know one's history well enough to recognise as evolution, a variation, when they saw it' (p. 58). Understanding of Walker's writing demands a preparedness to accept evolution, and a reader's willingness to follow the author's speculative revision of the world as we know it, for revision, re-evaluation, rethinking and possible transformations are the basis of her work.

Her first published work, *Once*, is a slim volume composed in feverish haste into which poems she packs a young lifetime. Short, often painful memories of rejection, frustration and friendship experienced as a student involved in the non-violent activities of the Student Non-violent Co-ordinating Committee (SNCC), are locked in frozen images like photographs in an album. Although foregrounding the experience of civil rights protest, they are also evidence of her concern to explore the problems unique to black women in a racist society. These themes are crystallised in her first novel, *The Third Life of Grange Copeland*,[5] which was published in 1970. The title of this novel reflects her attempt to historicise the present, in a narrative covering three generations of a family over almost a century, spanning a period of economic and political oppression. Her examination of the legacy for black women in terms of the sexual politics engendered in these decades, and her hope for future amelioration, are embodied in the girl-child Ruth Copeland: 'Yes, I believe in change; change personal and change in society'.[6] The potential of personal change as

personal is political

an agent for social change is enacted in the character of Ruth's grandfather, Grange, who eventually ensures Ruth's future by accommodating the past.

The narrative of the Copelands, with its potential for repeated tragedy, falls into three significant movements, producing a crisis at the end of the second and resolution in the last. The first concerns the consequences of Grange Copeland's defection from family responsibility when he can no longer stand the humiliation and misery of a share-cropper's life. His son Brownfield is left to struggle through a disintegrating childhood into young manhood and marriage to Mem, in which Brownfield begins to repeat the pattern of violence established by his parents' marriage. This first 'act' in the tragedy ends with the return of Grange to his homeland, to begin his 'second' life heralded by the birth of Ruth and a reawakening of Grange's capacity for love. In a narrative pattern which Walker will go on to use in later fictions she portrays a 'transformation' in Grange as stunning in its completeness as Celie's is in *The Color Purple*. In both of these novels the transforming agent is love. Grange's candid introspection forces him to accept his culpability for familial disunity, enabling him to blossom through love in his idyllic 'third' life spent caring for Ruth. Grange's love grows as Brownfield's jealousy develops into a corrosive and implacable hatred for his father and daughter, ending in tragic violence as Grange kills Brownfield and is himself shot to death by law officers. To ensure the wholeness of his granddaughter, Grange has to rid their lives of the cancer of hate and despair which had been his own legacy to Brownfield.

The tracing of a familial history is facilitated by Walker's manipulation of narrative time by use of flashbacks structured to engage our sympathy for a character and elucidate motivation for later actions. The burden of the Copeland past is carried by Brownfield, whose initial capacity for wonder is dulled by his neglected babyhood when 'for hours he was lost in a dull, weak stupor' (p. 7). Walker creates in Brownfield the bewilderment of a child's growing awareness of adult concepts, as he is insidiously infected by his father's overwhelming hatred of whites. With this comes a knowledge of all the divisiveness which has accumulated around skin colour. Grange's hatred is passed on to Brownfield who translates it into a perception of black inferiority: 'When he noticed this difference, one of odor and sound and movement and laughter, as well as of color, he wondered how he had not seen it before' (p. 81).

Brownfield, like Morrison's Breedloves, does not have the
protective insulation of parental love to shield him from feelings of
inadequacy. His only escape is into a fantasy, inspired by contact with
his visiting Northern cousins, of an idyllic family life in the purity of
snow, away from the negative social connotations of blackness. Ruth's
recognition of racist discrimination occurs when in a textbook
previously owned by a white child she sees under the picture of an
African: 'Note: A Nigger' (p. 186). She needs no fantasy escape, for
in her grandfather's home 'Ruth's room was a veritable sun of
brightness and yellow and white' (p. 197). The importance of familial
love and the tragic consequences of its withdrawal are evident in
Brownfield and also in Josie, whose cruel treatment at the hands of
an intractable father is also revealed in narrative flashback. She is
described as an 'overturned pregnant turtle beneath her father's foot'
and 'like a spider, deformed and grotesque beneath the panicked
stares of man' (p. 40) – images of bloated vulnerability which soften
our judgement of her.

By using the simple narrative device of flashbacks Walker
historicises her protagonists, fleshing out many incidents which give
meaning to the whole. What might seem to be trivial narrative details
become significant as the narrative develops, so that Mem's albino
baby who 'seemed a phantom baby, not the real thing' (p. 110),
doomed to die unmourned, is an echo of Star, Margaret's half-white
child. Both children are echoes in the minds of the black men of an
enslaved past which underline the economic impotence of their
present position. In father and son hatred of white oppression had
been internalised to find expression in violence against the women
they feel unable to protect. As Brownfield's dreams die he becomes
bent upon reducing Mem to his own level of despair: 'Even her
wonderful breasts dried up and shrank; her hair fell out and the only
good thing he could say for her was that she kept herself clean' (p. 58).

While Mem still had hopes of a better life, she planted flowers
which symbolised beauty and growth, and when she finally accepts
defeat in a shack, we are told: 'never again did she intend to plant
flowers in boxes or beds' (p. 112). Her abandonment of the
perpetuation of beauty signals her abandonment of the future. The
inescapable connection between time past, present and future is
acutely realised by Walker in her planting of narrative seeds which
have later significance. This is demonstrated in the differing
perceptions of the statue of the Confederate soldier as seen separately

by Brownfield and Ruth. Brownfield, still locked into a pre-Abolition mentality, notices only that the statue is still resolutely facing North, whilst Ruth's concern is that the hips of the stone soldier impede her view of the new public clock. This conjunction points to Brownfield's inability to see beyond a hated history, and to Ruth's view of the past as something which can stand in the way of the present and the future.

Mem's murder is also revealed in a flashback which shifts the narrative focus from Brownfield to Ruth, through whose eyes the horror is recalled: 'What Ruth remembered now with nausea and a feeling of cold dying, was Mem, lying faceless . . . in a pool of blood, in which were scattered around her head like a halo, a dozen bright yellow oranges' (p. 122). This shift to the perception of the child underlines Walker's narrative theme about the possible contamination of the new generation by the old, and possible redemption is implied in this halo image. Mem's killing on Christmas Eve is associated with Christ's, for Mem's death is the catalyst for the new life of Ruth and Grange.

In a time of reassessment again retailed by flashback, Grange has to come to terms with events in the North, where he had experienced intense racist hostility and a loss of identity, culminating in an event which marked the loss of his humanity. He is shamed by the memory of a pregnant white woman who drowns rather than accept the black hand he offered, which on rejection he failed to offer a second time. The significance of that experience for Grange's spiritual wholeness comes with the realisation that 'he could only teach hate by inspiring it' (p. 157). To pass on such hatred to Ruth would be to murder her capacity for love as surely as he had Brownfield's. Grange's moral reawakening is emphasised by contrast with the moral disintegration of his son Brownfield, who instead of feeling remorse for the killing of Mem becomes increasingly paranoic, rationalising his action and absolving himself of blame by convincing himself that she had become so ugly she deserved death. In contrast, Grange's redemption comes from acceptance that his own wife's suicide was the result of his own treatment of her. Walker's message in *The Third Life of Grange Copeland* is that this generational self-destruction must stop. The weight of history must be recognised but not become a burden. Walker's overriding directional purpose in this novel was to 'explore the relationships between parents and children: specifically between daughters and their father . . . And I wanted to explore relationships between men and women . . .' (*Interviews*, p. 197). These relationships are the mainspring of all narrative action and the vehicle through which Walker explores questions of racism and sexism. Although ultimately Grange is redeemed by his love for Ruth, Walker makes no attempt to condone his treatment of his wife or his responsibility for Brownfield's progress through a life which echoes his name: a brown field – with no promise of nourishing growth. Brownfield's fate is 'to become what he hated'. As he turns in hate from the birth of children for whom he can ill provide, Grange is touched by awe: 'Lawd knows the *whole* business is something of a miraculous event. Out of all kinds of shit comes something clean, soft and sweet-smellin'' (p. 71).

Walker examines the ambiguous relationship which her people have with the South – as the site of a hated history which they needed to exorcise, and as the place they loved as their American homeland. When Grange returns to the South he accepts that, although he hated certain aspects of Southern life, home would always be the place where he was born. The same sentiment is expressed by Brownfield, who returned because 'It was a sweet, violent peculiarly accommodating land' (p. 163). The violence of the South's history is enacted in the Copelands' interrelationships, and the sweet beauty of the land is revealed in Walker's description of the natural landscape. At the beginning of the novel, when Brownfield's innocence is as yet unimpaired, the language brims with domestic, natural imagery drawn from rural life. Uncle Silas' car has 'great popping headlights like the eyes of a frog' (p. 4) and to children's ears the conversation of labouring adults sounds 'like the sporadic humming of wasps' (p. 17). Even Grange's dilapidated shack resembles 'a sway-backed animal turned out to pasture' (p. 13). All this is seen by Brownfield under a sky which 'seemed a round muffler made of wool' (p. 6). As Brownfield journeys towards ultimate corruption in Baker County, the imagery changes to reflect his shattered innocence in a world wherein all is cracked, used up or threatened: the ugly Lorene is described as having 'a tongue showing through her lips like a snake' (p. 36); Ruth is born in a leaking, chilled shack on a drizzly November night, so far from the possibility of blue days and sunshine with which her parents' marriage had begun.

In contrast to this inauspicious entry into the world, Ruth's life with her grandfather is full of organised light and beauty. Grange fulfils the function of the 'ancestor' figure in Afro-American literature as he 'taught her untaught history through his dance; she glimpsed a homeland she had never known and felt the pattering of drums' (p. 134). Grange is able to supplement the inadequacies of Ruth's formal education. With a fund of story from his own folk-heritage Grange compensates for the deficiencies in a formal education wherein Ruth encounters the complacent ignorance of a white teacher who dictated the following note about Red Indians: 'Note: Our own American Indians. We saved from disease and wild primitive life. Taught them useful activities . . . They have also been known to make beads' (p. 186).

As he passes on his store of folk-tales, African magic and music to Ruth he gives her a legacy, which is not one of hate but joy in the richness of black culture. He is restored to spiritual health. Able to laugh again he tells of his own 'conversion' to religion and engages with Ruth in productive debate about black/white relationships. Strengthened by black cultural identity, Grange is able to say about white dominance: 'Shit! Nobody's as powerful as we make them out to be. We got our own souls, don't we?' (p. 207). Grange survives his own bitter teaching but is determined that 'to survive whole was what he wanted for Ruth' (p. 214).

Walker says that, although this novel is ostensibly about Grange, 'it is the women and how they are treated that colours everything' (*Interviews*, p. 192). This is borne out in the reading, for even Josie arouses sympathy because of her maltreatment at the hands of men. When in her determination to improve her lot Mem forces the drunken Brownfield to crawl in his own vomit at the point of a shotgun, we applaud her spirit as she 'opened her eyes like someone opening the lid of a coffin'. All the characters in *The Third Life of Grange Copeland* are engaged in a search for self through love, and are either destroyed by its rejection or survive through its blossoming. Even Margaret, subjected to weekly beatings by a despairing husband, has in her eyes 'a deference . . . that spoke of her love for Grange' (p. 20). Josie also seeks love and tries to buy it, then ends up selling a cheapened imitation of it. Even Brownfield tries to align himself with love in his marriage to Mem, whose sweet, sustaining love reminds him of his mother's. The 'prong' of romantic love which Hurston talks of in *Their Eyes Were Watching God* proves to be the destruction of the women. Even the once-adored Mem, the butt of Brownfield's frustration, is called eventually a 'Goddam rib-ridden *plow* horse' (p. 78), whilst Brownfield himself becomes a caricature of a field nigger, tugging at an imaginary forelock in the presence of whites at whose commands he jumps, with a 'Yassuh', which denies the murderous thoughts he harbours.

The opportunity to make amends is given to Grange Copeland in his 'third life' as a home-maker and surrogate mother. His masculine taste is reflected in a room 'filled with his smell, of tobacco and hay, and, lightly, orange wine' (p. 197), a mixture of wholesome smells contrasted with the sickening odour of Brownfield's alcoholic vomit. Ruth's life with Grange flourishes among the smell of fresh coconuts and grapefruit, and on Christmas Eve they make ambrosia and celebrate with home-made peach wine while Grange 'crowns' Ruth with a cabbage. Walker establishes both character and narrative significance by their association with sensory images, so that the jealousy-ridden Josie has an unpleasant smell, whereas Margaret smells of fresh milk. Ruth's nervously debilitated sister Daphne is contrasted with another sister, Ornette, whose skin has a 'luxurious orange smoothness' (p. 111). Ornette is called 'slut' so often by Brownfield that inevitably she lives up to the label. Only Ruth survives, although her earliest recorded words addressed to her father were when she boldly called him a 'sonnabit' (p. 108). Clearly Ruth is the only female Copeland to survive 'whole' as the final blood-letting purges all hatred. Her liberation is accompanied at the end of the novel with the intrusion into a hitherto countrified world of television and its reports on the freedom-marchers. Ruth embraces the hope of a new future for all blacks, as open-mouthed in wonder she watches black and white students march together. Hitherto her consciousness of Baker County had been coloured by the statue of a Confederate soldier in a permanent attitude of defiance, the courtroom, and a fixed black society. Now Ruth can anticipate a political as well as an emotional liberation.

In this novel Walker uses death as a device to liberate some characters and to redeem others. Never dramatically over-elaborated, it is described with the swift simplicity with which it often occurs in life. Margaret's suicide is unexpected and prosaically related, while Grange's death, like Mem's, is announced by a sudden burst of gun-fire. Mem's final act is to pray, whilst Grange, refusing to be a hypocrite, remains mute. Unable to accept Christianity, he does, however, salvage something developed in *Revolutionary Petunias*[7] – a feeling of humanity, 'of man-womankind as a God worth embracing' (*Interviews*, p. 205). This genderless concept of God is significant in Walker's continued exploration of the tyranny of gender construction, which she identifies as a destructive force in the interrelationships of black men and women: 'I am preoccupied with the spiritual survival, the survival whole of my people. But beyond that, I am committed to exploring the oppressions, the loyalties and the triumphs of black women' (*Interviews*, p. 193).

In 1974 a number of her short stories were published in one volume, *In Love and Trouble*,[8] which celebrate the strengths as well as the neuroses of black women. Her fictional women range from the adolescent Myop to the dying old woman in 'The Welcome Table', and within that embracing scope she creates women loving, revengeful, submissive and violent. In 'The Child Who Favored Daughter' her subject is the sexual politics produced by black enslavement. The tragic consequences of a complex intermingling of parental love and racial hatred seen in *The Third Life of Grange Copeland* are rehearsed again in the sexual jealousy of a father for a daughter, around whom clusters the associated hatred of his white employers and the love of a dead sister, so confused that: 'He could not forgive her the love she gave that knew nothing of master and slave' (p. 39). The story is presented in a mixture of poetry and prose in an attempt to make 'prose and poetry run together to add a new dimension to the language' (*Interviews*, p. 204). The child who dallies homeward admiring the flowers is identified with the Black-eyed Susans, whilst her father waits ominously fingering a love-letter and cogitating upon destroying young wasps. The father imagines his daughter is a serpent in his bosom, as he plans on 'singeing the wings of the young wasps before they get a chance to fly or sting him' (p. 37). The father, like Brownfield Copeland, has the unforgiving nature of a man who feels betrayed, and is bent upon a repetitious course of violence in which he had beaten his wife to death and which ends in the violent cutting off of his daughter's budding breasts. As the daughter submits to the inevitable beating and violation, her innocence is suggested by the madonna-like image of her as a 'vivid shape in blue and white' (p. 40). Once again Walker demonstrates how the black woman has to go on paying for the iniquities of sexual exploitation suffered in slavery.

In contrast to this destructive and perverted love of parent for child, Walker portrays the devotion of a single mother, Rannie Toomer, for her dying bastard child in 'Strong Horse Tea'. In a futile attempt to save the child who already 'made a small grave-like mound in the bed' (p. 89), Rannie turns to Sarah, the root-doctor of the black community, who prescribes horse urine. There is pathos and irony in the final scene as the young mother, in a thunderstorm, chases a galloping mare to catch the liquid in a plastic overshoe that has a hole in it, unaware that death has already come to her child. In 'Entertaining God' a child dies with equal swiftness and in similar isolation. There is an element of the grotesque in both of these stories, especially in the latter, where in his attempt to understand his now alien Black Muslim father the child worships a zoo gorilla. In three short movements a history is rehearsed which is both tragic and grotesque, as a family is destroyed by parental neglect of the needs of a child.

That Alice Walker was attracted to, yet repelled by, the Black Muslim movement is seen in a few of her stories. 'Everyday Use' explores the impact of Black Muslimism on parent–child relationships. In this story Walker admires Muslim attempts at improving conditions of rural blacks through agricultural reform, yet is suspicious of any alignment prompted by a hatred of whites rather than a love of blacks. The mother in the story has two daughters, the beautiful Dee who has joined the Muslims, and the crippled homebound Maggie. The mother is honest in her appraisal of herself as a fat, hard-working peasant, yet day-dreams of being a more glamorous mother for Dee, who swoops down like a bird of paradise to visit her family. The mother's re-evaluation of her daughters changes when they display their differing attitudes towards home-made quilts. Dee seizes upon them as 'Art' and would use them as wall-hangings, saying disparagingly: '"Maggie can't appreciate these quilts! . . . She'd probably be backward enough to put them to everyday use"' (p. 57). Walker's own conviction that the co-operative creation of quilt-making, later to emerge in *The Color Purple* as a seminal image, is living evidence of black women's sisterhood, determines the mother's action. Despite her lack of education the mother – who is perceptive enough to realise that Dee's comments indicate her moving away from, rather than towards, her community – thrusts the quilts towards Maggie. She is aware of the patronising attitude of Dee and her male companion Hakim-a-Barber, who take endless photographs of the shack and its occupants whilst exchanging eye-signals which exclude the family. There is satisfaction at the end of the story as Maggie smiles in appreciation and the mother is cured of her day-dreams as she thinks dismissively of Dee as 'Miss Wangero'.

The suspicion of possible conflict between the aims of the Women's Movement and the Black Muslim movement are raised again in 'Roselily', whose name embodies the images of passion and purity, as well as life and death. In an interesting experiment in narrative technique, Walker interleaves snatches from the wedding service with Roselily's inner thoughts. Each familiar phrase triggers off a train of associations which is ordered and disciplined by past experiences and future hopes. The inner monologue gives the story a dream-like quality as the bride plays her appointed part in the ritual and betrays the mental conflict created by two opposing motives: the first to find security with this Muslim husband, the other to resist the absolute submission to the male inevitable in such a marriage. In thought Roselily drifts from childhood when she 'played at' weddings to the reality of marriage to this man, whose militancy is born out of a hatred for whites which she does not share. In her effort to concentrate on the ceremony the mention of God forces her to try to imagine Him as black. On hearing the phrase referring to the joining of man and woman she immediately thinks of chains and bondage, whilst part of her mind tries to cling to the idea of Chicago as a place of freedom for her children. As the marriage service continues there is a deepening sense of Roselily's alienation from a husband who sees life in terms of black and white. Consciousness that marriage will remove her from her familiar country life into an alien city becomes so oppressive that even her wedding clothes feel irksome and unnatural, as she fearfully anticipates a bondage to husband and children locked away from sun and air. She claims no understanding of her husband's religion, and sees him paradoxically as a means of escape from toil into a prison of non-identity. Doubting her ability to 'love forever', she feels a rising panic described as 'a rat trapped, cornered, scurrying to and fro in her head, peering through the windows of her eyes' (p. 8). We are left feeling that circumstances have steam-rollered her into a marriage which is an absolute denial of her previous life as she rushes through the night with a man determined never to look back.

Walker addresses contemporary feminist debates concerning the compatibility between women's demands for wider opportunities in education and careers and the demands of marriage and motherhood, in 'Really, Doesn't Crime Pay?'. Like Marshall's 'The Valley Between', this story explores marriage as a site of female imprisonment. In an attempt to convey this in a mode traditionally employed in women's confessional writing, Walker tells the story by sandwiching

together a seemingly random selection of extracts from the protagonist's past and present diary. The reader is invited to share, to
eavesdrop on, the woman's most intimate thoughts which belie her
outward complaisance. The language used to create her sense of self
is vivid as she admits to being so externally depersonalised by her use
of sweet-smelling, good brand-name cosmetics, that she sees her
public life 'like a jar of cold cream on a mirrored vanity shelf' (p. 11).
Her private opinion of the new house provided by her husband is one
of pain rather than pride: 'The yard is a long undressed wound, the
few trees are bereft of foliage as hairpins stuck in a mud cake' (p. 11).
The images of raw pain and sterility underline the theme of multiple
betrayal, by a husband who cannot understand her need to write, and
a lover who steals and publishes one of her stories. She is imprisoned
by men, by Ruel who sees her fulfilment as bearing his children, and
Mordecai who has stolen her secret thoughts. The irony in the title is
two-fold. It is obvious that crime *has* paid Mordecai, whose literary
career is founded on a lie despite his professed search for Truth.
Similarly, the woman now lives a life of sly deceit as she applies a
careful cosmetic mask, while secretly swallowing the contraceptive
pill in the hope that one day Ruel will abandon his attempts at
fatherhood. Her murderous attack on her husband and her
consequent nervous breakdown are echoed in another story about a
woman whose own sense of inadequacy leads her to death. In 'Her
Sweet Jerome' we have the opposite of the svelte, well-groomed
woman diarist in the person of the brash, garish figure of Jerome's
wife. An ugly hair-dresser, she imagines herself pretty in her pathetic
attempts to hold the attention of a ruthless young husband whose
interest in her is financial. A fanatical adherent to the Black Muslim
movement, he is unimpressed by her lavish gifts and uses her money
to further political ends. There is grim humour as in her maddened
state she threatens imagined rivals, as she stalks the town looking for
her sweet Jerome's paramour. She discovers his secret love is in the
political books lying behind the bed where 'it was dusty and
cobwebby, the way the inside of her head felt' (p. 33). The violence
of her death as she screams in self-incineration is made more horrific
because of the futility of her life, epitomised by the fact that she
doesn't even know what the word 'revolution' means, unless it
represents the way her head was whirling.

The dream of Jerome is for a violent resistance to oppression, but
it is equally effective when prompted by a simple non-political act, as

in 'The Welcome Table'. The title is from a negro spiritual which invites all creatures to feast together in the sight of God. Although based upon her personal memories of being a freedom-marcher, Walker avoids the trap of over-sentimental treatment by the distancing use of an omniscient narrative stance. In telling the story of an old woman who wanders unwittingly into a church for whites only, she attacks the hypocrisy of a church which practises racism, and so throws mocking doubt upon the validity of the institution, though not the basic faith in God. The old woman is likened to a worn-out working animal, 'an old collie turned out to die' (p. 82), and the imagery used to describe her emphasises her Southern roots. Even her skin is 'the color of poor gray Georgia earth' (p. 82) and is like 'the bark of old pines' (p. 82). The old woman becomes a symbol of the oppression of all blacks: 'On her face centuries were folded into the circles around one eye, while around the other, etched and mapped as if for print, ages more threatened again to live' (p. 82).

She is seen by the whites as a danger to the sanctity of their worship, and her accidental presence is interpreted as the thin edge of a racial wedge. Although burning with 'righteous' indignation, the white congregation is described as being frozen and cold, only to feel warm again in the 'impartial' love of God as the old black woman is ejected. In a telling interrogation of the process of white Christianity, the old woman walks towards death following her vision of Jesus. Walker's interrogation of the relevance of the Christian religion in the lives of blacks is continued in 'The Diary of an African Nun', where she suggests that the Christian church has been used as a tool to tighten imperialistic power over African people: 'In this way will the wife of a loveless, barren, hopeless marriage broadcast the joys of an enlightened religion to an imitative people' (p. 118).

In this Walker reworks the ideas embodied in Hurston's depiction of the preacher John Pearson in *Jonah's Gourd Vine*, as the black nun, shrouded in white, is drawn towards the sound of pagan African drums, and inwardly contrasts the sterility of her marriage to Christ with the vital dancing of the black 'pagans'. Longing to be with the dancers, she struggles to resist the temptation to experience the reality that the drums imply. The powerful attraction of this African inheritance emerges again in 'The Revenge of Hannah Kemhuff', a story Walker dedicates to Zora Neale Hurston, in whose writing Walker had witnessed the literary effectiveness of black vernacular as a literary medium, and the power of Afro-American spirituality. An interesting narrative device in this story is the witness-narrator, allowing the 'I' of the story, Tante Rosie's assistant, to stand at times outside the story although she plays a crucial part in the final outcome. The narrator is aware that Tante Rosie's Voodoo powers are aided by her copious files on local residents yet, without claiming magical powers for Voodoo, Walker implies the power of Voodoo suggestion, as Tante Rosie's intended victim dies.

Not all the stories in this collection tell of unmitigated trials and tribulations, for some express a belief in a positive life-force which relieves the collection from total pessimism. Even 'The Flowers', in which Myop comes upon the skeleton of a lynched black man when she is collecting wild flowers, has a note of beauty as she picks a pink rose from near the skull. A similar beauty surfaces in 'We Drink the Wine in France', which records the adolescent love of a black girl for her Polish teacher of French who has survived a concentration camp. Harriet and her teacher have secret but separate longings for one another, unfulfilled except in dream. He is conscious that 'his odor is of ashes while hers is of earth and sun' (p. 125). She develops her idea that even out of the horror of slavery and the holocaust beauty can be salvaged and grow again. In this Walker celebrates – as she did in the story of Grange Copeland and in the first of her stories ever to be published, 'To Hell with Dying' – the power of love to redeem and regenerate.

In Love and Trouble foregrounds the problems experienced by black women from all walks of life, while *Meridian*, published in 1978, charts the impact made by the Civil Rights Movement on some women, fulfilling Walker's promise that 'My new novel will be about several women who came of age during the sixties, and were active (or not active) in the movement in the South' (*Interviews*, p. 197). *Meridian*[9] is Walker's memorial to the courage, strength and personal sacrifice made by her freedom-marching comrades whom the fictional Ruth Copeland joined. Walker's involvement as a student was with the SNCC, formed after a legal battle against Jim Crow laws had been won. The resistance to these laws had culminated in the demand by two black youths for service at the whites-only lunch counter of a Carolina store. A successful boycott of the store, where many blacks shopped, was organised, resulting in a dramatic loss in trading profits. This exercise in economic power resulted in new legislation giving blacks the right to eat in white restaurants – if they dared. Black students joined in the drive to persuade rural blacks to register as voters, in the hope that black civil rights would be won at the ballot box. *Meridian* records a young female student's experience of combating Jim Crow laws, and the mentality that had framed them. It is also Walker's rewriting of Toomer's *Cane*,[10] which had been seen by many as a unique celebration of black Southern culture, a supposition denied by Walker in 'The divided life of Jean Toomer', in *In Search of Our Mothers' Gardens*, pp. 60–6. In this she argues that in *Cane* Toomer believed he was 'memorialising' rather than celebrating a dying culture. Walker's self-appointed task was to show that, in spite of racist devaluation, this culture was far from dead, and the blacks were full of spirit. Not only does Walker rightly mistrust the motives of Toomer, a man who determined to 'live white', but she also believes that *Cane* had been falsely hailed as liberating. She points out that: 'Cane depicts primarily white people and never documents their racism in any way; it is as if Toomer believed an absence of black people assured the absence of racism itself' (*In Search Of*, p. 63). Walker's *Meridian* is her attempt to redress this omission. She concentrates not only on the lives of rural blacks, but on a woman, knowing that Toomer's own attitude toward black women had been one of condescension. The intertextuality of Walker's novel and Toomer's *Cane* and his poem 'The Blue Meridian', gives insight into her purpose. Meridian Hill's name is carefully defined by Walker to suggest Southernness, a reaching of a zenith in insight, and a capacity to embrace humankind. It also has significance in its connection with Meridian Hill Park, visited by Toomer, and renamed later as Malcolm X Park, in that *Meridian* articulates Walker's rejection of the violent revolution advocated by Black Muslims. It also implicitly interrogates the reasons behind a cultural acceptance of Toomer's one-and-only piece of sustained fiction, and the neglect of those by women like Hurston and Larsen.

This is a woman-centred novel in that Meridian Hill is the linking device between all other characters. By focusing on Meridian's various familial, emotional and political relationships, Walker presents a fictional woman whose acquisition of self-knowledge is perhaps a projection of Walker's own. The main characters form an eternal triangle between a black man, Truman Held, a black woman, Meridian, and a white woman, Lynne. Structured in three parts, the third part, 'Endings', suggests resolution of conflicts established in the first two, eventually celebrating a sisterhood across the colour divide, between Meridian and Lynne. In a non-chronological sequence which underlines Walker's own sense of history as a non-linear, seamless process, Meridian is glimpsed in various stages of development, from child, to student, mother and political activist. Time past and present are interwoven in the consciousness and presentation of Meridian, whose sense of self is defined through her memory of significant experiences. As in *The Third Life of Grange Copeland*, as well as in Paule Marshall's and Toni Morrison's writing, Walker's narrative perspective is an historical one, emphasising her conviction that personal identity depends upon a knowledge of familial and racial history. Meridian is a conscious link with the past, and at the end of the novel she accepts that, like the slave Louvinie, her role will be to sing of that past.

Walker's concern to retrieve and record her foremothers' contribution to her people's oral culture, and her perception of her own responsibility as an artist to enrich and perpetuate that process, have not diminished with time. The artist as poet, singer and seer, foregrounded in her later novel *The Temple of my Familiar*, is prefigured in the character of Meridian. Possessed by psychic powers inherited from an Indian foremother, Meridian falls into cataleptic trances, when she feels 'like a speck in the grand movement of time'. As a student she decorates her walls with photographs of rocks, clouds and hills which she claims she 'knew'. The spiritual inheritance of her people, carried by Meridian, marks her off as unique and intensifies the relationship with her father who also claims, like his African forebears, awareness of the ancestral dead. Mr Hill, a scholarly idealist, becomes symbolic of aloof wisdom, as he ponders Indian history in a room with windows 'like the eyes of an owl' (p. 45). From him, Meridian learns of the genocide and dispossession of the Indian, a knowledge which shapes her consciousness of the oppression of her own people. Her father, like Grange Copeland, identifies with the displaced Indian, but unlike him, does not seek to apportion blame: 'I never said either side was innocent or guilty, just ignorant' (p. 47). He gives back to the Indians land to which he has legal title when he discovers it is both an ancient burial ground and the site of ecstasy experienced by himself and his Indian ancestor, Feather Mae. Meridian, too, has out-of-body experiences which foreshadow Lissie's past reincarnation as a lion in *The Temple*. When emerging from a trance Meridian describes feeling her feet 'curl over the grass, as if her feet were those of a leopard or a bear' (p. 51).

Meridian inherits her father's spiritual awareness and his profound sense of racial oppression. From her mother, she gains insight into the peculiar burden of motherhood, against which she rebels. A teacher like her husband, Mrs Hill had quickly become over-burdened with children whom she accepts as an inevitable bondage. Living only for her children, Mrs Hill, 'a strong, silent woman who seemed always to be washing or ironing or cooking or rousing her family from naps', gives rise to a persistent sense of guilt in Meridian. The short chapter 'Gold' serves as a parable illustrating the mother–daughter relationship, in which the mother is too harassed to listen sympathetically to her child's account of buried treasure. Marriage and motherhood have destroyed the mother's capacity to dream as she uncomplainingly starches and irons her way through life. She never pauses to question her role as a black woman in a life where she passively submits to the 'Lord's Will'. Yet although Walker exposes Mrs Hill's unawakened political consciousness, she does not diminish her. Deftly moving from present to past, she enlarges our understanding of the mother by recounting her descent from a long line of enslaved women who had fought fiercely to have their children educated, like those celebrated in her poem 'Women':

> How they battered down
> Doors
> And ironed
> Starched white
> shirts

Indomitable mothers, marching warriors, they had blindly pushed

> Across mined
> Fields
> Booby-trapped
> Ditches
> To discover books
> Desks. (*Revolutionary Petunias*, p. 5)

Meridian admires the mother as a giant of fortitude, whose legacy to her is an endurance she could not, nor did she wish to, emulate. Meridian would weep to hear of her mother's childhood, but recognises that freedom exists only where choice can be exercised. Her ancestors, whose children could be taken from them to be sold, had not lived in an 'age of choice'. In deciding to give away the one child she bears, Meridian claims to exercise the choice denied her ancestors, an act that horrifies the mother as much as does Meridian's questioning of the assumptions generally made about motherhood.

When motherhood comes to Meridian with alarming suddenness, the chapter title 'Happy Mother' is an ironic denial of the reality, as the child bride begins to repeat her mother's experiences. Unlike Mrs Hill, Meridian does not accept childbearing with furious equanimity, and questions the social expectations of motherhood. The first assumption questioned is that motherhood is a fulfilling experience. For Meridian it is the opposite, bringing a sense of enslavement: 'Everyone who came to visit assumed she loved him – but he did not feel like anything to her but a ball and chain' (p. 63). Another assumption examined is that motherhood is accompanied by instant adoration of the offspring, and Walker expresses the feelings of many women, silenced by a fear that their thoughts of infanticide are unnatural:

> So this, she mumbled, lurching towards his crib in the middle of the night, is what slavery is like. Rebelling, she began to dream each night, just before her baby sent out his cries, of ways to murder him. (p. 63)

Meridian, who knew but questioned accepted social rules, did not associate childbearing with instant joy, or the marital embrace with pleasure. She had thought of marital sex as a sanctuary, a resting of pursuit from other males, only to find that even advanced pregnancy does not protect her from a husband determined to enjoy his conjugal rights. She feels she has no control over her own body or of her life's direction in an existence where she is defined by the roles of a wife and mother, both of which implied duties but no rights. Rejecting the notion that creativity is fulfilled in childbearing, she grows to regard her life as a living entombment. She is incensed by the insensitivity of those who ridicule women with very large families, and wonders why they cannot see that such women are 'being buried alive, walled away from – life, brick by brick'.

In despair at the disintegration of her own marriage, Meridian turns for solace to magazines such as *Real Romances*, which merely reinforce the gender structure against which she is rebelling, and exacerbate her resentment at the organised exploitation of women as sex objects. Walker castigates the popular media for its peddling of a fantasy world in which young girls are encouraged to believe in 'the dream of happy endings: of women who had everything, of men who ran the world'. The reality of life is a betrayal of these dreams of happiness for women, but the magazines reinforce the social reality that men are in control and that they are white. Already predisposed to feel oppressed as a woman, Meridian's sense of injustice is brought into sharper focus as she watches TV newsreels of the Civil Rights workers, whose ranks she joins. Yet underlying the euphoric faith that black and white together would overcome racial oppression lurks the deep unspoken taboo concerning interracial sexual relationships. These came to the fore in the 'freedom summer' of 1964, when SNCC was joined by another civil rights organisation, COFO (Council of Federated Organisations) and white students from the North were encouraged to join blacks in their protests in the South. 'Freedom' described the activities of black and white students who together rode in 'bus-ins' as a challenge to segregation in schools. It could also have been an apt description of the increased 'freedom' of interracial sexual alliances between the students. Walker is courageous enough to explore this sensitive area at a time when such alliances brought social ostracisation from both sides of the race divide. Black women were suspicious of a sexual freedom which seemed to them to mean that black men found it easier to sleep with white women. When Meridian's lover Truman shows sexual interest in a white female fellow activist, Meridian feels sexually betrayed. She is also bewildered. That a black man could desire a white woman is beyond her comprehension:

> As far back as she could remember, it seemed something *understood*: that while white men would climb on a black woman old enough to be his mother 'for the experience' white women were considered sexless, contemptible and ridiculous by all. (p. 103)

The gulf between black and white women has been deepened by their perception by men as sexual objects, in which the black woman has been negatively mythicised as being more sexually active and available than the white. Because of this Meridian had never viewed white women as sexual rivals and had grown up in ignorance of them as anything other than machines for the making of white babies. Having joined the movement against racism she discovers her own racial prejudice, as well as the sexism of her lover who, like Roselily's husband, wanted 'an attractive woman – but asleep', one who would make no claim to a life separate from himself.

Walker shows how political consciousness-raising, once initiated, cannot be limited. Meridian's original spur to action was racial oppression. Soon she recognised the equally oppressive sexism which is non-racial, affecting white and black women alike. Through the sexual relationships in the novel, and particularly in the rape of Lynne by Tommy Odds, in which he lived out his own personal sexual fantasy, Walker examines the hatred and violence which result from the fear of difference. Lynne's rape is an act of aggression perpetrated in misguided revenge. Tommy Odds hates Lynne's whiteness for what it represents, so that in urinating on her he pisses on the white race. The revulsion expressed for Lynne's violation is matched by Walker's arousal of pity for those whose hearts had been blunted by fanatical devotion to a single cause and whose humanity had been diminished by a nursing of racial hatred. Meridian voices this when she asks fellow students: 'Is there no place in a revolution for a person who cannot kill?' (p. 193). In a questioning of the methods advocated by militant Black Muslims such as Malcolm X, Walker suggests that violence, once unleashed, is difficult to control. In the turmoil of Wild Child's funeral the rioting students accidentally destroy their own totem, the magnolia tree Sojourner, under which the slave Louvinie's tongue is reputedly buried. The violence of racial hatred results in the senseless murder of Lynne's and Truman's child, and Meridian is able to offer the estranged parents a healing commensurate with her own sense of wholeness acquired through pain. Through her confrontation with racism and sexism in society Meridian had been forced into recognition of her own harboured race prejudice. Her re-evaluation of Lynne begins when they watch plantation sagas together on TV, which 'never delved into women's problems, black or white'. Sisterhood is born when Meridian conquers her sexual jealousy of Lynne, whom she learns to love 'totally free of possessiveness or contempt' (p. 175). Purged of the desire to blame Lynne for her colour or her sexuality, Meridian is cleansed by her willingness to forgive. She progresses towards a spiritual health matched by the physical deterioration she endures as her spiritual dis-ease is healed. To Truman, Meridian eventually passes on her cap, the symbol of her soldiering, knowing he too will have to undergo an agony if he is to emerge whole.

The message of *Meridian* is one of hope, of personal salvaging from a decade of conflict. This is in itself a cause of celebration, but the power of the novel depends as much upon the medium as the message, in the remarkable manipulation of a narrative full of unexpected time shifts and varied linguistic registers. It opens near the time when all action in the story is ended, then immediately moves backward to Meridian's student life ten years before. The intervening years are given substance in a series of episodes that could easily be detached and stand as short stories, held together by Meridian who is at the centre or on the fringe of each separate action, some of which are in the present, some in the past. Past and present are interwoven as Part 1 affords glimpses of those experiences, lived and ancestral, which had shaped the young Meridian. The same technique is employed in Part 2, where Truman's relationship with Lynne naturally slips into an account of her Jewish background and her parents' repudiation of her marriage to a black man. Time shifts enrich the texture of the novel, as layers of time and accrued experience are unpeeled to illuminate the present. By ignoring linear time Walker arouses sympathy and understanding for Lynne simultaneously in the reader and Meridian. Walker's conviction of the interrelatedness of the present and an historical past determines the way in which she reveals narrative facts. The murder of Lynne's child, Camara, is revealed before the fact of her birth, emphasising Walker's notion of history as the place where tragic seeds are planted. Part 3, although firmly dated as 1968, in fact covers the years that follow, all characterised by sudden death. Martin Luther King is joined in death by Camara and the drowned black boy whose body Meridian carries to the mayor's office. The experience of violent death intensifies Meridian's belief that life must be respected, so answering a question raised earlier about the right to kill. She rejects violence as a solution to human conflict.

The narrative structure and manipulation of time reflect the technology of the visual media. The all-pervasive TV camera bringing images directly into the home is imitated by Walker, who uses language as a zoom lens to probe deeper into the past and present lives of her characters. A decade of political assassinations is re-created in a series of action replays, all firmly rooted in the reality of television news coverage: 'Three small children were injured – no, a flash at the bottom of the screen announced them dead, several grown-ups were injured' (p. 67). The translation of the camera image into language, employed so effectively in her early poetry, re-emerges in her description of Truman and Lynne, captured in photographic stills. Lynne is described in the present tense – 'She is sitting on the porch steps' (p. 127) – and the portrait of the pair on a motor-cycle is a black-and-white snap-shot which blurs in passage. This camera technique combines with poetic prose to produce a perfectly controlled image. Her images throughout are startlingly apt. Mrs Hill's bottled-up frustration is expressed in her laundering, so that her children 'in their stiff, almost flexible garments . . . were enclosed in the starch of her anger' (p. 73). When Truman learns of Meridian's child, the breasts he had fondled suddenly seem like 'used jugs' (p. 140), and when he needs solace he sees her 'as a lifeboat receding into distance' (p. 138). As in her poetry, Walker employs strong sensory images which capture emotional as well as physical reality. The sexual advances of the funeral director, Mr Raymond, are more repulsive to Meridian when she thinks of his teeth 'covered in yellowish flannel', and his breath as 'nauseating as his whole mouth were a tunnel of sewerage' (p. 109). His assistant is a more successful seducer, with the aid of a persuasive voice 'more skilful than the suppleness of wrist required to extract blood from a cadaver's vein' (p. 61). The grotesque humour in this last image displays Walker's ability to convey scenes vividly, without missing the ludicrous that is never far beneath the surface of events, so that Eddie's promise to marry Meridian is given whilst he anxiously scrutinises the used condom for possible leakage. Her humour is earthy but not crudely offensive. Even in her use of the vernacular, crudity is modified by the situation. She comments on a black riot policeman who 'can't stand up to them no more than piss can fall upward' (p. 30), and when Meridian is supported by a friend in her decision to give away her baby, Dolores pointedly reminds Mrs Hill that 'the last time God had a baby He skipped too' (p. 86).

Linguistic variety and vivid imagery, coupled with her skilful manipulation of fictive time and narrative connections, are the hallmarks of Walker's immense talent as a teller of story. Intertextuality plays its part in her narrative art, as does her reworking of stories from slave history. Her determination to build on the efforts of slave ancestors and perpetuate their heritage as something of beauty, is seen in the interpolated story of the slave Louvinie, whose tongue, when cut out, looked like a 'thick pink rose-petal' (p. 34). Although destroyed in rioting, the tree Sojourner, named after the redoubtable nineteenth-century campaigner for black and women's rights, Sojourner Truth, begins sprouting again as 'The new part had grown out of the old' (p. 227). In this Walker emphasises the passing on to succeeding generations of the power of ancestral speech to effect reform. The tree's recovery of healthy growth coincides with Meridian's, linking her inextricably with an enslaved past to which she owes a duty. Narrative links are constantly made and reinforced by juxtaposing incidents which are examples of oppression, and force is added to their meaning by their deliberately non-chronological presentation. The circularity of historical process is underlined when an early chapter on political martyrs is explored further in the final part, 'Endings', in which Walker laments the speed with which people commercialise the good and noble with popcorn and Coca-Cola holidays. At the same time, questions raised earlier in Meridian's interior monologues concerning the validity of violence, are resolved. Meridian's answer, which reflects Walker's own pacifist stance, is to abjure violence absolutely, in the faith that the future for humankind rests on their capacity for love and mutual understanding as well as the ballot box.

Meridian fictionalises Walker's re-evaluation of the Civil Rights decade, and heralds a sharpening of her political analysis in the wake of the inevitable disillusionment in the years that followed. The ensuing divisions amongst blacks who advocated differing paths towards political liberation, as well as those amongst black women who found the Women's Movement incompatible to their needs, are addressed in *You Can't Keep a Good Woman Down*. This collection of stories has a more conscious theoretical thrust than the earlier *In Love and Trouble*, as by using the short story, letter or diary as narrative frameworks, Walker begins to clarify her political stance. Black feminists had in 1973 formed a separate feminist organisation, the National Black Feminist Organisation (NBFO), in response to a need not satisfied by the Women's and Civil Rights Movements. Their need for a non-sexist philosophy was not shared by many black male activists, and white women did not share their need for non-racism. The dilemma facing black women of Walker's generation was whether or not to prioritise racism as a focus for their energies, or sexism. If the former, they ran the risk of doing nothing to alleviate the sexist oppression of their women; if the latter, they faced the racist hostility they sensed in the predominantly white Women's Movement. Walker's solution was to move to a definition of herself as 'womanist' rather than 'feminist', in an attempt to avoid the narrowness often produced by definitions which are too narrowly focused. 'Womanist' in *In Search Of Our Mother's Gardens* is defined in four different ways, from the black idiomatic 'womanish' to the metaphorical 'womanist is to feminist as purple is to lavender'. She describes a 'womanist' perspective as a life-loving, non-sexually divisive one, 'committed to survival and wholeness of entire people, male *and* female'.

This appeal for 'wholeness' is exemplified in 'Coming Apart', an introductory essay to a book on pornography, penned as a narrative fable, in which Walker identifies pornography and racism as having the same root: both are a violent expression of assumed power. The story envisages a black woman reading essays by black women, when she discovers her husband's secreted store of pornographic material. In an effort to explain to him that pornography is demeaning to women, she reads extracts from the essays, and is met with familiar accusations of her own sexual and racial betrayal in her perceived alliance with whites and lesbians – Lorde, Teishe and Gardiner. The wife had never considered herself a feminist, but manages to persuade her husband that he colludes in his own degradation by the reading of pornography in which 'black women are depicted as shits' (p. 52). Walker argues that the black man must free himself from the cultural corruption of a white pornography which reinforces the exploitative nature of racism. The reduction of black woman to animal in pornographic representation is equated with the depiction of the black man who is 'defined solely by the size, readiness and unselectivity of his cock' (p. 53). The sexual abuse of black women, perpetuated in pornography, is not diminished in any way by the black man's freedom to ogle pornographic representations of white women. To imagine this, Walker argues, is to repeat the viciousness of white racists' abuse of power. Rape, whatever the colour of the raped or rapist, is violation.

The use of sexuality as an exercise in power was explored in the rape in *Meridian*. In 'Advancing Luna and Ida B. Wells' Walker admits that this fictional representation had caused her some torment. Walker's fears that this episode could be interpreted as a reinforcement of the white myth of the black man as insatiable sexual performer, are addressed to Ida B. Wells, who had spent her life protecting black men from accusations of rape and subsequent lynching. Walker justifies her inclusion of rape in her fiction because it is an inescapable, inexcusable fact in the experience of some women – a truth she could not pretend never happened. 'Advancing Luna', firmly rooted in 1965, records the idealism of her co-activists who thought they could change America 'because we were young and bright and held ourselves *responsible* for changing it' (p. 86). The fragility of interracial co-operation is exposed when Baraka's advice

– 'Rape the white girls. Rape their fathers' (p. 92) – is acted upon. Luna's rape might have been considered a political act, but Walker cannot condone it. No matter how, in the various endings, explanations and postscripts she gives to this story, she concludes that rape is never to be condoned. Her revulsion at sexual exploitation is expressed again in 'How did I get away with killing one of the Biggest Lawyers in the State? It was Easy?'. In a scenario depressingly reminiscent of the sexual exploitation in plantation slavery she portrays a young, urban, black girl who had become resigned to exploitation. Only when the girl's mother instigates legal action against the white seducer, and is consequently incarcerated as a patient in a mental institution, does the girl recognise the enormity of the white man's abuse. She shoots him. The victim has become the agent in a tale which challenges the stereotype of black woman as a permanently non-resistant focus for white men's lust. The notion of non-resistance is also exploded in 'Elethia', where Elethia with others steals and burns 'Uncle Albert', a supposed dummy but actually the stuffed body of a former slave which stands in an attitude of willing service outside a 'whites-only' restaurant. Uncle Albert had in life been anything but servile. All his teeth had been smashed out in his various attempts to escape his slave-holder. His stuffed, smiling effigy was a symbolic perpetuation of the white myth of willing black servitude, like the effigy Denver sees in the white man's house in Morrison's *Beloved*, and, as such, had to be destroyed. Revising the 'magnolia myth' begins with that destruction. A more difficult myth to dispel is that of Scarlett O'Hara, the enduringly manipulative white Southern belle, immortalised forever surrounded by ineffectual, admiring black servants. Using the letter form, Walker writes a story exposing the racism on which this characterisation is built. The split between black and white feminists is defined in the author's hostility towards a white feminist who, at a ball where guests dressed as the character they most admired, had come as Scarlett O'Hara.

You Can't Keep a Good Woman Down offers a retrospective view of the issues which preoccupied all black, and some white, women in the 1960s. Reflecting a shared concern in an age when the availability of abortion was increasingly demanded, Walker talks with conviction of the psychological repercussions for the woman who aborts an unwanted child. In 'The Abortion' a married woman decides to terminate a pregnancy, as a logical exercise of shared responsibility. Her husband, a political activist, joins her in attendance at a memorial service for a young girl killed in civil disturbance. Engrossed in political discussion with a black Mayoral candidate, he remains outside the church for the duration of the service. This apparent disregard for wasted life exacerbates the wife's growing suspicion that politics could not be divorced from the personal. There was no way for the husband to understand his wife's equation of Holly Monroe's death with that of their aborted child, just as in the assembly line of legally executed terminations, 'There was no way to explain to a man' the emotional anguish of the aborting mother. Walker knew from personal experience that the personal is political. Her marriage to a Jewish lawyer had been an act of political defiance as well as love. The impinging of the political on the personal is explored in 'Laurel', a fictionalised account of the narrator's affair with a white, married man, whose attentions persisted long after the affair ended. Contemplating the complexity of emotions experienced during the illicit affair, Walker admits that one was to satisfy her lust for adventure: '(I at least was not yet able to articulate how the personal is political . . . Viz, nobody wanted us to go to bed together, except us, and they had made laws to the effect)' (p. 108).

Out of her most personal and private concerns, Walker creates fiction wherein narrative tension and didactic purpose are held in equilibrium. The poignancy of 'A Sudden Trip Home' lies in the girl's grief at her father's death, coupled with her previous unwillingness to confront the source of their estrangement, which is her sense of shame at black men's seeming political impotence. The girl is unable to paint portraits of black men because she cannot bear to depict the defeat she sees in their faces, which was 'the defeat of black forever defined by white' (p. 135). Only the sight of her grandfather's dignified bearing at her father's funeral reminds her of a responsibility to forebears whose struggles had enabled her to be the only black student at a prestigious Northern college. To repay the debt she owes to ancestors who had fought to ensure her present opportunities, she resolves to stare down the 'rat' of racism by succeeding in, rather than abandoning, her college education. Political and personal responsibility are inseparable in this story, where the informing sentiment of regret at the character's lack of closeness to her father reflects Walker's own regret, expressed in 'Poem at Thirty Nine':

> How I miss my father
> I wish he had not been
> so tired

when I was
born[11]

Walker writes out of herself in an honest and increasingly self-
conscious way. What began as an expression of political ideology in
her early writing has developed into an ever-intensifying inward
probing of self, and a search for the connectedness of that self with
ancestors who began their American life as slaves. The poem
prefacing *Horses Make a Landscape Look More Beautiful* talks of her
'part'-Cherokee maternal foremother, and a paternal great-great-
grandmother who was raped by a white man – '(a "Walker",
perhaps?)'. Her own mixed ancestry could have made of Walker yet
another 'tragic mulatta', a fate she avoided because as a Southern rural
woman she was always sure of her black identity. The confusion of
those who could, and did, pass for white, like Jean Toomer, is also
the subject of 'Source', in which the character Anastasia has spent her
adult life trying to avoid the implications of racial divisions arising
from her light skin. She remembers growing up in a black community
but 'not resembling any of my friends', where blacks envied and paid
deference to her white skin while despising the whites to whom they
likened her. Black colorism makes Anastasia say, 'and oh, black
people were *so confused*'. Part of their confusion was fuelled by the
racist artefacts of white culture like the film 'Birth of a Nation' and
Styron's account of the rebel slave Nat Turner, in both of which
blacks were portrayed negatively. Anastasia's old college friend Irene
had never suffered such doubts about her racial identity, and had been
involved in an underfunded teaching programme catering mainly for
poor black women. It was this experience which convinced Irene that
because the white world offered them so little, the voices to which
poor black women most responded were those of the female slave
narratives with which they could identify. It was in these that their
education could begin. The complexities arising from centuries of
miscegenation and white cultural domination are presented as
barriers to the multi-racial dream Anastasia had entertained as a hippy
in San Francisco, but her search for a comfortable identity was still
in progress.

Clearly, as Walker's own perceptions have matured, her awareness
of the perils attendant upon embattled polarities – black and white,
male and female, homosexual and heterosexual – has moved her
towards a philosophy of peaceful co-existence. Her vision of 'health'

is not exclusively black, but co-operatively human. The wholeness and survival of her people, whilst still a goal, could only be achieved if attitudes towards difference were changed. In *The Color Purple*[12] she envisages human progress in terms of transformations made possible by the rejection of attitudes founded upon assumed superiority, whether it be of sex, race, nationality or even species. In 'Everything is a Human Being', in her collection of essays *Living By The Word*,[13] she reiterates the message of *The Color Purple* in which Celie's final letter is addressed to creation:

> Our primary connection is to the Earth, our mother and our father, regardless of who 'owns' pieces and parts, we are sisters and brothers to the 'four-legged' (and the fishes) and wings of the air, share the whole.' (*Living*, p. 148)

The encapsulation of her fictive messages in prose essays is a pattern of creativity established by Walker over the last decade. The informing impulse of her poetry and fiction is justified and explained in essays which are in some cases anticipatory, in others retrospective, but in either case always introspective. She displays readiness to face and counter criticism whilst explaining her creative process. The filming of *The Color Purple* brought her work to many who were unaware of her writing, and exposed her to hostility from blacks who felt the novel presented them in a degrading and stereotypical way. They objected to any suggestion of child-rape, incest or lesbianism within their community. On such grounds they wanted the novel banned from public libraries. One black magazine refused to publish it because 'Black people don't talk like that' (*Living*, p. 63). In 'Coming in from the Cold', Walker strenuously defends her novel and vouches for the authenticity of the language and Celie's voice. She goes even further in suggesting that Celie and Shug entered her mind as voices from the past, and that Celie was 'only one of a long line of ancestors who came to visit' (*Living*, p. 67). The intensification of her own spirituality and her deepening belief that everything in the physical world is divine, can explain her claim to an extraordinary personal sensitivity. In 'The Universe Responds', she realises that 'To some people who read the following there will seem to be something special or perhaps strange about me. I have sometimes felt this way myself!' (*Living*, p. 187). Perhaps this explains why she describes herself at the end of *The Color Purple* as author and medium, a disturbing definition for the critic to accept. 'Medium' in a spiritual sense means a mediating agent between the supernatural and the physical world; authorship implies interpretative imagination and skill in organisation and transcription of experience into the word, and I, like others, can only approach her writing with any critical certainty from that angle.

If indeed Walker's creativity was fed by supernatural voices, my only brief is to see how effectively these were made manifest by the author, not to judge their supposed source. In this *The Color Purple* stands up to examination as a highly crafted fiction, in which the voices of the sisters, Celie and Nettie, carry the burden of the narrative. Through their exchange of letters Walker creates and contrasts the worlds of Africa and the Deep South of America, and breathes life into characters whose existence is defined by their words and reported actions. Walker uses the once-fashionable epistolary narrative style initiated in the eighteenth century in Richardson's *Pamela*, which was copied and developed by the popular English woman novelist Fanny Burney. Both writers had used narrative letters to outline romance, and in so much as Richardson's story of Pamela is one of escape from attempted rape by a 'Mr B', and is a reinforcement of the powers of patriarchy and gender construction which Walker's novel interrogates, it is tempting to see that Walker was using this form very deliberately. It is also an apt device in that it reflects the traditional familial role of women as keepers of family history in their talk and letters. The fabric of the novel is made by the interweaving of letters which reveal the respective network of inter-familial relationships supported by each sister. Despite the differences in the sisters' language, as well as the experiences described, these letters are quilted into a rich and many-coloured pattern to produce an harmonious whole. In *The Color Purple* Walker re-creates the reassuring emotional resolution of the fairy tale, in which all evil witches, ogres and rapacious wolves are not so much defeated as transformed when their need to be oppressive is removed. Evil, it is suggested, comes from the accumulation of attitudes inculcated over centuries of ritualised oppression which are the inevitable consequence of an act of colonisation, whether it be of a nation, a race, or a sex.

In *The Color Purple* Walker celebrates the unsung creativity of black women described in the title essay in *In Search Of Our Mothers' Gardens*, where she claims: 'These grandmothers and mothers of ours were not Saints, but Artists, driven to a numb and bleeding madness by the springs of creativity in them for which they had no release' (p. 232).

Walker argues that the outlets for her enslaved ancestors' suppressed creativity were found in the planting of flowers, the making of church prayer mats, or in the co-operative creation of a quilt like that in 'Everyday Use'. Interestingly, while 'waiting' for *The Color Purple* to take form in her imagination, Walker says she herself was occupied in making a quilt that 'began to grow' in the same way that the fictional letters grew and were pieced together. Quilting is the reworking of discarded fragments of material into something new, original and pleasing. As an attempt to make sense out of seemingly disconnected pieces, it is both creative and therapeutic. It is while quilting that Celie takes her first step towards sisterhood when, ashamed of her advice to Harpo to beat Sofia, her 'sin' is forgiven by Sofia who suggests they make a quilt together out of old curtains. Shug becomes a member of this sisterhood when, convalescing with Celie, she idly picks up a piece of cloth and asks how to sew it. Eventually all three sew the quilt, the pattern of which is significantly called 'Sister's Choice'. Mary Agnes is added to this mutually supportive group whose composite self-esteem grows to the point where they can openly laugh together at their erstwhile oppressors – men:

> Shug look at me and giggle.
> Then us laugh sure nuff. Then
> Squeak start to laugh. Then Sofia
> All us laugh and laugh. (p. 171)

The smothered giggle grows into open laughter because the assumed superiority of the men has been debunked, the source of their power demystified. As the sisters' lives unfold over thirty years of letter-writing, both bear witness to oppression. Celie's early despoliation by the stepfather she thought was her natural father, has conditioned her to expect nothing for herself. Her low self-esteem is emphasised by her husband, Mr---, who tells her, 'You black, you pore, you ugly, you a woman. Goddam, he say. You nothing at all' (p. 175). Mr---'s view of Celie sums up the societal disadvantages of black women, as well as revealing how Mr--- had unquestioningly accepted the white man's view of power. When he tells Harpo to beat Sofia into wifely submission, he could be a white man talking of slave management: 'You have to let 'em know you got the upper hand. Nothing can do that better than a good sound beating' (p. 34). Harpo's role model for marriage is of aggressive, selfish masculinity in the shape of Mr---, who, in spite of his boasting, had lacked the courage to defy his own father and marry Shug. Harpo's love for Sofia is genuine, but he is bewildered by her refusal to fit the mould of wife cast by Mr--- and filled by Celie. Gender socialisation has conditioned Harpo into believing that his manhood is measured by his mastery of his wife, even if this entails beating. He has no way of dealing with the living reality of Sofia who, having learned to defend herself from numerous siblings, fights back. She tells Celie, whom she pities, 'A girl child aint safe in a family of men' (p. 38). She and her sisters had fought for equal status with their brothers, whose respect and fierce loyalty they had won. In the depiction of Harpo's marriage to Sofia, Walker repudiates the gender stereotyping which has stifled the development of both sexes. Harpo is not designed, mentally or physically, for wife-beating. He loves to cook and clean the house, whereas Sofia, dressed in Harpo's work-pants, is a competent maintenance worker in the house, happily nailing roof-boards. In this gender role-reversal Harpo is initially ill at ease, comfort-eating to the extent that his belly expands to the proportion of pregnancy, but his discomfort results from his sense that he is failing to meet the social expectations of what a man should do and be.

Although *The Color Purple* is firmly rooted in the life of a rural black community, where lives are shaped by interpersonal relationships, the weight of white institutions is ever present. The town government is white, the law is white, Sofia is imprisoned because she attacks a racist Mayor, Squeak is raped when she tries to intercede on Sofia's behalf with the white Sheriff, to whom she is distantly related. This particular outrage is cleverly turned to black advantage, when Squeak outwits the Sheriff by using the same survival strategy as the rabbit in the tar baby tale. Sofia is released into the custody of the Mayor's wife because the authorities are convinced she will regard this as a harsher punishment than imprisonment. As the folklore collected by Hurston reveals, black survival had depended upon such stratagems, just as it had upon an accommodation of Christianity. Hurston, to whose writing Walker had turned for verification of authentic Voodoo rites, questioned the relevance of white Christianity to blacks, as does Walker in *The Color Purple*. The bulk of Celie's letters are addressed to God, as the only Being in whom she could confide the horror of her rape and the burden of her marriage of convenience to Mr---. When she discovers that her abuser was not her natural father, her joy is accompanied by a feeling that God had ignored her suffering. At the same time, Nettie's description of life as a missionary in Africa reveals an increasing doubt about the relevance of Christian teaching to the Olinka people. She begins to decorate her Olinkan home with examples of their art in preference to portraits of a white Jesus. The debate between Celie and Shug about the nature of a personal God who is gendered and white is the pivotal point in Celie's transformation from drudge into self-possessed woman. She no longer writes to God, but to Nettie: 'Anyhow, I say, the God I been praying to is a man. And act just like all the other men I know. Trifling, forgitful, lowdown' (p. 164). Shug argues that the inscription of male dominance in Christian religion is a man-made perversion: 'Man corrupt everything, say Shug . . . Soon as you think he everywhere, you think he God. But he aint' (p. 168). Shug's concept of God is genderless and joyful, a creator who delights in creation and wants all creatures to share the joy of the color purple.

One of the joys extolled by Shug, which Puritan abhorrence of the flesh had castigated as sinful, is sexual pleasure. Walker engages with the taboo subject of female sexual satisfaction in her account of Celie's experience of heterosexual sex which had brought pain, abuse, exploitation but no pleasure. In their lesbian relationship Celie learns from Shug that the female body is beautiful and can receive as well as give pleasure. In this relationship Walker challenges the compulsory heterosexuality which dominates in Western society, and the proprietary attitudes involved in monogamous pairings which give rise to sexual jealousy. Notions of 'ownership' in sexual pairings are shown to arouse destructive jealousy. Celie is jealous of Shug's last fling with a young male lover, and only when she conquers this jealousy does she salvage the joy of reciprocal love.

In all of Walker's challenges to patriarchal attitudes and the gender construction which underpins these in *The Color Purple*, conflict is resolved as it is in fairy-tales. A facile solution to gender differentiation is offered in Celie's pants-making, which are comfortable because they are designed to fit everybody, but the truly fabulous element in *The Color Purple*, with its incredibly happy ending, is embodied in the transformations undergone by the characters. With the exception of Sofia, each one enters the story as a stereotype and leaves completely transformed. The agent for these miraculous changes is Shug Avery, who acts as bringer of light and health, yet she too undergoes a change, not in herself so much as in how she is perceived by others. She first enters Celie's life as a photograph, in which she is associated with the Biblical 'scarlet woman', a notion emphasised by the preacher who refers to her as 'slut, hussy, heifer and streetcleaner' (p. 60). Those who love her refer to her as 'Queen Honeybee', purveyor of life and sweetness, captured in her name 'Shug' for sugar. Always associated with the royal colour purple, she is beautiful and 'black as any sloe' (p. 19). She is not a promiscuous flirt, but a woman disappointed in a lover too weak to withstand parental pressure to marry her. As she evolves in the novel, Shug takes on deeper resonances of earth-mother and good fairy. Her given name was Lillie, a possible diminutive of the Black Lillith who pre-dated Eve as the mythical first wife of Adam. Her essential femaleness is emphasised in her large Memphis house, pink and full of elephants and turtles, suggesting her harmonious spiritual accord with the natural world. Her bed is round, and her dream is to build a grand gyrocentric house, an elaboration of Nettie's home with the Olinkas. Shug loves men and women with equal ardour, and functions in the novel as a guide and mentor to those whose capacity for love, of either self or others, is stunted by society. She encourages Mary Agnes to sing and discard the name 'Squeak', and Celie to find economic independence as the proprietor of the unlikely 'Folkpants Unlimited'. We might question the relevance of a capitalist enterprise as a suitable rejection of patriarchal society, but cannot refute that independence allows Celie to say, 'I am so happy. I got love, I got money, friends and time' (p. 183). Fortified with these new advantages, she leaves Mr---, the lazy, tyrannical husband, whose ability to command Shug's love is never explained, not even in sexual terms, as he seems to be unaware of how to arouse female desire. With Shug's temporary absence from their lives, Mr--- and Celie gradually form a loving relationship, cemented by their mutual love for Shug, and gradually Mr--- loses his ogreish aspect to become polite, considerate and in his own eyes a 'natural' man for the first time in his adult life. By this, we assume he means he is freed from gender assumptions, as he takes up the designing and sewing of shirts to accompany Celie's pants. Celie addresses him as Albert, and as they begin to talk, she concludes: 'Mr--- seem to be the only one understand my feelings' (p. 220). This is barely credible.

Harpo is also freed from the constraints of male gender construction to live as he wishes, finding happiness in housework and childcare. Only Sofia does not undergo a fundamental change. She had been strong in her sisterhood when she married Harpo: 'Sister' husband stand up with Harpo. Other sister sneak away from home and stand up with Sofia. Another sister came to hold the baby' (p. 32). Sofia can learn nothing from Shug, and possesses the Amazonian spirit which Angelou displays in her autobiographical self for, like Angelou, Sofia refuses to accept victim status. Even in the Mayor's household, which she dominates as Mammy to the daughter, she is the antithesis of the fictional, ever-loving black Mammy. She never professes love for Eleanor Jane, to whose offspring she also displays indifference. Sofia never denies that she would have preferred to live with and care for her own children. The servant/mistress roles of Sofia and Eleanor Jane are subtly reversed by Walker, giving power to Sofia in spite of her lack of freedom. In an episode exposing the ludicrousness of racism, the wife, whom Sofia had taught to drive, offers to drive Sofia to visit her children but, mindful of attitudes, insists that Sofia sits in the back of the car. Thus, to all intents and purposes, the white woman acts as chauffeuse to the black. Through Sofia, Walker explodes the comfortable white myth that black women adored their white employers and enjoyed serving them.

The novel concludes with resolution of all tensions, and the harmonious living together of all participants, including Nettie and Celie's 'lost' children. Although the issues addressed are firmly rooted in experience, this is not realist fiction. Events are manipulated to fashion an ideal world, where death is not allowed to obtrude, except the fortuitous one of Celie's stepfather that transforms her into an heiress. Not only has Celie discovered her Princess Charming, but she is rewarded with the pot of gold too. Potential tragedy is averted when the ship carrying Nettie back to America, reported sunk, returns safely. This report of possible death which seems to have no narrative purpose is explicable only if Walker intends to emphasise a fairy-tale 'happy ending'. This I believe is so. Nothing short of magic could have operated to enable Nettie to become mother to Celie's children, and wife to the saintly Samuel. However, incredible narrative coincidences characterise the resolution rather than the evolution of the fiction. Celie's suffering is not diminished by the happy ending, nor is the exposure of colonial despolation described in Nettie's letters. Some critics question the need for Nettie's letters at all, and point to the difference in language and experience they contain as a disuniting factor. This criticism is easily refuted by reference to the fact that the juxtaposition of the African and American worlds is a deliberate underlining of Walker's themes. These intercontinental letters serve to illustrate the connection between colonialisation and American racism, and also debunk the eulogising belief that everything African is intrinsically laudable.

Celie's letters, couched in the idiom of her rural language, move from bewildered ignorance to lively reportage of experiences through which she gains self-knowledge and esteem. In contrast, the formal, restrained language of Nettie's letters reflects her life with educated black missionaries. Even Nettie's letters, when rearranged chronologically, reveal the educative influence of Corinne and Samuel. Her first letter bears the traces of the black language of her childhood: 'when I left you all's house . . . when we was well out of sight . . . but my bundles was heavy . . . After while . . .' (p. 107). With the passage of years, Nettie's language becomes more grammatically correct and her voice takes on the tones of a patient educator. She explains to Celie, and the reader, that the supposed 'Dark' Continent had supported great civilisations, and that the Egyptians, as well as many Biblical characters, were black. Nettie expresses disquiet about missionary work when she realises that Africa had been plundered by colonial masters. Olinkan art had been stolen and displayed in European museums, and their oppression was ongoing under capitalistic concerns. At the same time Nettie is horrified at the barbarity of clitoridectomy, and the sexist discrimination inherent in tribal patriarchy. This particular aspect of African culture becomes the focus in Walker's last powerful novel, *Possessing The Secret Of Joy*,[14] published in 1992. Coming nine years after *The Color Purple*, this searing novel shows how Walker continues to explore areas of female experience which she recognises as oppressive. Nettie observes about Olinkan gender divisions that 'A girl is nothing to herself, only to her husband can she become something' (p. 132). Their sexism, she realises, is no different in origin from the racism the Olinkas encountered as a people. Through Nettie's letters Walker holds the African and American worlds in a productive tension. Each one illuminates the other, and eventually join in the miraculous reuniting of the sisters and their families. The concept of a large, intergenerational, genderless, harmonious family is Walker's vision of a strife-free world.

This marks a definite movement away from the public to the

privately political, and many readers might feel that Walker's dream places too much dependence on the assumed goodness of humanity. Her prefatory remarks to *Living By The Word*, published in 1988, describe this collection of essays as 'a map of my journeys and discoveries'. These 'journeys and discoveries' transcend the physical and are as much about the inner exploration of Walker's own self as records of her experiences as a much-travelled international writer and philosopher. In this writing she draws increasingly upon personal, spiritual reserves which might create a distance between herself and a readership who have come to expect from her a writing more obviously rooted in black life. Her concerns still spring from her people's American history, but have enlarged to become global. The essays range from an account of her denial of access to an imprisoned woman, Dessie Woods, to worrying over the neuroticism of a lonely horse. Her overriding concern is for the planet's survival in the Nuclear Age, and is the logical extension for a writer whose philosophy is that 'everything is divine'. The rigorous reassessment of herself, her life and her creative process, has led Walker away from realist fiction, ever deeper into magic realism 'away from sociology, away from the writing of explanation and statistics and further into mystery, into poetry and into prophesy' (*In Search Of*, p. 8). She has taken upon herself the role of prophetess as a natural extension of liberation. In 'Breaking Chains' she addresses her admitted homophobia, and defends the right of black women to write of anything they please, lesbianism included. In an effort to practise the generosity of spirit without which her New World will not exist, she describes how she re-examined her relation to the physical world. The result is vegetarianism, ecological awareness, and a continued condemnation of political oppression wherever she sees it. *Living By the Word* and *In Search Of Our Mothers' Gardens* document these concerns, and her novel, *The Temple of my Familiar*, attempts to conceptualise this philosophy in fiction. In this work, which she describes as a 'Romance', she abandons the realist fiction mode of her earlier work and moves into a visionary world inhabited in part by fictional characters from *The Color Purple*. Having built previous fictions on her belief that only with love can humanity survive, she attempts to realise a fictive world where this is universally practised. Believing that a gendered society has given rise to a gendered Divinity, in *The Temple* Walker deposes the male God questioned by Celie and Shug in favour of a non-hierarchical, genderless originator:

'The God discovered on one's own speaks nothing of turning the other cheek. Of rendering unto Caesar. But only of beauty and greatness of the earth, the universe, the cosmos' (p. 143).

In a fiction which ambitiously spans 500,000 years Walker offers a complete revision of the history of the human race. This is possible through the creation of Lissie, a woman who can remember a series of reincarnations going back to the dawn of time. Obviously speculative, this novel is a magical reinterpretation of how men had gained dominance in human affairs. Like *The Color Purple*, it ends with a fairy-tale happiness of mutual love between previously antipathetic men and women.

The quilting together of narrative strands within a structure where linear time is disrupted to create a sense of holistic and unbroken experience, is a sophisticated development of the technique used in *The Color Purple*, which began in realist fiction but was resolved by hopeful magic realism. The elements of Romance which gather to resolve Celie's story are not peripheral but central in *The Temple*. The cyclical, unbroken stream of life embodied in Lissie's reincarnations allows Walker to speculate upon an unrecorded history in which women were revered because of their spiritual kinship with the natural world:

> Our mothers taught us that in the old, old days, when they were their grandmothers and their grandmothers were old – for we are our grandmothers, you understand, only with lots of new and different things added – only women had been priests. (*Temple*, p. 47)

Lissie's memories of recorded and pre-history are not revealed chronologically, but piecemeal, culminating in a final taped message recorded before her most recent 'death', in which she remembers the Garden of Eden. Lissie's life stories include an account of how she and her mother were sold into slavery as an act of revenge by men whose original mother-worship had been destroyed. According to Lissie, African men had displaced women as priests because they were jealous of their power, and 'That is why, the ultimate curse against Africa/Mother/Goddess – motherfucker – is still in the language' (p. 63).

Within an encompassing vision of a spirituality which Walker believes is still there but untapped in an age of imperialism and commercialism, she sets in motion characters who had lost their sense of direction in the post-sixties years. She focuses on a teacher of history, Suwelo, who encounters the mysterious Lissie when he inherits his uncle's house. Suwelo stands as living demonstration of the failure of the 1960s to alter men's sexist attitudes. He also represents the psychic dis-ease seen by Walker as the inevitable consequence of a loss of contact with an ancestry whose existence was governed by their knowledge that they were merely part of, and not the purpose of, creation. In 'Lulls' in *In Search Of*, she laments that 'The bond of black kinship – so sturdy, so resilient, – has finally been broken in the cities of the North' (p. 195), destroyed by their entry into a man-made environment which suppresses the natural. It is no accident that in Suwelo Walker gives us a male teacher of history, which he persists in teaching not only from a male but from a white perspective. Walker's own experience of teaching illiterate black women about a history they had been taught to regard with shame, had made her aware of the need to revise that account of events from which women had been written out by white men. Walker is disillusioned by the failure of the post-sixties generation of men like Suwelo, whom she sees as having failed women:

> For all their activities and political development during the sixties, all their understanding of the pervasiveness of oppression, for most men, the preferred place for women had remained at home; the preferred position for women, wherever they were, supine. (*Temple*, p. 28)

Fossilised within a false reading of the past, Suwelo's marriage to Celie's granddaughter cannot flourish because he cannot rid himself of the generations of white oppression which he perpetuates in his teaching. An alternative vision of history is provided by the glittering pop-guitarist Arveyda, whose artistic creativity is channelled into the singing of unrecorded folk-history, and whose marriage is fulfilling. He with his wife Carlotta and her mother Zede, who had made their living making and selling traditional feathered Indian capes, has not rejected a cultural past which continues to give spiritual nourishment.

The scenario for Suwelo's struggle to break the chains of white cultural colonisation is established in the first of the six parts of the novel. Here the main actors in the story are introduced, with no authorial direction about their interconnection which is only tantalisingly revealed as the narrative unfolds. Readers' expectations of a traditional linear plot involving the sympathetic following of a main protagonist are completely and deliberately disrupted. Such an empirical and phallocentric interpretation of human existence would not be compatible with Walker's gyrocentric vision. As in life, where each individual lives a personal 'history' which cannot be separated from the totality of human experience, so Walker's characters enter the narrative to tell their stories, then disappear to make way for others. The web of narrative is woven from a collection of voices, none of which is allowed to predominate, drawing the reader ever deeper into an imagined past. Walker compels the reader to interrogate and suspend all previous assumptions about narrative structure, and demands an active attention. This process enables the reader to internalise the connection between Zede's and Lissie's stories. Zede is living evidence of the oral history of her South American people, and Lissie's stories describe the subversion and suppression of that culture under a Western, capitalistic, patriarchal order which is depicted as being as spiritually destructive for men as it is for women. The African character Ola in *The Temple* is shown to die because he cannot accept the oppressive nature of his country's patriarchal government, and Zede's lover, Jesus, who is appalled at man's despoliation of the world, suffers a similar fate. Jesus' 'bleeding' when trees were cut occurs because his physical self is still spiritually connected with the rest of the created world, and his essence had not suffered the destructive division of separation. Walker suggests that this spiritual separation of humanity from Nature led to a destructive polarisation in social organisations, of which the construction of gender division is one. That Jesus' essence was as much female as male is seen in his guarding in his village of three stones, which when arranged in a pyramid or triangle is women's sign for peace.

Of paramount importance in Walker's novel is the stress she lays upon the responsibility of the artist, whether male or female, to speak out loudly in defiance against oppression. On artists, Arveyda says, 'fell the responsibility of uniting the world' (p. 122). Arveyda recognises this to be an awesome task, but one he feels capable of fulfilling. One can assume that in writing this novel, Walker felt in the same way. Walker's placing of this responsibility for change on the shoulders of artists, is reminiscent of that carried by the Harlem writers, except her interpretation of that duty widens it from a racial to a universal one. She rejects any idea of an exclusivity in this process in her belief that creativity is not centred in a coterie of artists – Locke's 'talented tenth' – but in every single human being, each of whom possesses a unique creativity. Her essay on the unrecognised creativity of her female ancestors emphasises her conviction that men have prioritised their own at the expense and neglect of women's, and have created a canon and an aesthetic which is diminished in the process. In the case of Suwelo, his refusal to acknowledge the gender domination in the history he teaches, has so suppressed his own capacity for imaginative thought that he cannot attempt revision: 'But he did not want to change the way he thought of Africa. Besides, when he wanted insight into Africa he'd read a man' (p. 172). Suwelo could not accommodate the change in his wife after her visit to Africa, for this would entail a revision in attitudes for which he had lost the aptitude. The capacity for a spiritual awareness which Suwelo had allowed to be stifled is only released in *The Temple* when characters tune into and listen to the natural world. Walker suggests in this fiction that humanity has been educated out of that facility, exemplified in the sterility of the propagation of a body of knowledge such as Suwelo was teaching. A spell as a university lecturer leaves the African Ola convinced that human progress is only made when people learn to 'love each other freely, regardless of tribe' (p. 185). In her examination of gender division Walker concludes that the roots of division are the same as the 'otherness' recognised by Ola in tribal divisions.

To reinforce the message that pre-historical African spirituality survives, and is perpetuated in the culture of women, Walker introduces the diaries of a 100-year-old white woman, which record the story of M'Sukta. The sole survivor of a destroyed tribe, M'Sukta lives in the Natural History Museum, endlessly weaving the traditional cloth of her people, knowing that her tribe's spirit survives so long as the cloth is woven. That Walker is committed to the continued survival of black culture is evident in all that she has written, but she has no desire to see this become atrophied like M'Sukta's, or to be regarded as a separate artefact as Dee had seen the quilt in 'Everyday Use'. Her wish is that the informing spirituality of her people's culture will survive to be *lived* and not be pigeonholed into the realm of academic or social history. Her fear that the women's culture which has been so assiduously reclaimed in recent years is in danger of becoming a middle-class ghetto is expressed in her treatment of Suwelo's wife, Fanny. After her African sojourn has opened her eyes to the emptiness of her marriage, Fanny not only divorces Suwelo, she disengages from a women's studies course, to become a masseuse, believing that physical, rather than intellectual, contact is the true source of healing. The unenlightened atmosphere of racism and sexism in the university is described by Fanny in her explanation to Suwelo: 'in the administration office at the college I had to explain about blacks; to you and the other men I had to explain about women' (p. 315). The blind divisiveness of a perception governed by difference, so powerfully argued in Audre Lorde's essays, is conveyed in Lissie's posthumous message to Suwelo. In this, she confesses that in past lives she had existed as a white man, and as a lion. This illustration of the commonality of spirit in all things reinforces Walker's message that we all need 'parent knowledge', rather than the knowledge gained from formal education. Carlotta, whose affair with Suwelo eventually brings his and Arveyda's worlds together, sums up this attitude. Talking of universities, she asks: 'Who needs more of the kind of people colleges produce? They're all consumers really. No matter what they study. What they're successful at is shopping' (p. 370).

Walker is consistent in this novel in her repetition of her belief that spiritual health is possible for all who listen to ancestral voices. The industrial Western world, she says, has closed its ears firmly to these voices. She endorses the view of artistic responsibility to which Arveyda gives utterance and subscribes to his definition of the artist as messenger

The deliberate intertextuality of *The Temple* and *The Color Purple* lies not only in the issues raised and explored but also in the continued presence of Celie and Shug, whose family history and development from where *The Color Purple* ends, is sketched in. In her most recent novel, *Possessing the Secret of Joy*, intertextuality is intensified in that the Tashi who appears in *The Color Purple* is the protagonist, although the reader does not need knowledge of Tashi's fictive past to understand her situation. In her address to the reader in *Possessing the Secret* Walker says: 'Though obviously connected, *Possessing the Secret of Joy* is not a sequel to either *The Color Purple* or *The Temple of my Familiar*', but a picking up of 'those characters and events that refused to leave my mind. Or my spirit.' The danger of an undermining of the artistic integrity of the single text is obviated by Walker in *The Temple*, in that she gives a brief recapitulation of Celie and Shug's previous story, and the story of Tashi in *Possessing the Secret* is firmly rooted in female experience in the Africa and America and Europe of today. Walker's transportation of characters between fictions gives reader satisfaction in that she supplies further answers to questions raised. In *The Temple* we learn that Shug and Celie, like Morrison's ancestor figure Baby Suggs in *Beloved*, have continued their spiritual journey by forming a church, in a tradition of 'long standing among Black women'. Shug and Celie have become the ancestor figures in Walker's fictional world, in their continued presence in the writer's consciousness, and Tashi is the symbol of how far from being won is the battle against female subordination. Walker's spiritual identification with her characters is so complete that she can say, 'Certainly I recognise Tashi as my sister'.

For a reader familiar with the span and evolution in Walker's writing the dynastic development of female characters is logical and convincing, although I feel that her early and later fictions might appeal separately and differently to different readerships. As Walker has moved continually deeper into the envisioned world of her own creation her appeal might be increasingly to those initiated by acquaintance with all her other writing. I think that the incorporation of Shug, Celie and their descendants must puzzle those who come to this novel as a fresh experience and complicate understanding of what is a very complex narrative. *The Temple* demands a high level of reader sophistication to handle the diversity of characters, and their interrelationships, as well as shifts in time and location. Experimental in form and content, this novel deliberately does not allow the reader to settle into any comfortable relationship with any of the established novelistic conventions. It offers a challenge to many assumptions that lie beneath critical evaluation, and I feel it is best approached from a feminist critical stance. As a revision of history from a womanist perspective it is both compelling and stimulating. A warning about unsympathetic interpretation, whether it be from a male or a white viewpoint, is prefigured in 'Saving the life that is your own', where she talks of the occupational hazard faced by artists, and here it is safe to assume she is thinking particularly of black women, whose models are in short supply:

> Deadlier still to the artist who lacks models is the curse of ridicule, the bringing to bear on an artist's best work, especially his or her most original, most strikingly deviant, only a fund of ignorance, and the presumption that, as an artist's critic, one's judgement is free of the restrictions imposed by prejudice, and is well-informed, indeed, about all the art in the world that really matters. (*In Search Of*, p. 4)

This would have served as answer to the hostile reviews *The Temple* received in the British press. This novel is original, is strikingly deviant, and I cannot presume to approach it without the prejudicial weight of my own critical and cultural assumptions. It is, nevertheless, consistent in its development of Walker's initial use of her immense talent as a storyteller to celebrate the beauty and uniqueness of black women which have been enlarged to encompass all. It is an arresting fiction in which Walker's power as a storyteller is as compelling as ever. Her characters stir the imagination, her situations startle the reader out of complacency. Certainly it demands and rewards a Jamesian 'careful perusal' of attention. The issues of racism, sexism and spirituality, though not exclusive to Walker, are certainly raised in a unique manner, and as befits Romance, are resolved in harmonious forgiveness. Suwelo's reward for breaking traditional modes of thought is to live as Shug's Mr--- does, in an atmosphere of non-competitive, non-proprietorial comfort with all of those with whom he had been previously out of spiritual contact.

The Temple exemplifies Walker's belief that involvement in struggle is the source of creativity and that if an artist refuses commitment then she will never discover 'Some kind of larger freedom'. Walker's own 'larger freedom' has enabled her to engage more and more with areas of human experience which have gone unrecorded or undiscussed, and her success as a writer means that she is heard by more and more people. In *Possessing the Secret of Joy* she dares to discuss the genital mutilation of clitoridectomy. She tells the reader:

> It is estimated that from ninety to one hundred million women and girls living today in African, Far Eastern and Middle Eastern countries have been genitally mutilated. Recent articles in the media have reported on the growing practice of 'female circumcision' in the United States and Europe, among immigrants from countries where it is part of the culture. (p. 266)

The horror of such a revelation comes in Walker's afterword to her novel, and is more effective there because it shocks the reader into an awareness that the hideousness of Tashi's fictional experience is a daily occurrence for some women today.

Possessing the Secret of Joy sees Walker returning to a realist mode in fiction: to have treated this subject in any other way would have been unthinkable. Even just *reading* the unelaborated, factual description of the physical consequences of clitoridectomy makes the female reader writhe in imagined pain: 'There were premenstrual cramps; cramps caused by the near impossibility of flow passing through so tiny an aperture as M'Lissa had left, after fastening together the raw sides of Tashi's vagina with a couple of thorns' (p. 62).

The enormity of the 'cleaning out' of the female genitals, the subsequent sewing up, and the supposed 'success' when the husband painfully manages penetration, is not left to reader imagination. And yet, although the subject-matter is painful, the manner and style of the narrative is not. This novel is less discursive, more economic and concentrated than any of her previous novels, in its focus upon one issue and the consequences it had for a woman and her close family. Once again the narrative is created by the weaving of a non-chronological relation of events in three continents, Africa, America and Europe, as told by different participants in Tashi's tragic story. The voices are relayed as letters, confessional statements to the psychiatrist – first supposedly to Carl Jung in Switzerland, then to a black woman psychiatrist in America – or as testimony in the court case in which Tashi is accused and found guilty of murder. Her intended (but not actual) victim was the old African woman M'Lissa, who had performed the genital operation on Tashi and whose previous bungling of the same surgery had killed Tashi's sister. Tashi was bent on revenge against this old woman whom she also holds responsible for her own life of physical pain and the emotional pain caused by her husband's affair with a Frenchwoman. Tashi accepts responsibility for M'Lissa's death, and is executed in Africa where her supposed crime had taken place, welcoming release from a life which had been a torment.

It is on her return to Africa that Tashi, whose American name 'Evelyn' was symptomatic of her fractured life and murdered capacity for sexual pleasure, realises in her conversations with M'Lissa that both she and her mutilator had been pawns in a male game of power. In her previous writing Walker has explored the consequences of her ancestors' enslavement, and in *Possessing the Secret of Joy* she identifies the source of racial and gender oppression as being the same: 'I recognised the connection between mutilation and enslavement that is at the root of the domination of women in the world' (p. 131). In her story of Tashi's life Walker shows that M'Lissa and Tashi had been manipulated in a political game, to fulfil their male political leader's urging that the customs and culture of their tribe should be continued as a sign of their independence from colonial masters. Tashi's scarification described in *The Color Purple* had been willingly undergone by Tashi as a way of maintaining a threatened tribal identity, but this is as nothing compared to sexual mutilation. Clearly, whilst Walker's writing, like Hurston's, Morrison's, Lorde's and Marshall's, stresses the Afro-American need to celebrate their African culture, this is one part of that tribal culture which is seen as a hideous barbarity, and one she would not want continued. Walker is at pains to tell the reader that this is not a feature of African culture alone, and comments that Christianity had not spoken out against it. In her last communication from the condemned cell, to the long-dead mistress of her husband, Tashi-Evelyn writes:

> They circumcised women, little girls, in Jesus' time. Did he know? Did the subject anger or embarrass him? Did the early church erase the record? Jesus himself was circumcised; perhaps he thought only the cutting done to him was done to women, and therefore, as he survived, it was all right. (p. 260)

That the circumcision of the male in some cultures on the grounds of hygiene, which did nothing to impair male sexual pleasure, could not compare to the removal of the female clitoris, is self-evident. Walker points out that clitoridectomy is another form of the social control of women by men. In case any white European women have forgotten, she reminds them that such mutilation was practised in Victoria's Britain as a 'cure' for female hysteria. The denial by men to women of masturbatory pleasure is one way of denying them sexual autonomy and preserving their own.

Clitoridectomy is the removal of women's 'secret of joy' and the connection between this as an act of oppression against women as monstrous as the subjugation of a people because they are black, is made in the epigraph to the text: 'There are those who believe Black people possess the secret of joy, and it is this that will sustain them through any spiritual or moral or physical devastation'. At the end of *Possessing the Secret of Joy* Walker defines this secret in a particular and political way. In a message which articulates her stand against female circumcision, as well as sexual and racial oppression, she tells the reader in block letters that '*RESISTANCE* IS THE SECRET OF JOY!'

In this fiction Walker takes as material how sexual practice is related to social control and points to the reverberating consequences of interference with sexuality. One consequence of the sewing up of the female genitalia was that men practised anal sex with their female partners. Walker chillingly suggests that we should ponder this when considering the particularly rampant spreading of AIDS in some of the African countries. Her concerns as a writer have not been limited to the racial politics in America, but have widened, although her preoccupations as a writer are still clearly focused in her female protagonists. She writes about women in whose continued resistance to oppression, of which her writing is a part, lies a hope for human improvement. Her artistic creed, expressed by Arveyda in *The Temple*, is that 'the pain he brought to others and to himself – so poorly concealed in the information delivered – would lead not to destruction, but to transformation' (*Temple*, p. 122). Walker's writing addresses those areas of life in which transformation is needed, and in this she does not speak only to black women.

Conclusion

> Thematically and stylistically, the tone of the fiction of the early eighties communicates the sense that women of color can no longer be perceived as marginal to the empowerment of all American women and an understanding of their reality and imagination is essential to the process of change that the entire society must undergo in order to transform itself.[1]

Barbara Christian's claim for the power of black women as a force for change is not an empty one. Today the writing of black women can no longer be considered as marginal either to the struggles of all women, black or white, or to the American literary canon. The award to Toni Morrison of the 1993 Nobel Prize for Literature is an acclamation of her tremendous talent as a writer. It also marks a recognition that the black woman as a writer has moved from the margins to the very centre of world literature. The empty space where Toni Morrison had listened in vain to hear 'the interior life' of the female has been amply filled by a variety of voices from women of colour. Fifty years separate the births of Zora Neale Hurston and Alice Walker, in which short space of time black women writers in America speak loud and clear to all prepared to listen. The often ambiguous but undoubtedly individual voice of Hurston has been joined by those of such as Marshall, Lorde, Angelou, Morrison and Walker, each of whom has taken up and amplified issues with which Hurston had engaged. Each one has her own distinctive tone, manner or modulation, but they have an agenda in common, although their prioritisation of issues in that agenda may be different. In spite of the disparity in their economic, educational, cultural and familial circumstances as well as geographic locations, there is a unity in their efforts to speak about, to and for, women. Of course they speak as black women, for whom the construct of gender has been exacerbated by race, but in their constant reaffirmation of the feminine principle which has been denied or subdued in our social organisation, they speak for white women too.

Beginning as *black* women, they have interrogated the notions of gender by which women have been subordinated and silenced. Fixed notions about the woman's role as mother, or indeed the need for a woman to be a mother at all, have been investigated from a variety of angles by these writers. In this they have dared to explore the ambiguities of female sexuality and in so doing they have expressed the previously inexpressible: the taboo facts in female experience which can encompass lesbianism, female rape and incest. In a sustained attack upon those literary stereotypes which were reinforcements of the negative socialisation of black women, they have succeeded in foregrounding women in general, bringing them out of the margins into the mainstream of life and literature. This they have done by giving us women-centred novels and essays, enabling an expression of the world as it is perceived by the female. As black Americans they have all begun with a consciousness of racial oppression which they have not been content merely to describe, but in their often painful probing of experience for meaning have offered an explanation of the human motivation which lies beneath any attempts to define and so control any 'other' which is perceived as 'different'. In their depiction of male/female relationships they clearly expose the injustice to women of sexism, yet whilst women-loving, they are not men-hating, but urge a reassessment of the relation between the sexes based upon the idea of sharing rather than domination. The inscription of power within any relationship is a source of dis-ease, and the notion of masculine dominance, as demonstrated in the writing of many black women, has been achieved by the stifling of the feminine within the male. In his essay 'The Master's pieces', Louis H. Gates Jr tells of how moved he was by a paper, 'Mama's Baby, Papa's Maybe', given at Cornell University by Hortense Spillers, the black feminist critic. One sentence from that paper sums up the importance of this reassessment: 'It is the heritage of the *mother* that the Afro-American male must regain as an aspect of his own personhood – the power of "yes" to the "female" within'.[2]

The search for self-definition beyond those imposed by race or gender has enabled those writers whose work I have examined to identify a matrilineal source of strength and joy, which they celebrate in the ancestral mothers who inhabit their fictions. The tapping into the spirituality of African foremothers is demonstrated as an essential ingredient in the recognition of communal identity, without which self-esteem does not flourish. Each of these writers has identified a need to reclaim and perpetuate their distinctive black cultural heritage as a source of pride and beauty. The pioneering work done by Hurston in this area has been capitalised upon by those writers who came later, in whose work is incorporated the myths, magic, music and stories of illiterate and enslaved ancestors. This in itself fills another empty space in the canon, where the voice of the poor and underprivileged of both genders should be, for each of these women has taken these people as subject. Their protagonists have been in the main drawn from the ranks of the disadvantaged, and when economic improvement has made these fictive characters affluent, their creators have warned of the danger in embracing such capitalist affluence at the expense of losing cultural identity. However, this is not to suggest that they have been positing an acceptance of economic disadvantage as a way to preserve integrity: the ghetto is never depicted as inviting, but a warning is given about what can be lost in the climb out. It seems to me that what are being stressed in their writing are all those distinctive cultural elements which black people can bring to the definition of what it *is* to be American, to emphasise the multi-cultural richness which racism denies.

Pride in their blackness is no greater than delight in their femaleness, both of which are seen to be causes for celebration, and in these shared preoccupations they can be seen as parts in a continuum of inherited black culture. The delight in wordplay and the power of language which is attested to in the oral folklore collected by Hurston has lost none of its vividness in its translation into the printed word. First and foremost, each of these writers is a skilled wordsmith and consummate teller of stories. However, the power of language to transform as well as entertain is exercised, for their texts emanate from lived experience, however imaginatively portrayed. They take creativity seriously, and none views nor portrays life from an ivory tower. Their serious interrogation of racial and sexual politics is not confined to the lonely act of writing, nor do they see these issues as being separable from the ideological, territorial or religious struggles on the world stage. Toni Morrison does not see her function as novelist and academic as exclusive or non-political. In the collection of essays on the Anita Hill/Clarence Thomas investigation which she edited, she brings together the voices of academics from different disciplines, sexes and races as evidence that the American academia was not suffering from 'paralysis' or 'intimidation'. Refusing to accept any idea that the academic and the artist had no place in the political, she says in her introductory essay: 'In matters of race and gender, it is now possible and necessary, as it seemed never to have been before, to speak about these matters without the barriers, the silences, the embarrassing gaps in discourse'.[3]

Audre Lorde has warned of the danger of keeping silent, whether it be about racism, sexism or homophobia, acknowledging the power of language which lies in the power of naming. With a refreshing curiosity these writers have looked again at the world, in which they see everything as sacred but nothing as sacrosanct; there are no 'givens' which go unchallenged, whether it be in custom or religion. Alice Walker's latest fiction on female genital mutilation is an instance of this and is evidence of the potential for transformation which Barbara Christian identifies as the power of black women writers. This power, I feel, is in direct relation to the reader's recognition of the hitherto sensed but unspoken: the holes in discourse where women's voices should have been. Because of this, a feminist reading of their texts is productive. They *do* interrogate the canon, they *do* contribute to an existing literary tradition in women's literature, and they *do* offer a distinctive female voice.

As writers they have inherited a tradition of protest against injustice which was a strong factor in both black oral culture and the early writing of the newly literate black women in the nineteenth century. They have taken the strands of that culture and given them extra strength and definition, and these they have melded into the literary models already existing in the dominant white culture. In this process they have enriched and diversified existing form and expression, by the inventiveness of their language and imagination. Not content with the realist mode of fiction they have, in their move into magic realism, found new ways to translate the female experience into fiction. They have reinterpreted history in their defiant rejection of linear narrative time, and have interrogated assumptions about the nature of women by giving answers to Freud's question about 'what did women really want?'. All of these are sound reasons in answer to the question with which I began, 'Why do white students enjoy the writing by black American women?' In final answer to my other question about why do we, as white teachers, want to teach these works, I will endorse what Louis H. Gates Jr says about his own reasons:

> My task, as I see it, is to help guarantee that black and so-called Third World literature is taught to black and Third World and white students by black and Third World and white professors in heretofore white mainstream departments of literature, and to train students to think, to read, to write clearly, to expose false uses of language, fraudulent claims, and muddled arguments, propaganda, and vicious lies . . .[4]

If it's good enough for Louis H. Gates, it's good enough for me.

Notes

Introduction

1. Claudia Tate (ed.), *Black Women Writers at Work* (Harpenden, Oldcastle Books, 1985) (p. 121).
2. Barbara Smith, 'Towards a black feminist criticism', in J. Newton & D. Rosenfelt (eds), *Feminist Criticism and Social Change* (New York, Methuen, 1985).
3. Elaine Showalter, 'Review essay: Literary criticism', in *Signs* (Winter, 1975).
4. Elaine Showalter, *Sister's Choice: Tradition and change in American women's writing* (Oxford, Clarendon Press, 1991).
5. Michèle Barrett, *Women's Oppression Today* (London, Verso, 1980).
6. Hélène Cixous, 'The laugh of the Medusa', in Marks E. & de Courtivron, *New French Feminisms* (Brighton, Harvester Press, 1981), p. 257.
7. *op. cit.*, p. 157.
8. bell hooks, *Ain't I a Woman: Black women and feminism* (Boston, 1982).
9. J. Newton & D. Rosenfelt (eds), *Feminist Criticism and Social Change* (New York, Methuen, 1985), p. xvii.
10. Elizabeth Meese & Alice Parker (eds), *The Difference Within: Feminism and critical theory* (Philadelphia, John Benjamins Publishing Company, 1989).
11. Barbara Christian, 'Trajectories of self-definition', in Marjorie Pryse & Hortense Spillers (eds), *Conjuring: Black women, fiction, and literary tradition* (Bloomington, Indiana University Press, 1985).
12. Alice Walker, *In Search of Our Mothers' Gardens* (London, Women's Press, 1984).
13. Paul Lauter, 'Race and gender in the shaping of the American literary canon: a case study from the twenties' in J. Newton and D. Rosenfelt (eds), *Feminist Criticism and Social Change* (New York, Methuen, 1985), pp. 19–45.
14. Elaine Showalter, *op. cit.*, p. 6.
15. Virginia Woolf, *A Room of One's Own* (Harmondsworth, Penguin, 1945).
16. Houston A. Baker Jr, 'When Lindbergh slept with Bessie Smith', in Meese & Parker, *op. cit.*, p. 94.

17. Pryse & Spillers, *op. cit.*, p. 3.

18. Edith Wharton, *The House of Mirth* (London, Penguin, 1982). ◾

Chapter 1

1. Selwyn R. Cudjoe, 'Maya Angelou and the autobiographical statement', in Mari Evans (ed.), *Black Women Writers* (London, Pluto Press, 1985), p. 6.

2. Stephen Butterfield, *Black Autobiography in America* (Amherst, University of Massachusetts Press, 1976), p. 12.

3. Former slaves were interviewed by the WPAF (Works Progress Administration Federal) Writers Project. Useful examples are to be found in Dorothy Sterling (ed.), *We Are Your Sisters* (Ontario, Penguin, 1984).

4. Marjorie Pryse, 'Zora Neale Hurston, Alice Walker, and the "Ancient Power" of Black Women', in Marjorie Pryse & Hortense Spillers (eds), *Conjuring: Black women, fiction and literary tradition* (Indiana University Press, 1985), p. 5.

5. Harriet Jacobs, *Incidents in the Life of a Slave Girl Written by Herself*, edited by L. Maria Child (Boston, 1861).

6. Harriet Beecher Stowe, *Uncle Tom's Cabin* (Boston, 1851).

7. Stephen Butterfield, *op. cit.*, p. 3.

8. *Narrative of the Life of Frederick Douglass*, pub. 1845. Douglass was born a slave in 1818. His autobiography brought in fame in Europe as well as America. In 1848 he took part in the Seneca Falls Convention in New York, which inaugurated the Women's Rights movement in America. He was an active abolitionist and champion of black people. He became the most respected and prominent black man of his time. He died in 1895.

9. Charlotte Brontë, *Shirley* (London. 1849).

10. William L. Andrews (ed.), *Sisters of the Spirit: Three black women's autobiographies* (Bloomington, Indiana Press, 1986), p. 1. (Hereafter cited as *Sisters*.)

11. Pryse & Spillers, *op. cit.*, p. 35.

12. Houston A. Baker Jr, *Long Black Song* (Charlottesville, University of Virginia Press, 1972).

13. David Brion Davis, *The Problems of Slavery in Western Culture* (Ithaca, New York, Cornell University Press, 1966), p. 43.

14. Zora Neale Hurston, *The Sanctified Church* (Berkeley, California, Turtle Island Foundation, 1983).

15. Harriet Wilson, *Our Nig* (Toronto, Random House, 1983). First published by George C. Rand & Avery, September 1859. (Hereafter cited as *Nig*.)

16. Introduction by Henry Louis Gates to Harriet Wilson's *Our Nig* (Vintage, New York, 1985), p. ii.

17. Mrs Seacole, *The Wonderful Adventures of Mrs Seacole in Many Lands* (Bristol, Falling Wall Press, 1984). First published by James Blackwood, July 1857. (Hereafter cited as *Seacole*.)

18. Ellen Harper, *Iola Leroy or Shadows Uplifted* (first published in Philadelphia, 1893).
19. Barbara Christian, 'The uses of history: Frances Harper's *Iola Leroy or Shadows Uplifted*', in Barbara Christian, *Black Feminist Criticism* (London, Pergamon Press, 1985), pp. 165–70.
20. LeRoi Jones (Imamu Baraka), *Blues People: Negro music in white America* (New York, William Murrow & Co., 1963), pp. 60–81.
21. Alice Walker, interview in John O'Brien (ed.), *Interviews with Black Writers* (New York: Liveright, 1973), p. 208.

Chapter 2

1. Nathan A. Huggins (ed.), *Voices from the Harlem Renaissance* (Oxford, Oxford University Press, 1976).
2. Du Bois, W. E. B., 'Of Mr Booker T. Washington and Others', from *The Seven Souls of Black Folk* reprinted in Julius Lested (ed.), *The Seventh Son: The Thought and Writing of W. E. B. Du Bois* (New York, Random House, 1971), Volume 1, p. 74.
3. Alain Locke, 'The New Negro' (Huggins, *op. cit.*), p. 47.
4. Quoted in James O. Young, *Black Writers of the Thirties* (Baton Rouge, Louisiana State University Press, 1973), p. 65.
5. Franz Boas, *Race Language and Culture* (New York, Macmillan, 1940), p. 51.
6. James Weldon Johnson, Foreword to 'Challenge', Vol. 1, March 1934, in Huggins, *op. cit.*, p. 390.
7. Young, *op. cit.*, p. 135.
8. Houston A. Baker Jr, *Long Black Song* (Charlottesville, University Press of Virginia, 1972), p. 135.
9. Ralph Ellison, *Shadow and Act* (New York, New American Library, 1966), p. 172: '[folk-lore] . . . embodies those values by which the group lives or dies. These drawings may be crude, but they are nonetheless profound in that they represent the group's attempt to humanise the world. It's no accident that great literature, the products of individual artists, is erected upon so humble a base.'
10. Michael G. Cooke, *Afro-American Literature in the Twentieth Century* (New Haven, Yale University Press, 1984), p. 32.
11. Langston Hughes, *The Big Sea*, quoted in Huggins, *op. cit.*, p. 370.
12. Robert E. Hemenway, *Zora Neale Hurston: A literary biography* (London, Camden Press, 1986), p. 38.
13. Langston Hughes, *The Big Sea*, in Huggins, *op. cit.*, p. 380.

Chapter 3

1. Alice Walker, *In Search of Our Mother's Gardens* (London, Women's Press, 1984), pp. 93–116. (Hereafter cited as *In Search Of.*)

2. Zora Neale Hurston, *The Sanctified Church* (California, Turtle Island Foundation, 1986), p. 7. (Hereafter cited as *S. Ch.*)
3. Ralph Ellison, *Shadow and Act* (New York, New American Library, 1966), p. 172.
4. Robert E. Hemenway, *Zora Neale Hurston: A literary biography* (London, Camden Press, 1986). (Hereafter cited as *ZNH*.)
5. Zora Neale Hurston, *Dust Tracks on a Road* (London, Virago, 1986), p. 43. First published in 1942 by Lippincourt in New York. (Hereafter cited as *Dust Tracks*.)
6. Michelle Wallace, 'A Black Feminist's Search for Sisterhood', in Gloria T. Hull, Patricia Bell Scott, Barbara Smith (eds), *But Some of Us Are Brave* (New York, Feminist Press, 1982), p. 5.
7. Barbara Christian, *Black Feminist Criticism* (Oxford, Pergamon Press, 1985), p. 72.
8. Langston Hughes, 'The Negro Artist and the Racial Mountain', in *The Nation*, 1926.
9. Franz Boas, *Race Language and Culture* (New York, Macmillan, 1940), p. 16.
10. Houston A. Baker Jr, *Long Black Song* (Charlottesville, University Press of Virginia, 1972).
11. Richard Dorson, *Negro Folk-Tales in Michigan* (Cambridge, Mass., Harvard University Press, 1956), p. 187.
12. Zora Neale Hurston, *Mules and Men* (Bloomington, Indiana University Press, 1978). (Hereafter cited as *M&M*.)
13. J. Mason Brewer, *American Negro Folklore* (Chicago, Quadrangle Books, 1968), pp 3–4.
14. Joel Chandler Harris (1848–1908), born in Georgia where he was apprenticed to Joseph Addison Turner to learn the printing business, on a plantation near Eatonton. There he visited slave quarters where he heard black folk stories. He re-told these in *Uncle Remus: His songs and sayings* (1880), *Nights with Uncle Remus* (1883), *Uncle Remus and His Friends* (1892), *Tar Baby* (1904). His narrator was his creation – Uncle Remus.
15. A. P. Davis and M. W. Peplow (eds), *The New Negro Renaissance* (New York, Holt Rinehart, 1975), pp. 252–4.
16. 'Jooking' from 'jook' – a place to eat and drink; 'bookooing' from Beaucoup, meaning to show off.
17. The earth was raked clear of weeds then a pattern was raked on to the earth.
18. Angela Davis, *Women Race and Class* (London, Women's Press, 1986).
19. Zora Neale Hurston, *Tell My Horse* (New York, Harper & Row, 1990).
20. Buchi Emecheta, *Head Above Water* (London, Fontana, 1986).
21. Zora Neale Hurston, 'How it feels to be colored me', in Alice Walker (ed.), *I Love Myself* (New York, Feminist Press, 1979), p. 127.
22. Introduction to Zora Neale Hurston, *Moses, Man of the Mountain* (Urbana & Chicago, University of Illinois Press, 1984), p. xiv. (Hereafter cited as *Moses*.)

23. Zora Neale Hurston, *Jonah's Gourd Vine* (New York, Lippincourt, 1934). Quoted in Hemenway's introduction to *Mules and Men*. (*Hereafter cited as JGV.*)

24. Nancy Tischler, *Black Masks: Negro characters in modern Southern fiction* (Pennsylvania, Pennsylvania University Press, 1969) p. 158.

25. Letter from Hurston to James Weldon Johnson (April 1934) quoted in Larry Neale's introduction to the 1971 edition of *Jonah's Gourd Vine* (New York, J. B. Lippincott), p. xii.

26. Ibid., *JGV*, p. xx.

27. Anne Rayson, in her article 'The novels of Zora Neale Hurston', *Studies in Black Literature*, Vol. 5 (Winter 1974), pp. 1–10, points out that Hurston does nothing new in her use of a Bible story. She is merely repeating the success of Roark Bradford's parody, *Ol Man Adam and his Chillun*, in which Adam is Africanised and all dialogue is in black dialect. However, Rayson does show that Hurston's use of source material is more sophisticated than Bradford's and that her characters are rounder. Whereas Bradford's novel is a parody, *Moses: Man of the Mountains* is not, although Hurston was adept at using that literary device. Her outrageous *Book of Harlem* illustrates her mastery of the form, as she depicts the progress of a young black in Harlem:

> 5. And his raiment was very glad, for he had sojourned in the city of Babylon, which is ruled by the tribe of Tammany. And his garments putteth out the street lamps, and the vaseline upon his head, yea verily the slickness thereof did out-shine the sun at noonday. (*Spunk*, p. 76)

Rayson's argument that this novel is not a parody is a convincing one.

28. Ellease Southerland, 'Zora Neale Hurston: The Novelist – Author life/works', *Black World*, August 1974, pp. 21–30.

29. Zora Neale Hurston, *Their Eyes Were Watching God* (London, Virago, 1986). (Herafter cited as *Eyes*.)

30. Zora Neale Hurston, 'How it feels to be colored me' (see n. 20), p.153.

31. Darwin T. Turner, *In a Minor Chord* (Carbondale, South Illinois University Press, 1971), p. 90.

32. Lorraine Bethel, '"This Infinity of Conscious Pain": Zora Neale Hurston and the Black Female Literary Tradition', in Gloria T. Hull, Patricia Bell Scott and Barbara Smith (eds), *But Some of Us Are Brave* (New York, Feminist Press, 1982), p. 179.

33. Arna Bontemps, quoted in Turner, *op. cit.*, p. 95: 'Miss Hurston deals very simply with the more serious aspects of Negro life in America – she ignores them.'

34. Quoted in Lorraine Bethel's '"This Infinity of Conscious Pain": Zora Neale Hurston and the Black Female Literary Tradition', *But Some of Us Are Brave*, pp. 176–88, from Mary H. Washington (ed.) *Black Eyed Susans: Classic stories by and about black women* (Garden City, NY, Doubleday, 1975).

35. Zora Neale Hurston, collected short stories in *Spunk* (California, Turtle Island Foundation, 1985).

36. Nella Larsen, *Quicksand* (New York, Alfred A. Knopf, 1928).

37. Nella Larsen, *Passing* (New York, Alfred A. Knopf, 1929).
38. S. J. Walker, 'Zora Neale Hurston's *Their Eyes Were Watching God: Black novel of sexism*', in *Modern Fiction Studies*, 20 (Winter 1974–5), pp. 519–27.
39. John O'Brien (ed.), *Interviews with Black Writers* (New York, Alfred A. Knopf, 1964), p. 205.
40. Zora Neale Hurston, *Seraph on the Suwanee* (New York, Charles Scribner's Sons, 1948). (Hereafter cited as *Seraph*.)
41. Richard Wright was competing with Hurston for a reading public. His protest novel *Native Son* was published in 1940, two years before Hurston's autobiography, and was much more outspoken in its attack upon white racism than Hurston was in *Dust Tracks*. One reason for Hurston's reticence was that her book was published after America's entry into the Second World War and passages in which she criticised American expansionist policies were excised. Ann Petry's novel *The Street* was published in 1946, and reflects the bleak disillusionment of life in the Northern black ghettos. Both Wright and Petry used the European literary mode of Naturalism to frame their protests.

Chapter 4

1. Audre Lorde, *Zami* (London, Sheba Feminist Press, 1984).
2. Paule Marshall, *Merle* (London, Virago, 1985), p. 11.
3. Paule Marshall, *Browngirl, Brownstones* (London, Virago, 1982). (Hereafter cited as *Browngirl*.)
4. Paule Marshall, 'The Valley Between', in *Merle* (n. 2), pp. 16–24.
5. Paule Marshall, *Soul Clap Hands and Sing* (New York, Chatham N.J., Chatham Bookseller, 1961).
6. Paule Marshall, 'Reena', in *Merle*, (n. 2), pp. 73–91.
7. Paule Marshall, 'To Da-Duh, in Memoriam', in *Merle* (n. 2), pp. 96–106.
8. Paule Marshall, *Praisesong for the Widow* (London, Virago, 1983). (Hereafter cited as *Praisesong*.)
9. Paule Marshall, *The Chosen Place, The Timeless People* (New York, First Vantage Books/Random House, 1984). (Hereafter cited as *Chosen Place*.)
10. Audre Lorde, *Sister Outsider* (New York, The Crossing Press Feminist series, 1984). (Hereafter cited as *Sister*.)
11. Audre Lorde, *The Cancer Journals* (London, Sheba Feminist Publishers, 1985). (Hereafter cited as *Journals*.)
12. Claudia Tate, *Black Women Writers at Work*, (Harpenden, Oldcastle Books Ltd, 1985), p. 115.
13. Audre Lorde, 'From the House of Yemanja', in *The Black Unicorn* (New York, W. W. Norton & Co., 1978) p. 6.
14. Audre Lorde, 'A Litany for Survival', *ibid.*, p. 32.
15. See Hélène Cixous, 'The Laugh of the Medusa', in Elaine Marks and Isabelle de Courtivron (eds), *New French Feminism* (Brighton, Harvester Press, 1981), pp. 245–64.

Chapter 5

1. Claudia Tate, *Black Women Writers at Work* (London: Pluto Press, 1985), p. 6.
2. Estelle C. Jelinek (ed.), *Women's Autobiography in America: Essays in criticism* (London, Indiana University Press, 1980). (Hereafter cited as *Jelinek.*)
3. Maya Angelou, *I Know Why the Caged Bird Sings* (London, Virago, 1984), p. 265. (Hereafter cited as *Caged Bird.*)
4. Stephen Butterfield, *Black Autobiography in America* (Amherst, University of Massachusetts Press, 1974), p. 212.
5. Horatio Alger's published titles included *Tom the Bootblack*, *Jed the Poorhouse Boy*, *The Errand Boy*, *From Boy to Senator*, *Nelson the Newsboy*, indicating the rags-to-riches themes of his work. He was born in 1833 and died in 1899.
6. Maya Angelou, quoted in Tate, *op. cit.*, p. 7.
7. Regina Blackburn, 'In Search of a Black Female Self', in Jelinek, *op. cit.*, p. 134.
8. Maya Angelou, *And Still I Rise* (London, Virago, 1986), p. 72.
9. Maya Angelou, *Gather Together in my Name* (London, Virago, 1985). (Hereafter cited as *GT.*)
10. Maya Angelou, *Singin' and Swingin' and Gettin' Merry Like Christmas* (London, Virago, 1985). (Hereafter cited as *S&S.*)
11. Maya Angelou, *Heart of a Woman* (London, Virago, 1986). (Hereafter cited as *HOAW.*)
12. Maya Angelou, *All God's Children Need Travelling Shoes* (London, Virago, 1987). (Hereafter cited as *AGC.*)
13. Mari Evans (ed.), *Black Women Writers* (London, Pluto, 1985), p. 31.
14. Michelle Wallace, *Black Macho and the Myth of Superwoman* (London, John Calder Ltd, 1979).
15. Sondra O'Neil, in Mari Evans, *op. cit.*, p. 35.
16. The Autobiography of Malcolm X (Canada, First Ballantine Books, 1992). First published in 1965, this was written 'as told' to Alex Haley by Malcolm X.
17. The Black Muslim movement began in America in Detroit in 1930 when a mysterious mullah, W. D. Farad Muhammed, appeared there and began to preach that the biblical Adam was black, and that a malicious Yacobus had genetically engineered the evolution of white humans, who were white devils. Muhammed established a Muslim church, gathered disciples and disappeared as mysteriously as he had arrived. His main follower, Elijah Poole (later to call himself Elijah Muhammed) declared himself to be the new messenger of Islam. With Malcolm X as a devoted lieutenant the Muslim numbers greatly increased, with places of worship appearing in many Northern cities, including Chicago and New York. Elijah Muhammed preached a hatred of whites as the devil incarnate. He expected his followers to neither smoke nor drink, and to observe strict sexual morals. Malcolm X and he fell out when it was revealed that Elijah Muhammed was the father of several illegitimate babies born to him by Black Muslim women.

18. L. R. Berzin, *Neither White Nor Black* (New York University Press, 1978), p. 3.
19. Maya Angelou, 'Phenomenal Woman', *And Still I Rise* (n. 8), p. 9.

Chapter 6

1. Claudia Tate, *Black Women Writers at Work* (Harpenden, Oldcastle Books Ltd, 1985), p. 122.
2. Toni Morrison, *The Bluest Eye* (London, Triad/Panther, 1981).
3. Toni Morrison, *Sula* (London, Triad Grafton, 1982).
4. Interview Morrison gave to the BBC, transmitted on Radio 4 in 'Kaleidoscope' on 24 February 1988. (Herafter cited as BBC Interview.)
5. Ellen Moers, *Literary Women* (London, Women's Press, 1978).
6. Elaine Showalter, *A Literature of Their Own* (London, Virago, 1978).
7. Barbara Christian, *Black Women Novelists: The development of a tradition 1892–1976* (Westport, Connecticut, Greenwood, 1980).
8. Toni Morrison, *Beloved* (London, Chatto & Windus, 1987).
9. Toni Morrison, *Jazz* (London, Chatto & Windus, 1992).
10. Toni Morrison, *Song of Solomon* (London, Triad Grafton, 1980). (Hereafter cited as *Song.*)
11. Toni Morrison, *Tar Baby* (London, Triad Grafton, 1983).
12. E. Franklin Frazier, *The Negro Family in the United States* (Chicago, University of Chicago Press, 1966), p. 38.
13. BBC interview (see note 4).
14. Gerda Lerner, *Black Women in White America* (New York, Pantheon, 1971), pp. 60–3.
15. Michelle Wallace, *Black Macho and the Myth of Superwoman* (London, John Calder, 1978), p. 15.
16. Dorothy Sterling, *We Are Your Sisters* (New York, W. W. Norton & Co., 1984), p. 25. (Hereafter cited as *Sisters.*)
17. *Ibid.*, p. 39.

Chapter 7

1. Alice Walker, *In Search of Our Mother's Gardens* (London, Women's Press, 1984), pp. 119–29. (Hereafter cited as *In Search Of.*)
2. Alice Walker, *Once* (New York, Harcourt Brace and World Inc., 1968).
3. Alice Walker, *The Temple of my Familiar* (London, Women's Press, 1989). (Hereafter cited as *Temple.*)
4. Alice Walker, *You Can't Keep a Good Woman Down* (London, Women's Press, 1982).
5. Alice Walker, *The Third Life of Grange Copeland* (New York, Harcourt Brace Jovanovich Inc., 1971).
6. John O'Brien (ed.), *Interviews with Black Writers* (New York, Liveright, 1973). (Hereafter cited as *Interviews.*)
7. Alice Walker, *Revolutionary Petunias and Other Poems* (New York, Harcourt Brace Jovanovich Inc., 1971).

8. Alice Walker, *In Love and Trouble: Stories of black women* (New York, Harcourt Brace Jovanovich Inc., 1974).
9. Alice Walker, *Meridian* (London, Women's Press, 1982).
10. Jean Toomer, *Cane* (first published New York, Liveright, 1923).
11. Alice Walker, *Horses Make a Landscape Look More Beautiful* (London, Women's Press, 1985), p. 32.
12. Alice Walker, *The Color Purple* (London, Women's Press, 1984).
13. Alice Walker, *Living by the Word* (London, Women's Press, 1988). (Hereafter cited as *Living*.)
14. Alice Walker, *Possessing the Secret of Joy* (London, Jonathon Cape, 1992).

Conclusion

1. Barbara Christian, 'Trajectories of self-definition', in Marjorie Pryse and Hortense Spillers (eds), *Conjuring* (Bloomington, Indiana University Press, 1985).
2. Quoted in Louis H. Gates Jr, *Loose Canons* (Oxford, Oxford University Press, 1992), p. 42.
3. Toni Morrison, *RACE-ing, JUSTICE, En-GENDERing POWER* (*New York, Pantheon Books, 1992*), *p. xxx.*
4. *Gates, op. cit.,* p. 80.

Bibliography

Andrews, William L. *Sisters of the Spirit: Three black autobiographies*, Bloomington, Indiana University Press, 1986.

Andrews, William L. *Six Women's Slave Narratives*, Oxford, Oxford University Press, 1988.

Angelou, Maya. *I Know Why the Caged Bird Sings*, London, Virago, 1984. First published USA, Random House, 1969.

Angelou, Maya. *Gather Together in my Name*, London, Virago, 1985. First published USA, Random House, 1974.

Angelou, Maya. *Singin' and Swingin' and Gettin' Merry Like Christmas*, London, Virago. 1985. First published USA, Random House, 1976.

Angelou, Maya. *Heart of a Woman*, London, Virago, 1986. First published USA, Random House, 1981.

Angelou, Maya. *All God's Children Need Travelling Shoes*, London, Virago, 1987. First published USA, Random House, 1986.

Angelou, Maya. *And Still I Rise*, London, Virago 1986. First published USA, Random House, 1978.

Baker, Houston A., Jr. *Long Black Song*, Charlottesville, University Press of Virginia, 1972.

Bigsby, C.W.E. *The Second Black Renaissance: Essays in black literature*, Westport, Connecticut, Greenwood Press, 1980.

Boas, Franz. *Race, Language and Culture*, New York, Macmillan, 1940.

Brewer, J. Mason. *American Negro Folklore*, Chicago, Quadrangle Books, 1968.

Butterfield, Stephen. *Black Autobiography in America*, Amherst, University of Massachusetts Press, 1974.

Christian, Barbara. *Black Feminist Criticism*, Oxford, Pergamon, 1985.

Christian, Barbara. *Black Women Novelists*, Westport, Connecticut, Greenwood Press, 1980.

Clarke, Robert. *History, Ideology and Myth in American Fiction*, New York, Macmillan, 1984.

Cooke, Michael G. *Afro-American Literature in the Twentieth Century*, New Haven and London, Yale University Press, 1984.

Davis, Angela. *Women, Race and Class*, London, Women's Press, 1986.

Davis, A.P. and Peplow, M.W. (eds). *The New Negro Renaissance*, New York, Holt, Rinehart, 1975.

Davis, David Brion. *The Problems of Slavery in Western Culture*, Ithaca, New York, Cornell University Press, 1986.

Dorson, Richard. *Negro Folk-Tales in Michigan*, Cambridge, Massachusetts, Harvard University Press, 1956.

Ellison, Ralph. *Shadow and Act*, New York, Random House, 1964.

Emecheta, Buchi. *Head above Water*, London, Fontana, 1986.

Evans, Mari. *Black Women Writers*, London, Pluto Press, 1985. First published by Anchor Press/Doubleday, New York 1984.

Fisher, Dexter. *The Third Woman: Minority women writers in the US*, Boston, Houghton Mifflin, 1980.

Frazier, Franklin E. *The Negro Family in the United States*, Chicago, University of Chicago Press, 1966.

Gates, Louis Henry, Jr. *'Race', Writing and Difference*, Chicago, University of Chicago Press, 1986.

Gates, Louis Henry, Jr. *Loose Canons: Notes on the culture wars*, Oxford, Oxford University Press, 1992.

Gloster, Hugh. *Negro Voices in American Fiction*, New York, Russell & Russell, 1945.

Gomme, George Laurence. *Folklore as an Historical Science*, London, Methuen, 1908.

Harper, Ellen. *Iola Leroy or Shadows Uplifted*, Oxford, Oxford University Press, 1988.

Harris, Kevin. *Sex, Ideology and Religion*, Brighton, Wheatsheaf Books, 1984.

Hemenway, Robert. *Zora Neale Hurston: A literary biography*, London, Camden Press, 1986. First published by the University of Illinois Press.

hooks, bell. *Aint I a Woman: Black women and feminism*, London, Pluto Press, 1981.

Huggins, Nathan (ed.). *Voices from the Harlem Renaissance*, Oxford, Oxford University Press, 1971.

Huggins, Nathan (ed.). *Black Odyssey*, New York, Random House. 1977.

Hull, Gloria T., Scott, Patricia Bell, and Smith, Barbara (eds). *But Some of Us are Brave*, New York, Feminist Press, 1982.

Humm, Maggie. *Feminist Criticism*, Brighton, Harvester Press, 1986.

Hurston, Zora Neale. 'Crazy for this Democracy', *Negro Digest*, Dec. 1945.

Hurston, Zora Neale. *Dust Tracks on a Road*, London, Virago, 1986. First published by J. B. Lippincott, 1942.

Hurston, Zora Neale. *Their Eyes Were Watching God*, London, Virago 1986. First published by J. B. Lippincott, 1937.

Hurston, Zora Neale. *Jonah's Gourd Vine*, J. B. Lippincott, 1971. First published by Lippincott, 1934.

Hurston, Zora Neale. *Tell My Horse*, J. B. Lippincott, 1938.

Hurston, Zora Neale. *Moses, Man of the Mountain*, Urbana & Chicago, University of Illinois Press, 1984. First published by J. B. Lippincott, 1939.

Hurston, Zora Neale. *Mules and Men*, Bloomington, Indiana University Press, 1984. First published by J. B. Lippincott, 1935

Hurston, Zora Neale. *The Sanctified Church*, Berkeley, California, Turtle Island Foundation, 1983.

Hurston, Zora Neale. *Seraph on the Suwanee*, New York, Charles Scribner's Sons, 1948.

Hurston, Zora Neale. *Spunk: Selected short stories*, Berkeley, California, Turtle Island Foundation, 1985.

Jelinek, Estelle C. (ed.). *Women's Autobiography: Essays in criticism*, London, Indiana University Press, 1980.

Jones, LeRoi. *Blues People: Negro music in white America*, New York, William Murrow & Co., 1963.

King, Helen M. 'The Black Woman and Women's Liberation', *Ebony*, March 1971.

Larsen, Nella. *Quicksand* and *Passing*, London, Serpent's Tail, 1989.

LaRue, Linda. 'The Black Movement and Women's Liberation', *The Black Scholar*, May 1970.

Lerner, Gerda (ed.). *Black Woman in White America*, New York, Pantheon, 1973.

Lester, Julius (ed.). *The Seventh Son: The thought and writing of W. E. B. DuBois*, Volumes 1 and 2, New York, Random House, 1971.

Lorde, Audre. *Sister Outsider*, New York, The Crossing Press Feminist Series, 1984.

Lorde, Audre. *The Cancer Journals*, London, Sheba Feminist Publishers, 1985. First published by Spinsters Ink.

Lorde, Audre. *The Black Unicorn*, New York, W. W. Norton & Co., 1978.

Lorde, Audre. *Zami*, London, Sheba Feminist Press, 1984. First published by Persephone Press Inc., 1982.

Malcolm X. *The Autobiography of Malcolm X*, New York, Ballantine Books, 1992.

Marks, Elaine and Isabelle de Courtivron (eds). *New French Feminism*, Brighton, Harvester Press, 1981.

Marshall, Paule. *Merle and Other Stories*, London, Virago, 1985. First published New York, Feminist Press, 1983.

Marshall, Paule. *Browngirl, Brownstones*, London, Virago, 1982. First published in Great Britain by W. H. Allen & Co., 1960.

Marshall, Paule. *Soul Clap Hands and Sing*, New York, Chatham N.J., Chatham Bookseller, 1961.

Marshall, Paule. *The Chosen Place, The Timeless People*, New York, First Vantage Books, Random House, 1984.

Marshall, Paule. *Praisesong for the Widow*, London, Virago, 1983. First published by G. P. Putnam's Sons, New York, 1983.

Mays, Benjamin E. *The Negro's God*, New York, Negroes University Press, 1969.

Meese, Elizabeth and Parker, Alice. *The Difference Within: Feminisim and critical theory*, Volume 8, Philadelphia, John Benjamins, 1989.

Miller, Ruth. *Backgrounds to Black American Literature*, Scranton, Chandler Publishing Co., 1971.

Morrison, Toni. *The Bluest Eye*, London, Triad Panther, 1981. First published by Chatto & Windus, 1979.

Morrison, Toni. *Sula*, London, Triad/Grafton, 1982. First published in Great Britain by Chatto & Windus, 1980.

Morrison, Toni. *Song of Solomon*, London, Triad/Grafton, 1980. First published in Great Britain by Chatto & Windus, 1978.

Morrison, Toni. *Tar Baby*, London, Triad/Grafton, 1983. First published in Great Britain by Chatto & Windus, 1981.

Morrison, Toni. *Beloved*, London, Chatto & Windus 1987.

Morrison, Toni. *Jazz*, London, Chatto & Windus Ltd, 1992.

Morrison, Toni. *RACEing, JUSTICE, EnGENDERing POWER*, New York, Pantheon, 1992.

Newton, J. and Rosenfeld, D. *Feminist Criticism & Social Change*, New York, Methuen, 1985.

O'Brien, John (ed.). *Interviews with Black Writers*, New York: Liveright, 1973.

Petry, Ann. *The Street*, London, Virago, 1986. First published in Boston by Houghton Mifflin, 1946.

Porter, Dorothy B. *Early Negro Writing*, Boston, Beacon Press, 1971.

Pryse, Marjorie and Spillers, Hortense J. (eds). *Conjuring: Black women, fiction and literary tradition*, Bloomington, Indiana University Press, 1985.

Rayson, Anne. 'The Novels of Zora Neale Hurston', *Studies in Black Literature*, Volume 5, Winter 1974, pp. 1–10.

Robinson, Lillian S. *Sex, Class and Culture*, Methuen, 1986. First published by Indiana University Press, 1978.

Seacole, Mrs. *The Wonderful Adventures of Mrs Seacole in Many Lands*, Bristol, Falling Wall Press, 1984. First published by James Blackwood, July 1857.

Sellers, Susan (ed.). *Feminist Criticism: Theory & practice*, Hemel Hempstead, Harvester Wheatsheaf, 1991.

Showalter, Elaine (ed.). *The New Feminist Criticism*, London, Virago, 1986.

Showalter, Elaine (ed.) *Sister's Choice: Tradition and change in American women's writing*, Oxford, Clarendon Press, 1991.

Smith, Valerie. *Self-discovery & Authority in African-American Narrative*, Cambridge, Massachusetts, Harvard University Press, 1982.

Southerland, Ellease. 'Zora Neale Hurston: The novelist/author life/works, *Black World*, August 1974.

Sterling, Dorothy. *We Are Your Sisters*, New York, W. W. Norton & Co., 1984.

Szwed, John F. *Black Americans*, Voice of America Forum Lectures, 1970.

Tate, Claudia. *Black Women Writers at Work*, Harpenden, Oldcastle Books, 1985.

Tischler, Nancy. *Black Masks: Negro characteristics in modern Southern fiction*, Pennsylvania, Pennsylvania University Press, 1967.

Toomer, Jean. *Cane*, New York, Liveright, 1975. First published by Liveright in 1923.

Turner, Darwin T. *In a Minor Chord*, Carbondale, Southern Illinois University Press, 1971.

Walker, Alice. *Once*, New York, Harcourt Brace and World Inc., 1968.

Walker, Alice. *The Third Life of Grange Copeland*, New York, Harcourt Brace Jovanovich Inc., 1971.

Walker, Alice. *Revolutionary Petunias and Other Poems*, New York, Harcourt Brace Jovanovich, 1971.

Walker, Alice. *In Love and Trouble: Stories of black women*, New York, Harcourt Brace Jovanovich Inc., 1974.

Walker, Alice. *Meridian*, London, Women's Press, 1982. First published New York, Harcourt Brace Jovanovich, 1976.

Walker, Alice. *Good Night, Willie Lee, I'll see You in the Morning*, London, Women's Press, 1987. First published New York, Dial Press, 1979.

Walker, Alice. *You Can't Keep A Good Woman Down*, London, Women's Press, 1982.

Walker, Alice. *In Search of Our Mothers' Gardens*, London, Women's Press, 1984. First published New York, Harcourt Brace Jovanovich, 1983.

Walker, Alice. *The Color Purple*, London, Women's Press, 1984. First published New York, Harcourt Brace Jovanovich, 1983.

Walker, Alice. *Horses Make A Landscape Look More Beautiful*, London, Women's Press, 1985. First published New York, Harcourt Brace Jovanovich, 1984.

Walker, Alice. *Living By the Word*, London, Women's Press, 1988.

Walker, Alice. *The Temple of my Familiar*, London, Women's Press, 1989.

Walker, Alice. *Possessing the Secret of Joy*, London, Jonathon Cape, 1992.

Walker, Alice (ed.). *I Love Myself: A Zora Neale Hurston reader*, New York, Feminist Press, 1984

Walker, S. Jay. 'Zora Neale Hurston's *Their eyes were watching God*', *Modern Fiction Studies*, 20, Winter 1974/5.

Wallace, Michelle. *Black Macho and the Myth of Superwoman*, London, John Calder, 1978.

Washington, Booker T. *Up From Slavery*, London, Penguin, 1986.

Washington, Mary Helen. *Any Woman's Blues*, London, Virago, 1981. First published New York, Anchor Books, 1980.

Washington, Mary Helen. 'The Black Woman and Women's Liberation', *Black World*, August 1972.

Wilson, Harriet E. *Our Nig*, Canada, Random House, 1983. First published by George C. Rand & Avery, Sept. 1859.

Woolf, Virginia. *A Room of One's Own*, Granada Publishing Ltd., 1977. First published by Hogarth Press, 1929.

Wright, Richard. *Native Son*, London, Penguin, 1972. First published by Victor Gollancz, 1940.

Wright, Richard. *Black Boy*, London, Gollancz, 1947.

Young, James O. *Black Writers of the Thirties*, Baton Rouge, Louisiana State Press, 1973.

Index